NEW ECONOMIC SPACES:
NEW ECONOMIC GEOGRAPHIES

New Economic Spaces: New Economic Geographies

Edited by
RICHARD LE HERON
University of Auckland, New Zealand
JAMES W. HARRINGTON
University of Washington, Seattle, USA

Routledge
Taylor & Francis Group

LONDON AND NEW YORK

First published 2005 by Ashgate Publishing

Reissued 2018 by Routledge
2 Park Square, Milton Park, Abingdon, Oxon OX14 4RN
711 Third Avenue, New York, NY 10017, USA

Routledge is an imprint of the Taylor & Francis Group, an informa business

First issued in paperback 2018

A Library of Congress record exists under LC control number: 2005008491

Notice:
Product or corporate names may be trademarks or registered trademarks, and are used only for identification and explanation without intent to infringe.

Publisher's Note
The publisher has gone to great lengths to ensure the quality of this reprint but points out that some imperfections in the original copies may be apparent.

Disclaimer
The publisher has made every effort to trace copyright holders and welcomes correspondence from those they have been unable to contact.

ISBN 13: 978-0-815-39065-7 (hbk)
ISBN 13: 978-1-138-61996-8 (pbk)
ISBN 13: 978-1-351-15264-8 (ebk)

Contents

List of Tables

List of Figures

List of Contributors

Ji-Sun Choi, Associate Researcher, Regional Innovation Team, Science and Policy Institute (STEPI), 26f., Specialty Construction Center 395-70, Sindaebang2-dong, Dongjak-gu, Seoul 156-714, Korea. E-mail: choijs@stepi.re.kr Dr. Choi's research interests focus on the spatial impact of digital economy and e-commerce, the geography of innovation, the regional spillover of research and development and regional innovation system.

Tamsin E.C. Davies, Ms., Department of Geography, University of Wales, Swansea, Singleton Park, Swansea SA2 8PP, United Kingdom. E-mail: t.e.c.davies@swan.ac.uk Ms. Davies research interests focus on University – industry interaction and the transfer, translation and transformation of knowledge between different scientific spaces, and the circulation of knowledge in peripheral regions.

Marcus A. Doel, Professor, Department of Human Geography, The University of Swansea, Singleton Park, Swansea SA2 8PP, United Kingdom. E-mail: m.a.doel@swansea.ac.uk Professor Doel's research interests span post-structuralism, spatial theory, and post-Marxist political economy.

Hadi Dowlatabadi, Canada Research Chair, Professor of Applied Mathematics, Global Change and Integrated Assessment, Institute for Resources, Environment and Sustainability, The University of British Columbia, 216-1924 West Mall, Vancouver. E-mail: Hadi.D@ubc.ca Professor Dowlatabadi's research interests focus on the interface between human activity and natural systems and the challenge of policy design in complex multi-stress environments.

Melanie Feakins, Assistant Professor, Department of Geography, University of Southern Carolina, Columbia, South Carolina 29208 USA. E-mail: Feakins@gwm.sc.edu Ms. Feakin's research interests focus on economic transformations in post-socialist worlds, discourses and practices of trust and certification as governance for transnational economic connections.

Martina Fromhold-Eisebith, Dr., ARC Seibersdorf Research GmbH, Systems Research Technology-Economy-Environment, A-2444 Seibersdorf, Austria. E-mail: martina.fromhold@sbg.ac.at Dr. Fromhold-Eisebith's research interests cover technology oriented regional development, innovation systems in Europe and Asia, the economic geography of qualified labour migration, MNCs.

Jay D. Gatrell, Assistant Professor, Department of Geography and Women's Studies, Indiana State University, Terre Haute, Indiana, USA. E-mail:

gejdg@isugw.indstate.edu Jay is an economic geographer with interests in economic development theory and practices.

James W. Harrington Jr., Professor and Chair, Department of Geography, The University of Washington, Seattle, Washington 98105 USA. E-mail: jwh@u.washington.edu James W. Harrington's fundamental interest is in sub-national regional economic development. He currently pursues this with a focus on labor occupations, and the lens of formal and informal institutions.

Roger Hayter, Professor, Department of Geog4321`aphy, Simon Fraser University, Burnaby, British Columbia VV5A 1S6, Canada. E-mail: hayter@sfu.ca Professor Hayter's research interests focus on industrial location dynamics and regional industrial transformation, the forest sector, Japanese MNCs.

Baruch A. Kipnis, Professor, Department of Geography, The University of Haifa, Israel. E-mail: baruch@univ.haifa.ac.il Professor Kipnis' research interests include the dynamics of contemporary urban and economic spaces.

Richard Le Heron, Professor of Geography, School of Geography and Environmental Science, The University of Auckland e-mail: r.leheron@auckland.ac.nz Professor Le Heron's current research focuses on post-structural political economy, globalizing processes and agri-food restructuring, socio-scientific institutions and nature-society relationships and sustainable development pathways.

Hiroyasu Motoki, Dr. Department of Geography, Nippon Institute of Technology, Gakuendai, Miyashiro, Saitama, 345-8501, Japan. Email: mtk@an.email.ne.jp Dr Motoki is researching the changing economic geography of Japan.

Raul Pacheco, Researcher on Environmental Issues, Center for Applied Innovation on Competitive Technologies (Centro de Innovacion Aplicada sobre Tecnologias Competitivas, CIATEC), Omega 201 Fraccionamiento Delta, Leon, Guanajuato 37545, Mexico. E-mail: rpacheco@ciatec.mx Mr. Pachco's research interests focus on adaptive system responses to external pressures that include environmental regulatory mechanisms.

Sam Ock Park, Dean and Professor, College of Social Sciences, Seoul National University, Seoul 151-742, Korea. E-mail: parkso@snu.ac.kr Professor Park's research interests focus on industrial restructuring, regional innovation systems, E-commerce, innovative cluster and knowledge based economy in Korea and the Pacific Rim.

Jerry Patchell, Dr. Division of Social Sciences, Hong Kong University of Science and Technology, Clearwater Bay, Kowloon, Hong Kong. E-mail: sopatch@ust.hk Patchell's research interests focus on how firms and related institutions work together, how this occurs in the vertical relations among firms in various industries in Japan, the horizontal relations among winegrowers in Bordeaux, Napa and Chianti, university-industry collaboration, and environmental consequences of supply chains.

Guy Penny, Dr., Socio-Environmental Scientist, National Institute of Water and Atmospheric Research (NIWA), Auckland, New Zealand. E-mail: g.penny@niwa.co.nz Dr. Penny's research interests focus on Human-Environment relations, rural/indigenous commuities and sustainable resource use, knowledge systems, social and economic processes and their geo-cultural contexts.

Kevin G. Rees, Dr., Department of Human Geography, The University of Swansea, Swansea, United Kingdom. E-mail: k.g.rees@swansea.ac.uk Dr. Rees' research interests embrace corporation collaboration, institutional learning and intellectual property, especially in knowledge-based industries, and a critical evaluation of government technology policies aimed at promoting regional economic development.

Neil Reid, Associate Professor of Geography and Director of Master of Liberal Studies Program, University of Toledo, Toledo, Ohio, USA. E-mail: nreid@utnet.utoledo.edu Neil's research interests include the spatial dynamics of foreign direct investment and the locational determinants of territorial industrialization.

Tim Reiffenstein, Assistant Professor, Department of Geography, Mount Allison University, Sackville, New Brunswick, Canada E-mail: treiffen@mta.ca Assistant Professor Reiffenstein's research interests focus on contemporary and historical geographies of industry, with a focus on the evolution of Japanese innovation systems, and bridging the evolutionary economics and science studies literature by way of geography.

Bongman Seo, Dr. Visiting Assistant Professor, Department of International Relations and Geography, Florida International University, DM 432 Uiversity Park, Miami FL 33199, United States of America. E-mail: seob@fiu.edu Assistant Professor Seo's research interests focus on financial geography, contemporary East Asian development, alternative economies, and network analyses techniques.

Yufang Shen, Professor, The Yangtze Basin Development Institute, East China Normal University, Shanghai 200062, China. E-mail: syf200062@yahoo.com Professor Shen's research interests focus on the assessment of the investment environment, industrial distribution and redistribution, industrial linkages and networks, regional development and regional coordination, globalization and regional intergration, mechanism of endogenous development, Shanghai as a world megalopolis, Yangtze Valley, Yangtze Delta, regional planning and development.

Atsuhiko Takeuchi, Professor, Department of Geography, Nippon Institute of Technology, Gakuendai, Miyashiro, Saitama, 345-8501, Japan. E-mail:

atu@nit.ac.jp. Professor Takeuchi's research interests focus on the regional dynamics of industry in Japan.

Shuang-Yann Wong, Associate Professor, Department of Humanitites and Social Studies Education, National Institute of Education, Nanyang Technological University, 1, Nanyang Walk, Singapore 637616. E-mail: sywong@nie.edu.sg. Associate Professor Wong's research interests focus on Southeast Asia economic development, ASEAN cooperation, local government planning and practices, banking and finance of Singapore and Malaysia, Singapore foreign investments, overseas Chinese of Southeast Asia.

Tong Xin, Dr. Assistant Professor, Department of Geography, Peking University, Beijing, 100871, P.R. China. E-mail: tongxin@urban.pku.edu.cn. Dr. Tong's research interests focus on the geography of information technology in China.

Chapter 1

Describing, Studying, and Creating New Economic Spaces

James W. Harrington and Richard Le Heron

This volume brings together empirical examples from Asia, Europe and North America, to illustrate and understand the ways in which institutional, technological and policy innovations have created and attempt to affect the location of economic activity and the nature of economic development. We use the phrase 'new economic spaces' for the resultant patterns, and 'new economic geographies' for the several ways in which observers attempt to understand them.

More formally, we asked each author to address the constitutive processes of new economic and institutional spaces and the theoretical, methodological and policy-engaging practices of emerging economic geographies. As our writing and reading has progressed, we found we could encapsulate our purposes into three deceptively simple questions relevant to any investigation, and important to any citizen:

- What's going on?
- How can we understand it?
- How can we make a difference?

Of course, 'What's going on?' is easy to ask and difficult to answer. Whatever is going on within and among our national and regional economies, it changes rapidly. However, it probably changes no more rapidly than 'how we understand it' – the frameworks, concepts and methods academics have employed to describe it. Perhaps our role is to develop as many different lenses as possible, through which to view the kaleidoscope of regional economic activities and interactions. It certainly seems to be our lot to do so.

Sam Park opens with suggestions of what's going on and how we might study these processes. He suggests that the innovations noted above yield new economic spaces that have important informational and virtual geographies, as well as literal geographies. Our study of them should analyze economic activities in relation to other social, cultural, political and institutional processes in and across places. These processes create specific nexuses of physical and virtual connections and geographic control.

Such an emphasis on multidimensional processes and virtual relationships leads us to new interpretations of popular concepts. Clustering, for example, need not be construed as geographic clustering. Information and control systems have allowed clustering and the communication of tacit knowledge within newly industrializing countries, linked to the world's economic control centres. Networks, and even social embeddedness, can be understood as non-local as well as local, implemented through facilitative vehicles such as proximity, interaction, cultural affinity, corporate encouragement, or worldwide communities of practice. Such research requires interviews, participant-observation, multiple types of data collected at multiple scales and tracing the interactions among different sorts of actors.

Operation of New Economic Spaces

We first turn to economic geographers' longstanding interest in corporations and the dynamics of the industries in which they compete, as primary actors and processes in (re)creating economic spaces.

Roger Hayter, Kevin Rees, and Jerry Patchell promulgate the 'large firm' as an ideal type, distinct from global or multinational firms and from small or medium-sized firms. As an ideal type, large firms retain their entrepreneurial origins and local embeddedness, but combine these with economies of scale and scope. As such, they can become a source of external economies and technological leadership for a region. Hayter and colleagues argue that this is the case in the technology-intensive sectors of metropolitan Vancouver, British Columbia. Tim Reiffenstein presents a study of Hamamatsu, Japan, home of the three largest electronic musical instruments firms. He sees radical technological change as the major influence on the industrial and spatial organization of the musical instruments sector, and the processes by which technological change is accomplished as the major influence on where and how successful systems of innovation operate. Specifically, the manner in which knowledge is published (e.g., journals vs. patents) affects how and by whom it are used. Melanie Feakins investigated corporate outsourcing. Her case study is of the software outsourcing clusters in St. Petersburg, Russia. In terms of the operation of outsourcing relationships, she asks whether the increasing importance of process standards and certification influences the adoption of processes by cluster participants.

Recognizing that a key dimension of economic activity is the flow of capital, Bongman Seo examines the global movements of syndicated credit. In part because of the Asian financial crisis of the late 1990s, North American and Western European lenders have maintained a strong lead in international credit syndications. Shuang-Yann Wong also focused on a credit institution, Singapore's United Overseas Bank. Founded in 1917, UOB is one of only two locally owned banks in Singapore. UOB will to change from a commercial bank to a financial holding company, with a substantial investment-banking portfolio. Wong emphasizes the social construction of economic change: the bank's actions are determined jointly by culture, personalities and regulation. Corporate actors can have substantial differences in their perception of and reaction to government and economic regulatory change.

Yufang Shen's focus is on FDI, rather than flows of credit. Shen undertook a regression analysis of FDI flows, international trade and GRP growth per province in China's Yangtze Valley. This very large and varied area contains both a world city (Shanghai) and very peripheral regions, and points to the importance of provincial regulation and relative location in determining the effect of international capital flows.

Three chapters emphasize the importance of representation in and of new economic spaces. In his study of dairy and sheep industries in New Zealand, Guy Penny focuses on how the major agents for farmers and processors represent their interests and the pressures they face. Pressured by major changes in international trade regimes, global production chains and consumer markets, these actors have attempted cooperation across their linked sectors – while working within physical-environmental constraints of New Zealand agriculture. Jay Gatrell and Neil Reid attempt to characterize the self-representation of Toledo, Ohio as a self-conscious economic space. Maintaining that 'culture' can be interpreted as the 'local' processes and practices that mediate the local outcomes of global processes, they investigated the actions and reactions of Chrysler, labor representatives, and local government as Chrysler engaged in a publicized process of location decision making. They conclude that the economic development process is 'expressive', explicitly and deliberately giving meaning to places, in order to create a coalition of other firms, labor and community. At the scale of personal self-representation through lifestyle decisions, Baruch Kipnis employs the 'value-stretch' model to identify how people assess and value their work, leisure and consumption. Given the popular accounts of hyper-consumption and hyper-differentiation in Israeli society, he asks whether work, leisure and consumption values vary by age, class, or gender.

Three chapters remind us that economic activities have physical environmental origins and implications. Xin Tong looks at international recycling and waste products from the electronics industry. China has become the largest destination for international shipments of electronic wastes, even as China's electronics sector grows by leaps and bounds. Refurbishing used equipment and recycling e-waste have become important economic activities in rural areas of coastal China, given international differentials in environmental regulations; low Chinese labour costs for recycling activities; high cost of and growing demand for raw materials for electronics manufacturing; and high demand for refurbished electronic hardware in China. She suggests that evolving standards in the regulation and pricing of industrial wastes may move the region from the victim of 'ecological dumping' to a key economic participant in 'international recycling'.

Atsuhiko Takeuchi and Hiroyasu Motoki developed two case studies of environmentally degraded industrial districts in Japan, to illustrate the importance of economic history, physical setting, and political and social culture on environmental outcomes. Redevelopment of Tokyo's Kawasaki District and western Japan's Kitakyushu District provide examples of new economic spaces carved out of old, at great expense, to take advantage of local human resources and new physical infrastructures. Local economic and social histories and global market pressures also influenced the reactions of industrial actors in the two Mexican leather/footwear districts studied by Raul Pacheco and Hadi Dowlatabadi.

They show that the interplay of economic geographies with their physical environment needs to be explored by observation, by econometric study, and by teaming with other researchers.

Studying New Spaces: New Economic Geographies?

We then present three chapters that suggest ways of approaching the study of economic spaces. Martina Fromhold-Eisebeth provides a thoughtful review of the concepts 'creative-innovative milieux' and 'social capital'. She uses published information to generate a short empirical example with which to illustrate the utility of using the two concepts in conjunction. The phrase 'social capital' denotes neither a specific geography, nor a specific unit of analysis, nor a specific purpose. By opening up the concept of social capital in these three ways, the concept of social capital becomes a fairly powerful conceptual and empirical tool for situating the operation of regional innovative milieux.

Just as any stylized fact or generalized concept is doomed to fall short of the mark, any readily available data source is similarly doomed. Marcus Doel, Kevin Rees, and Tamsin Davies deconstructed the practice of citing previous patents within new patent applications. In the process, they cast serious doubt on the utility of a popular data source used to investigate technological change. They suggest that what this data source could actually tell us is something about which we should be more concerned than we have been! They conclude that patents are not a very good measure of innovative activity, patent citations are not a very good measure of scientific linkages among innovations, and patent citations are probably even a worse measure of scientific linkages among places. They eschew studying patents as a proxy for innovativeness, and suggest studying patenting as one indicator of the institutional practices of innovation.

Roger Hayter proposes going back to the future, using the framework of 'dissenting institutionalism': 'dissenting' in the sense of rejecting the individual basis of neoclassical economics or the determinacy of marxism. He suggests that not only institutionalism, but also the region (as the geographic locus of institutions) should be the empirical focus of new economic geography.

For any investigation of economic spaces (virtual or geographic) to gain understanding, the investigator must ask least these questions: Who holds agency? What are the temporal dynamics of any situation under study? How can we undertake explicitly multi-scalar analyses?

Creating New Economic Spaces via New Economic Geographies

How might our research and writing affect economic actors and activity? Do our research practices make a difference? In other words, does economic geography have a role in shaping new economic spaces?

First, under-specified concepts and processes make for poor public policy. Ji-Sun Choi provides an overview of Korean industrial policy, primarily to illustrate the over-reliance on the academic concept of 'clusters'. She argues and shows that the cluster concept is vague, applied to every case, and overly fashionable. Indeed, it is ironic that a concept based on processes of spatial concentration has become the cornerstone for a government strategy for reducing the geographic concentration of the Korean economy!

Richard Le Heron examines recently published reviews of economic geographic practice and suggests that these reviews ignore the practice (performance) of academic work and its effects. He argues that rather than merely studying new economic spaces, we can be a conscious part of their creation by making our projects and purposes explicit, and recognizing the importance of how we engage in research, writing and teaching. An important first step is to appreciate, write about and teach about the varied sites in which economic geography is being practiced – by corporations and governments, yes, but also by households, community groups and labour organizations. It's a large, heterogeneous world, and there are many examples of activities and organization of economic activity that we need to bring to light – to enrich our sense of what's possible.

Acknowledgements

In the preparation of the book a number of people willingly provided professional assistance and expertise. For this we are very grateful. We acknowledge in particular the extensive copy editing by Christina Kaiser in early stages of the book, research assistance by Marama Le Heron and generous secretarial support by Beryl Jack.

Chapter 2

Network, Embeddedness, and Cluster Processes of New Economic Spaces in Korea

Sam Ock Park

Introduction

Since the early 1990s, the nature of research in economic geography has been reshaped with a refiguring of the concept of 'economic' in economic geography. The terminologies of 'geographical turns' in economics and 'cultural turns' and 'relational turns' in economic geography are all related with the theoretical and empirical advances and debates in the new economic geographies. In the new economic geographies, the concept of 'economic' is not regarded as singular, uni-dimensional, deterministic, and aspatial because the economic activities are analyzed in relation to other social, cultural, political, and institutional processes in society and space (Yeung, 2003).

New economic geographies in recent years seem to be closely related to the emergence of new economic spaces resulting from the dynamic processes beyond economic motivation in the information society and knowledge-based economy. 'New' in the new economic spaces is the resulting spaces from the development of Information and Communication Technology (ICT) and new production, business, and innovation systems, and globalization. New economic spaces are not just new industrial spaces, but include services, consumption and distribution spaces as well as production spaces. New economic spaces include both physical spaces and electronic spaces of economic activities and are regarded as relational and network spaces in the global society. Due to the relation between the emergence of new economic geographies and the new economic spaces, understanding the processes constituting new economic spaces is an important issue for understanding changes in the nature of economic geography.

This chapter examines the processes of emerging new economic spaces in the global society in the digital era. The processes of the emerging new economic spaces are examined in the context of network and embeddedness. Two contrasting 'new economic spaces' in Korea, are then considered. Finally, the paper concludes with some policy implications.

Networks, Embeddedness and New Economic Spaces

Economic activities in space evolve in relation with social, cultural, political, and historical developments as well as with the pressures of pure economic rationality. Accordingly, economic activities are dynamic over time and space. Networks are regarded as relational processes among diverse agents of economic activities over space (Dicken et al., 2001). Networks also can be viewed as 'social spaces for communication and information exchange' (Murphy, 2003, p. 174).

In the mass production systems, inter-firm networks were critical for understanding the economic activities over space. In the knowledge-based economy and information society, networks are beyond the inter-firm networks and embraces inter-personal relations, supplier-customer relationship for material transactions, relations with diverse organizations such as producer service firms, universities, and public institutions. These networks contribute significantly learning processes, promote knowledge spillover, and provide context for knowledge creation or innovation (Bunnel and Coe, 2001; Malecki, 1997; Malecki and Oinas, 1999; Yeung 2000a). In the contemporary era, 'the process by which this creative knowledge and economic learning occurs is an ever-more important element of economic development' (Boggs and Rantisi, 2003, p. 111). Individuals or public organizations can be key actors in the networks. The interactions of key actors are very important for evolving the new economic spaces. The actors are, however, still 'viewed as operating within a context of institutions, norms and rules which condition their choices and relations, i.e. within a broader system which is constituted by both structure and agents' (Boggs and Rantisi, 2003, p. 111).

The network space is not limited to local area: it can be extended to regional, national, or global space (Park, 1996). Accordingly, the networks have spatial dimension that can be easily seen from the knowledge creation and transfer (Park, 2003). Tacit knowledge (TK) is very difficult to describe or communicate and remains more or less exclusively within the individual, the group or the whole organization. The transfer of TK can take place at a local level where firms share the same values, background and understanding of technical and commercial problems (Maskell and Malmberg, 1999). Since common language, observation, imitation and practice are necessary for the transmission of TK, individual interaction is localized within a limited area, which represents both geographical and cultural proximity. Proximity, both in terms of geographical and cultural aspects, provides access to local relational networks for the creation and transfer of TK. However, it should be noted that regular face-to-face contacts could be maintained over long distances if the necessary technological preconditions and communication channels exist (Grotz and Braun, 1997). For the interaction of TK over a long-distance, long-distance trip of the key able person who can transfer the TK is necessary. It is common of a long-distance trip of engineers or managers in multinational firms in order to interact of TK with foreign counterparts or affiliates. Due to the importance of spatial proximity in the transfer of TK, place is critical for knowledge creation and innovation. Only limited places in the economic spaces have possibilities for knowledge creation and innovation because TK is important for innovation and can be created and transferred only in limited places.

The key goal of the interaction of TK in a place is the codification of the TK with development of new products or processes. In many innovation centres, there are intensive interactions of TK and continuous codification of the knowledge (CK). Once TK is codified, the CK may become ubiquitous and TK is becoming more important as codification increases (Maskell and Malmberg, 1999; Sturgeon, 2003). Development of modular production networks in Silicon Valley is a good example of the codification process through the socialization of TK (Sturgeon, 2003). The transformation of the TK into CK makes possible to transfer of the knowledge over long-distance and then to promote globalization. The development of ICT has made CK more ubiquitous because it has made easier to transfer of the CK through Internet. Codification of the knowledge not only promotes the globalization but also contributes to integrate various centres of economic activities on a global scale. In this aspect, Sturgeon (2003) argues that codification of TK is the mechanism that weaves specialized agglomerations into global-scale production systems.

Traditionally production linkages were the focus of study in industrial networks. However, there are diverse contents of networks in the new economic spaces. In addition to material flows through production networks, flows of knowledge and technology, capital, manpower, advanced services, and strategy and power are realized through networks over economic spaces (Park, 2002). The flows can be accomplished not only by formal but also by informal institutions. Murphy (2003), for example, emphasizes the importance of informal institution in the networks in the case study of manufacturers in Mwanza, Tanzania showing three types of networks spaces: credit accessing relations; reputation-building relations; and information acquiring relations. Diverse contents of networks and types of networks in the economic spaces are driven by multiple and overlapping rationalities or logics (Ettringer, 2003; Murphy, 2003). There is no doubt that trust and power relations are important in the formation of the diverse networks over the economic spaces.

Economic actions and outcomes are affected by actor's dyadic relations and by the structure of the overall network of relations, representing embeddedness of economic behavior on social relations (Grabher, 1993). Accordingly, networks are closely related to the social embeddedness of economic action. The concept of embeddedness reconstructed by Granovetter (1985) following Polanyi's (1944) seminal work has made a significant impact on what is called 'new economic sociology' and on the understanding the organization of new economic spaces. According to Granovetter (1985, p. 485), the economic behaviors of firms are 'so constrained by ongoing social relations that to construe them as independent is a grievous misunderstanding'. This concept significantly contrasts with the 'under-socialized' view of economic action in the neoclassical economics and neoclassical location theory in economic geography, where economic decisions are made to secure optimum solution with regard to maximum profit. Since the early 1990s, the embeddedness concept has been introduced in economic geography such as studies of industrial districts, spatial agglomerations, regional development, spatial transfer of manufacturing technologies, etc. (Dicken and Thrift, 1992; Park, 1996; Yeung, 2000b). Especially, during the last decade, many studies on new economic geography have examined the social embeddedness of economic action and business networks of industrial firms in various spatial scales (more recent reviews, see Ettringer, 2003; Murphy, 2003; Storper and Salais, 1997; Yeung, 2000b; 2003).

In general, local embeddedness of economic action has been emphasized in the empirical studies such as industrial districts and industrial clustering. However, the application of the concept of embeddedness is not limited to local area. Economic actions can be embedded in organizational structure without embedding in local areas. Decision-making on capital investments, employee relations, and outsourcing advanced services in branch plants of multinational firms located in peripheral areas in the initial stage is embedded in the parent company's business culture and strategies. In this case, non-local embeddedness is also important. For example, branch plants in periphery invested from a parent company located in core region were embedded in parent company organization and strategy in term of technology, industrial relations, and qualified labour relations in the initial development stage in Korea (Park and Markusen, 1995). Technological upgrading of Hsinchu Science Park in Taiwan through ethnic connections between Silicon Valley and Hsinchu by transferring capital, skill, and know-how embedded in Silicon Valley and by facilitating collaborations between specialist producers in the two regions is a good example of global networks over long distance (Saxenian and Hsu, 2001).

Two Contrasting Cases in Korea: Kangnam and Sunchang

Most people may regard that the importance of networks and embeddedness in the spatial clustering and dispersal can be applicable only to the advanced economies and they are not applicable to peripheral areas even in the information society. However, I argue in this paper that the processes of new economic spaces are applicable even in the peripheral areas. I would like to introduce two contrasting region in Korea: one is most developed and innovative place, Kangnam in Seoul; the other is most underdeveloped region in Korea, Sunchang-gun in Jeonbuk province.

Gangnam, southern part of Han River in Seoul, has been newly developed since 1970s and has become Seoul's new core for economic activities with numerous modern high-rise office buildings. Since the late 1980s advanced services such as software, engineering, advertising, and design services has concentrated in the Gangnam area (Park and Nahm, 1998). The concentration trend has culminated since the financial crises in 1997 with agglomeration of new start-ups in high tech and software sectors. Along the Teheran Road, which across the Gangnam district from west to east, many large IT firms and new start-ups located in this area (Shin, 2001). 'Teheran Valley' has been named along the Teheran Road due to the overwhelming concentration of IT firms, advanced service firms and other high tech firms. Currently, more than 2700 venture firms (new start-ups in high tech or knowledge-intensive sector) are concentrated in Gangnam area, which is more than 20 per cent of the total venture firms in Korea. Foreign direct invested producer services are also concentrated in Seoul. The concentration of new start-ups, high-tech firms, R&D institutions of private firms in Gangnam area made the area as an innovation centre in Korea.

Local networks and embeddedness are strong in this area. There are strong inter-firm networks and collaboration within Gangnam and Seoul. Collective learning processes with formal and informal meetings can be regarded as a distinct culture of Gangnam. There are no leading research universities within Gangnam, but top ranking research universities and various private R&D centres are located in Seoul. Gangnam can be regarded as a learning region in Korea with continuing processes of collective learning through intensive local networks. It should be noted that information infrastructure of the Gangnam area is excellent and diverse international conferences and exhibition are held in convention centres or hotels in Gangnam area.

The sources of tacit knowledge form an interesting story. About one third of the responded firms regard that R&D activity within firms is the most important source for acquisition of tacit knowledge regarding product and process technology (Figure 2.1). However, personal relations and inter-firm relations are also important sources of the knowledge. For product technology, more than one quarter of firms regard the personal relations of the CEO and related employees as the most important sources for the tacit knowledge. More than 16 per cent of the firms consider suppliers or customers are important sources for tacit knowledge.

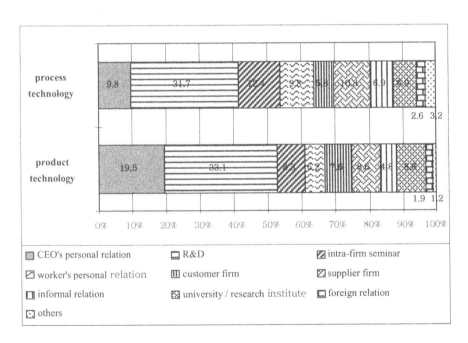

Figure 2.1   Source of Tacit Knowledge of Product and Process Technology

Source: Based on interview surveys in 2002.

Figure 2.1 shows that formal and informal relations with personnel and institutions are more important sources for acquisition of tacit knowledge for product and process technology than are formal R&D activities. This result is consistent with the survey result of OECD (1999a and 1999b), in which R&D shares only 33.5 per cent of the breakdown of innovation expenditures of the OECD countries. Networks of key economic actors are important in Gangnam. Entrepreneurs in Gangnam area have on average two formal meetings and three informal meeting per month. There are many informal meeting groups such as E-Business Club, Software Industry Club, Network Communication Club, Venture Leaders Club, I-Partnership and so on. In these informal meetings, many entrepreneurs, engineers, university professors, and venture capitalists gather to share their information and knowledge.

Overall, firms in Gangnam area have strong localized networks of innovation even though they have the innovation networks in other various spatial scales such as regional, national, and international levels. Their economic behaviours are embedded culturally and socially in Kangnam. They have significant international networks of innovation, especially with the USA, but the collective learning processes within Gangnam area are more important for innovation than national and international networks, representing localized innovation systems based on local networks and embeddedness are evolving.

Sunchang is located in a mountainous and peripheral area in southwestern Korea. Its population has continuously decreased since 1970s. Agriculture has been the key economic sector and traditionally major agricultural products in this area were tobacco, red pepper, and diverse mountainous vegetables and fruits. Gochoojang, thick soypaste mixed with red pepper, has been famous products of Sunchang because of its distinct taste with fermentation process. Most of the houses have made their own Gochoojang.

Since late 1990s the production system of the Gochoojang has been significantly changed. On the one hand, Daesang company, one of large company in food industry of Korea, established a branch plant in Sunchang to produce standardized Gochoojang under the brand of 'Sunchang Gochoojang' with quality control and maintaining the traditional taste. Daesang company has advertised the quality of Sunchang Gochoojang and has continued R&D activities in order to replicate quality when introducing automated mass production system. The case of Daesang shows that production technology of a large company is linked to local resources and culture. That is, the CK of the Daesang company is linked to locally embedded TK and resources.

On the other hand, Sunchang County designed a complex in order to gather together in one place the traditional Sunchang Gochoojang makers. The County allowed skilled persons, who have a license to make traditional Gochoojang with more than 10-year experience in making the traditional Gochoojang, to move their households into the complex. Fifty-four households moved in to make their own specialized traditional Gochoojang. They have their own market to sell their products and also started to sell their products through Internet to consumers in large cities.

Sunchang County also established a research lab in the complex to support quality control of the traditional Gochoojang. In the research lab, four researchers (one Ph.D., one doctoral student, and two with a Master's degree) conduct quality control and research to develop new products using one of local resources-raspberry. The idea to use raspberry instead of bean as an input material of fermentation originated from the fact the raspberry-wine, which is produced locally in Sunchang using the local raspberry in recent years, is good for health. In order to develop new Gochoojang using raspberry, the researchers frequently contacted local traditional Gochoojang makers, engineers of Daesang company, and survey Internet website to gather information and knowledge. The researchers also sought information from the faculty in Jeonbook National University located in Jeonjoo, about 60 km distance from Sunchang. Locally embedded resources and knowledge are networked with non-local institution to secure the development of the new product. In this case, local networks and embeddedness are continuously linked to non-local institutions, suggesting possibility of developing innovation and production systems even in the underdeveloped peripheral areas.

There is no surprise in the development of local innovation systems in Gangnam based on local networks and embeddedness. However, the Sunchang case suggests a new paradigm in the organization of production systems and economic spaces is emerging even in the peripheral areas, with respect to developing new ideas based on intensive local and non-local networks.

Conclusion

The new economic spaces are the result of processes of economic activities organized by actors whose economic behaviours are embedded in social relations, culture and environment over space and time. Accordingly, economic activities in the space evolve in relation with social, cultural, political, and historical developments as well as with pure economic rationality. The new economic spaces are dynamic over time with continuous processes of networking among agents in society over space and embedding into the social, cultural, and political structure of society. Innovation clusters are linked to each other in the global space economy beyond the regional or national boundary. They are linked into production centres with dispersing modular production systems and integrated into the global production networks.

The new paradigm in the organization of economic spaces and production systems is emerging even in the peripheral areas. The role of key economic actors in the organization of the new economic spaces is tremendously important in the digital era. The emerging new economic spaces are also closely related to the new techno-economic paradigm based on the development of ICT. Accordingly, supplying and maintaining qualified human capital and talent are critical for the development of innovation systems and for regional development.

New economic geographies have better opportunity to contribute to public policy because of their reflexive and pluralistic nature. Even in the peripheral regions, the process oriented analysis on new economic spaces can be useful to suggest appropriate policy directions and regional innovation strategies. The policy makers should consider the development of an environment for attracting qualified labour power and facilitating interactions of economic agents in addition to the provision of ICT infrastructure as one of the more important strategies in the information society. Developing diverse regional innovation systems considering the processes of new economic spaces is also an important strategy for regional development even in the peripheral regions (Park, 2001). However, because the new economic spaces are now dynamically emerging, more theoretical and empirical studies are required to understand clearly the process of the new economic spaces and to suggest appropriate policy directions for regional growth and development.

References

Antipode, 32(2) (2001), Special issue on 'Debating Economic Geography'.

Boggs, J. S. and Rantisi, N. M. (2003), 'The "Relational Turn" in Economic Geography', *Journal of Economic Geography*, 3(2): pp. 109-116.

Bunnell, T. G. and Coe, N. M. (2001), 'Spaces and Scales of Innovation', *Progress in Human Geography*, 25: pp. 569-589.

Dicken, P. and Thrift, N. (1992), 'The Organization of Production and the Production of Organization', *Transactions, Institute of British Geographers*, 17: pp. 279-291.

Dicken, P., Kelly, P., Olds, K., Yeung, H.W.C. (2001), 'Chains and Networks, Territories and Scales: Towards a Relational Framework for Analyzing the Global Economy', *Global Networks*, 1: pp. 89-112.

Ettlinger, N. (2003), 'Cultural Economic Geography and a Relational and Microspace Approach to Trusts, Rationalities, Networks, and Change in Collaborative Workplace', *Journal of Economic Geography*, 3(2): pp. 145-172.

Grabher, G. (ed.) (1993), *The Embedded Firm. On the Socioeconomics of Industrial Networks*, London, New York: Routledge.

Grannovetter, M. (1985), 'Economic Action and Social Structure: The Problem of Embeddedness', *American Journal of Sociology*, 91: pp. 481-510.

Grotz, R. and Braun, B. (1997), 'Territorial or Trans-Territorial Networking: Spatial Aspects of Technology Oriented Cooperation within the German Mechanical Engineering Industry', *Regional Studies*, 31(6): pp. 545-558.

Journal of Economic Geography, 3(2) (2003), Special issue on 'Relational Economic Geography'.

Malecki, E. J. and Oinas, P. (1999), *Making Connections: Technological Learning and Regional Economic Change*, Aldershot: Ashgate.

Malecki, E. J. (1997), 'Entrepreneurs, Networks, and Economic Development: A Review of Recent Research', *Advances in Entrepreneurship, Firm Emergence, and Growth*, 3: pp. 57-118.

Maskell, P. and Malmberg, A. (1999), 'Localized learning and industrial competitiveness', *Cambridge Journal of Economics*, 23: pp. 167-185.

Murphy, J. T. (2003), 'Social Space and Industrial Development in East Africa: Deconstructing the Logics of Industry Networks in Mwanza, Tanzania', *Journal of Economic Geography*, 3(2): pp. 173-198.

OECD (1999a), *Managing National Innovation Systems*. OECD, Paris.

OECD (1999b), *Boosting Innovation: The Cluster Approach*. OECD, Paris.

Park, S. O. (1996), 'Network and Embeddedness in the Dynamic Types of New Industrial Districts', *Progress in Human Geography*, 20 (4): pp. 476-493.

Park, S. O. (2001), 'Regional Innovation Strategies for Regional Development in the Knowledge-Based Economy', *Geojournal*, 53: pp. 29-38.

Park, S. O. (2002), 'Local and Global Networks of Innovation', in Alvstam, C. and Schamp, E. (eds), *Linking Industries Across the World: Process of Global Networking*.

Park, S. O. (2003), 'Economic Spaces in the Pacific Rim: A Paradigm Shift and New Dynamics', *Papers in Regional Science*, 82(2): pp. 223-247.

Park, S. O. and Markusen, A. (1995), 'Generalizing New Industrial Districts: A Theoretical Agenda and an Application from a Non-Western Economy', *Environment and Planning A*, 27: pp. 81-104.

Park, S. O. and Nahm, K. B. (1998), 'Spatial Structure and Inter-Firm Networks of Technical and Information Producer Services in Seoul, Korea', *Asia Pacific Viewpoints*, 39(2): pp. 209-219.

Polanyi, K. (1944), *The Great Transformation*, New York: Holt, Rinehart.

Saxenian, A. and Hsu, J. Y. (2001), 'The Silicon Valley-Hsinchu Connection: Technical Communities and Industrial Upgrading', *Industrial and Corporate Change*, 10(4): pp. 893-920.

Shin, C. H. (2001), *Clustering Information Technology Industries in Seoul*, SDI 2001-R-20, Seoul Development Institute.

Storper, M. and Salais, R. (1997), *Worlds of Production: The Action Frameworks of the Economy*, Cambridge, MA: Harvard University Press.

Sturgeon, T. J. (2003), 'What Really Goes on in Silicon Valley? Spatial Clustering and Dispersal in Modular Production Networks', *Journal of Economic Geography*, 3(2): pp. 199-225.

Yeung, H. W. C. (2000a), 'Embedding Foreign Affiliates in Transnational Business Networks: The Case of Hong Kong Firms in Southeast Asia', *Environment and Planning A*, 32: pp. 201-222.

Yeung, H. W. C. (2000b), 'Organizing "The Firm" in Industrial Geography. Part 1: Networks, Institutions and Regional Development', *Progress in Human Geography*, 24: pp. 301-315.

Yeung, H. W. C. (2003), Practicing New Economic Geographies: A Methodological Examination, *Annals of Association of American Geographers*, 93(2): pp. 445-466.

Chapter 3

High Tech 'Large Firms' in Greater Vancouver, British Columbia: Congregation without Clustering?

Roger Hayter, Kevin G. Rees and Jerry Patchell

Introduction

This chapter addresses the potentials of high technology (high tech) activities in the Vancouver metropolitan area of British Columbia, Canada. This sector is key to the region's re-definition of itself as a different if not new kind of economic space. Expectations in this regard are legitimate. Vancouver metro is a large, fast growing and high-income community offering diverse amenities, superior educational infrastructure and a highly skilled labour. Vancouver metro is a major port, a gateway to the Pacific Rim, is in the same time zone as Silicon Valley and two hours drive from Seattle and Microsoft's research and development (R&D) campus. To a significant degree Vancouver metro's high tech base derives from entrepreneurial initiatives. These initiatives and associated policy hopes, however, are at a crucial threshold. While high tech activities in Vancouver metro have grown considerably in recent years, the growth has been from a small base and its sustainability is in question (Rees, 1999).

The chapter's assessment of high tech activities in Vancouver metro focuses on 'large firms' (Hayter et al., 1999; Patchell et al., 1999). Large firms (LFs) define a distinct business segment whose characteristics combine attributes of small and medium sized firms (SMEs) and giant multinational corporations (MNCs). Thus LFs are entrepreneurial and focused in specific product markets, similar to SMEs. Simultaneously, LFs exploit economies of scale and scope to operate internationally through exports and even direct foreign investment (DFI), similar to MNCs. LFs are dynamic and innovative, able and willing to grow beyond the limits and comfort levels associated with SMEs, and to compete with MNCs in global market niches. Yet, LFs remain committed to their home localities because of involvement by founders and decision-makers who typically connect to local educational and research institutions, and help shape local technology policy. Whether local embeddedness of LFs is further reflected in links with local suppliers is another matter. LFs may either constitute the leaders of localized clusters or networks of closely related activities or operate largely independently of local supply connections, part of a congregation of firms but not a tightly knit cluster. Whatever the case, we argue that LFs anchor local high tech activities, especially in new or changing economic spaces such as Vancouver metro that are not the home bases for giant high tech firms.

Elsewhere we refer to LFs as 'ideal types' of business segmentation and heuristically explored their behaviour in specific sectoral settings within Japan and the USA (Hayter et al., 1999; Patchell et al., 1999). Here we elaborate on LFs (across the high tech sector) from a local development perspective. Conceptually, we explore the theme of LFs as 'big firms locally' in which 'big' refers to dynamism, innovation and local impacts, and not simply to size. Empirically, the study draws on several sources of information, notably original surveys of high tech firms in the biotechnology and telecommunications industries of Vancouver metro (Rees, 1999; 2004), interviews with selected LFs in 2002 and 2003, provincial government sponsored studies that define British Columbia's (BC) high tech sector (BC Stats, nd), and a new 'high tech map' of BC (Calyniuk, 2003). We conceive of high tech activities as comprising relatively research-intensive activities, investing at least 5 per cent of sales in R&D and product design activities.

The chapter initially discusses relationships between LFs and local development. It then provides a brief historical background on Vancouver metro's economy, a general review of the general characteristics of the region's high tech activities, and finally looks at local firms that qualify or potentially qualify as LFs. We conclude by reflecting on the nature of Vancouver's high tech economy as a cluster or congregation.

Large Firms as Big Firms Locally

The dual model of business segmentation, in which a few giant, powerful MNCs dominate groupings of SMEs is part of economic geography's consciousness. Indeed, the dual model defines a significant reality that MNCs and SMEs are different kinds of institutions, each with their own rules and conventions, strategies and structures and each with vastly different social consequences. Simultaneously, the resilient size distribution of firms that characterises industrial economies suggests that if business segmentation exists, the dual model over-simplifies segmentation processes. Thus pioneering studies from various national and cultural contexts have argued persuasively that there is an important middle segment (comprised of LFs) that cannot be easily categorised as SMEs or giant MNCs. In the USA LFs have been called 'little giants' (Kuhn, 1992), *chuken* or 'backbone firms' in Japan (Nakamura, 1990), and 'hidden champions' in Germany (Simon, 1992). In Canada, Steed (1982) refers to 'threshold firms' that are on the cusp of crossing a boundary between SMEs and a qualitatively different, likely bigger organisational type.

These apparently independent studies recognise a new segment of firms. As 'ideal types', these LFs share important characteristics that distinguish them from SMEs and giants. Ideal types of LFs are conceived as entrepreneurially organized firms that employ highly trained, functionally flexible workforces to produce specialised product mixes for international markets, often buttressed by branch plant operations. In their market niches LFs are typically global market leaders with global marketing networks and are committed to ongoing research, development and innovation. Simon calls LFs hidden champions because they are scarcely known outside of their own market niches. Nakamura refers to LFs as backbones because of their dynamic contributions to jobs, investment and innovation in the sectors in which they operate. For Kuhn, LFs provide a 'loyal opposition' that offsets the power of the true giants and ensure more competitive markets, wider consumer choice and democratic socio-economic systems.

As a distinct segment, LFs share the entrepreneurialism and flexibility of SMEs with an ability to exploit economies of scope and scale in supplying products and services to global markets. But it is not simply their entrepreneurial nature that distinguishes LFs from giants. While giants seek competitive advantage by seeking cost leadership or product differentiation across a *wide range* of goods, LFs seek more *focused* cost leadership or differentiation on a limited set of goods. LFs typically focus core technologies to limited product ranges to drive down costs by intensifying economies of scale or to gain advantages through differentiated innovations that exploit economies of scope within their specialist fields. LFs retain this focus even as they expand internationally.

The recognition of LFs implies a triad model of business segmentation where the boundaries between segments are more permeable than characterised in the dual model. In the latter model, the only connections between segments reflect the domination of the giants over SMEs, for example by acquisition or threats of acquisition. The triad model raises the real possibility of firms moving between segments ('upwards and downwards'), for the giants to be opposed by LF competition and for LFs to become giants. In this regard, if giants impose powerful barriers to small firm growth, the emergence of LFs must be based on some competitive advantage dominated by giants, most obviously realised through know-how based innovations. Giants can establish property rights over their existing knowledge through patents and brand names and reinforce this protection through marketing and production networks. However, LFs define a dynamic segment of firms that are fundamentally driven by innovation. As committed innovators, LFs can similarly protect the know-how they create and they need not succumb to acquisition threats from giants. Thus LFs exploit innovations to break out of the SME segment and to maintain their competitive advantages vis-à-vis the giants. In contrast, many giants are expansion driven while the majority of SMEs remain small, whether from internal preference or market dictates.

Recognition of LFs and the triad model of business segmentation have profound implications for local development. First, and perhaps foremost, LFs require economic geography to broaden its way of thinking about local development and policy, traditionally dominated by the giant firm-SME duality. Industrial location policy, for example, originated as attempts to re-direct branch plants from core regions to designated regions. Subsequently, policies were introduced to promote indigenous potentials and locally controlled SMEs. Recent interest in production systems, industrial districts and inter-firm relations has parallel policy concerns for promoting clusters of firms. Yet, even this literature primarily distinguishes core-firm-based and SME controlled production systems and still typically depicts giants firms as dominating and exploiting SMEs. The growing interest in inter-firm learning is also typically conceptualized within giant-SME relations, disregarding the distinctive role of LFs. The very existence of LFs relies on the ability to internally harness innovation-driven competitive advantages and derive dominating shares of important niche markets that are typically global in scope. Explicit awareness of LFs encourages a more sophisticated, nuanced understanding of relationships between industrial organization and local development than is provided by the dual model.

From the perspective of local development, LFs as learning systems can be expected to contribute directly to skill formation, innovation and value added developments that offer hope for income maintenance and perhaps for progressively increasing incomes. Where LFs become sizeable they can be 'big locally', especially in their home region where they may employ a thousand people and generate sales in the billions. These impacts are multiplied when LFs become committed to local regions and forge local linkages. LFs are big enough to organize their own extensive social divisions of labour and become a source of entrepreneurial spin-offs.

LFs collectively contribute to a dispersal of decision-making control, especially in comparison to the giants. On the basis of the size distribution of firms more LFs than giants are to be expected with greater possibilities for dispersal. Indeed, there is evidence that the location preferences of LFs and giants for their head-offices are considerably different and that in practice LFs are more dispersed. In the USA, for example, the Top 500 corporation head-offices are strongly concentrated in relatively few leading cities. In contrast, the headquarter locations of 100 'little giants', as listed by *Business Week* in 1993, are more dispersed among small towns and suburban areas of larger metropoles. In the German context, a central claim of Simon (1992, p. 122) was that Germany's hidden champions had strong location preferences for relatively small and remote places, including 'towns that most Germans had never even heard of'. The preference for remote communities reflects a desire 'to develop self-reliance on technical competence' through an internal division of labour and for developing close interdependencies between management and labour, as well as the strong ties of the founder. In this view, operations in isolated locations help protect proprietary knowledge and allow firms to control vital processes that are judged important from a quality and a security point of view.

LFs play a special role in the development of high tech activities in new economic spaces or the development of new high tech activities in old economic spaces. New locations can attract branch operations of giant high tech firms involving manufacturing and/or R&D. Even in the case of R&D units, however, concerns continue to be expressed about their contribution to long term local technological capability. The problem with SMEs in developing new high tech activities in a locale is their smallness; a large number of independently driven SMEs are required to exert notable collective impacts. LFs, however, are big locally and have wide ranging location preferences even with respect to their most sophisticated activities. For regions without home grown giants their presence may well be crucial for sustained development of high tech activities. This chapter now considers these ideas contextually in the new economic space of Vancouver metro, and the region's evolving high tech sector.

General Characteristics of High Tech Activities in Vancouver Metro

Vancouver metro has developed high tech activities to help replace its declining industrial base centred around forest products. This 'old' industrial economy, that featured sawmilling, other wood processing activities, equipment supply and engineering services, had itself established Vancouver metro as a classic new economic space within global capitalism late in the nineteenth century. Especially since the early 1980s, the BC's forest sector experienced deep-seated restructuring. Vancouver metro, however, was economically and socially buoyant, a diversified 'post-modern' city (Ley, 1980), whose population growth is fuelled by in-migration from the rest of Canada and elsewhere. A diversified range of small secondary wood processing firms have become increasingly important in Vancouver metro and provide connections to the city's resource history (Rees and Hayter, 1996). Vancouver metro has also attracted other specialised industries that have re-defined it as an economic space, notably tourism as illustrated by the cruise ship industry; a film industry with studios in Vancouver, Burnaby and North Vancouver; and a high tech industry. We turn now to the high tech activities of Vancouver metro (Figure 3.1).

Although Vancouver metro's resource base was associated with a large-scale export-oriented commodity culture, it rested on a distinct innovation system with sophisticated levels of engineering know-how in various public and private sector organizations. Resource exploitation required all kinds of adaptive R&D and imaginative engineering solutions. Only a few corporations invested in in-house R&D but there were various industry association and government laboratories. BC Hydro was an important provincial crown corporation that accumulated high levels of engineering expertise in the 1960s. The provincial university system expanded at this time beyond the University of British Columbia (UBC). In addition, vibrant engineering consulting and capital equipment supply industries that were themselves export oriented by the 1960s supplied technology across the resource industries. The demise of these manufacturing and service firms, primarily in Vancouver metro, constitutes BC's first failure to retain a (local) high tech sector.

The immigrant-entrepreneurs who first stimulated the resource sector on a large-scale also established pioneering forms of contemporary high tech activities in BC. Donald Hings began as an inventor by developing the 'walkie talkie' in remote areas of BC in the 1930s before its use in World War 2 (Hanson, 2001). Spillsbury Communications (founded 1940) also pioneered radio communications in BC, as did Lenkurt Electric (founded 1949). The latter eventually 'morphed' into the R&D arm of BC Tel (now Telus) to become MPR Teltech, with each firm emerging as an early local leader. Glenayre was established in 1963 (in general machinery) and by 1969 had chosen to focus on electronics. By the 1980s Glenayre was a high tech (LF) firm in BC, becoming the world's largest manufacturer of pagers. Until its closure in 1999 Glenayre employed about 300-400 engineers and a manufacturing workforce. The founding of MacDonald Dettwiler (MD) in 1969 most effectively symbolizes the emergence of a modern high tech industry in Vancouver metro. UBC Engineers Bob MacDonald and Norm Dettwiler were stimulated to establish their company as a way of employing engineering graduates in BC, especially as BC Hydro was then beginning to downsize its operations. Since then, MD has engaged in satellite communications among other activities to become the flagship high tech LF in BC.

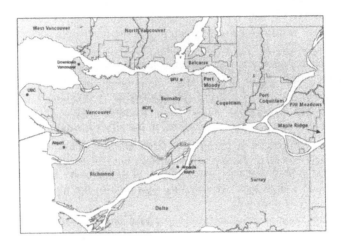

Figure 3.1   Vancouver Metro: Main Municipalities

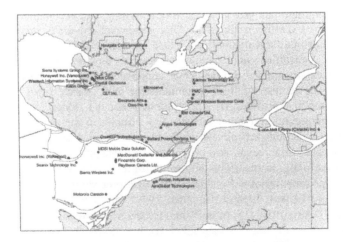

Figure 3.2   Location of BC's Top High Tech Firms, 2003

Bearing in mind the difficulties of precise calculations of size, available reports indicate recent growth of BC's high tech sector. According to BC Stats (nd) employment in the sector grew from 27,240 in 1988 to 41,350 in 1995. High tech's share of the BC economy rose from 1.8 per cent of provincial GDP in 1988 to 2.6 per cent in 1995. Mike Volker, Director of Simon Fraser University's (SFU) Industry Liaison Office, has stated that in 2001 BC's high tech sector directly employed over 60,000 people and contributed 3.9 per cent of provincial GDP. Vancouver's total workforce in 2001 was about 1 million. Another study estimates that the forest sector directly employed 21,000 people in Metropolitan Vancouver in 1996 and contributed about 1.7 per cent to provincial GDP (The Chancellor Partners, 1997).

High tech activities in Vancouver metro dominate the provincial scene (BC Stats, nd). In 1995, 66.7 per cent of high tech establishments in BC were in Vancouver metro and another 10.5 per cent were in the Victoria area (and still more on southern Vancouver Island as a whole). Further concentrations are found in the inner suburbs within Vancouver metro. The distribution of BC's top 20 high tech firms, for example, favours locations within Burnaby and Richmond (Figure 3.2). This is similar to the distribution of telecommunication firms (Rees, 1999).

High tech activities in Vancouver metro are strongly research, design, information, software and/or service oriented. High tech manufacturing is not significant and is probably declining. Many of Vancouver's high tech firms have failed to make profits or generate revenues. Rees (2004) identifies this situation in Vancouver metro's emerging biotechnology sector where the solely research based process is lengthy and costly and has resulted in most firms accruing substantial deficits. Vancouver metro also lacks a large-scale pharmaceutical manufacturing facility. Vancouver metro's highest profile non-profitable high tech firm is Ballard Energy, a fuel cell developer. Some products generate revenues (e.g. power supply units in Japan) but the firm has never been profitable and does not anticipate overall corporate profitability for at least ten years.

Although the high tech sector in Vancouver is relatively small it is remarkably diverse. BC Stats (nd) noted that 3 service industries generated 73.1 per cent of the $5.1 billion revenue generated by high tech in BC in 1995, namely engineering services (36 per cent), computer and related services (23 per cent) and science and technical services (16 per cent). A more sophisticated categorisation of BC's high tech activity by Calyniuk's (2003) maps high tech activities into nine main (and diverse) groups; software, telecommunications and wireless communications, electronics and peripherals, life sciences, energy technologies, services, new media, semiconductors and advanced manufacturing.

The provincial government had hopes for a high tech transportation sector in the 1990s and sought to replace its ageing fleet of coastal ferries by building a new fleet of 'fast ferries' based on Australian technology. Three were built, principally in North Vancouver, briefly put into service in 2000, but because of cost over-runs and poor performance, the ferries were phased out after costs of nearly $500 million. The provincial government also sought to stimulate high tech manufacturing in a rapid transit system for Vancouver metro. Thus it subsidized Bombardier, a Montreal-based MNC, to manufacture the train cars for the rapid transit system in a factory in Burnaby. Yet, very few cars were needed, anticipated export orders never materialised and the factory is now closed.

A prior provincial government initiative was the so-called Discovery Park Policy (1979). Discovery parks were established adjacent to the campuses of UBC in Vancouver, Simon Fraser University (SFU) and the British Columbia Institute of Technology (BCIT) in Burnaby, and the University of Victoria (Victoria). While the intention was to provide low-rent infrastructure for small firms that could draw on the expertise of the universities and BCIT, the impacts were minimal. In 1991, however, Discovery Park Inc was re-mandated to allow sales of land within the Discovery Parks so firms could own their land and buildings.

Provincial policy can claim to have been rhetorically supportive and mildly facilitative of high tech activities in Vancouver metro. Yet compared to other jurisdictions its efforts are minor and the most important direct initiatives have been failures. The federal government has provided tax incentives for R&D but these are available across the country and its direct stimulus to BC's high tech sector can be ignored. BC's high tech activity is very much 'home grown' and dependent on the private sector.

Diversity and Fragmentation of Vancouver Metro's High Tech Sector: A Large Firm Perspective

While Calynuik (2003) sought to reveal high tech clusters and specialisms in Vancouver metro, we suggest that diversity and fragmentation are more appropriate defining features of it's high tech sector. Thus Rees (1999; 2004) critically examined the clustering qua localised networking assertion within the context of the (new) biotechnology and (longer established) telecommunications industries, the former corresponding to Calyniuk's life sciences and the latter to both telecommunications and wireless communications, and electronics and peripherals. Rees found most firms had strong local entrepreneurial roots and many had important contacts with specific local research institutions, such as UBC and the BC Cancer Research Institute. Nevertheless, Rees (2004) found the degree of local networking even within these clusters to be limited, and that non-local networks were vitally important to the R&D activities of emergent and established firms.

Reference to the largest 20 high tech firms across all sectors, as ranked by sales and employment according to Calynuik (2003), provides further insights into the structure of high tech activities in Vancouver metro (Table 3.1). The BC based firms range in size from sales of just over $1 billion in 2001 (Creo) to $57 million (Ballard) while the pure, non-direct sales generating R&D operations of firms such as IBM are ranked only with respect to employment. The firms, none of which are multinational high tech giants, vary in the extent to which their employment is located in Vancouver metro. With the special exception of Telus (known as the 'telephone company' for BC and Alberta), the largest high tech operations in Vancouver metro range from around 325 to 1500 jobs.

Table 3.1   The Top 20 High Tech Companies in BC, 2001

2001 Revenue ($000)			2001 Employment		
Rank	*Company*		*Rank*	*Company*	
1.	Creo Inc.	1,018,225	1.	Telus Corp.	25,752[1]
2.	Macdonald, Dettwiler and Assoc	481,300	2.	Creo Inc.	4,050
3.	PMC-Sierra Ltd.	346,200	3.	IBM Canada	-
4.	Xantrex Technology Inc.	170,000	4.	Ballard Power Systems	1,300
5.	Seanix Technology Inc.	152,000	5.	Crystal Decisions	1,703
6.	QLT Inc.	129,470	6.	MacDonald Dettwiler	2,225
7.	Pivotal Corp.	128,800	7.	Electronic Arts Canada	
8.	Sierra Systems Group Inc.	128,760	8.	PMC Sierra	1,099
9.	AimGlobal Technologies	123,000	9.	Avcorp Industries	400
10.	Creation Technology Inc.	94,199	10.	Raytheon Canada	1,500
11.	Avcorp Industries Inc.	93,300	11.	QLT Inc.	336
12.	Sierra Wireless Inc.	92,480	12.	Creation Technologies	650
13.	MDSI Mobile Data Solutions	89,956	13.	MDSI Mobile Technologies	325
14.	Argus Technologies	79,000	14.	Sierra Systems Group	909
15.	Aston Group	76,000	15.	Westech Information	-
16.	Power Measurement	70,000	16.	E-One Moli Energy	-
17.	Navigata Communications	61,549	17.	Top Producer Systems	-
18.	Fincentric Corp.	61,100	18.	Honeywell Inc.	2,800[2]
19.	Microserve	58,750	19.	Motorola	1,000[2]
20.	Ballard Power Systems	57,000	20.	Glentel	-

Source: Mainly T-Net British Columbia.
[1] Telus is based in Western Canada; [2] Corporate Canada-wide employment. For the other firms, employment is predominantly or wholly concentrated in BC.

The ranking of 'large' firms purely in terms of employment and sales does not equate to LFs as an ideal type of business segment as discussed previously in the paper. Indeed, on the employment rankings, we argue that there are just two 'classic' LFs that closely approximate the ideal type, Creo and MacDonald Dettwiler (MD), while Electronic Arts (EA) is a 'virtual' LF (Table 3.2). Thus EA functions as a (local) LF, although it is foreign owned. There are, however, a number of locally based firms that have recently grown rapidly and may be regarded as potential' or emergent LFs. In addition, there are a number of subsidiary operations and the above-mentioned anomalous Telus.

Table 3.2   Segmentation of Largest Vancouver-based High Tech Firms

Company	Segmentation Type
1. Telus	'Regional Giant' in telecommunications and wireless communications.
2. Creo	Classic LF in electronics and peripherals category.
3. IBM Canada	Subsidiary of US-based computer giant in software category.
4. Ballard	Emergent LF in energy technologies category.
5. Crystal Decisions	Subsidiary of US-based LF in software category.
6. MacDonald Dettwiler	Classic LF in software category.
7. Electronic Arts	Virtual LF in software category.
8. PMC Sierra	Main R&D arm of US-based LF in semiconductor category.
9. Avcorp Industries	Medium sized firm in advanced manufacturing category.
10. Raytheon	Subsidiary of US-based giant in electronics and peripherals, and advanced manufacturing categories.
11. QLT	Emergent LF in life sciences category.
12. Creation Technologies	Emergent LF in electronics and peripherals category
13. MDSI	Emergent LF in software and telecommunications categories.
14 Sierra Systems	Emergent LF in telecommunications and wireless categories.
15. Westech Info Systems	Medium sized firm in software category.
16. E-Moli Energy	Subsidiary of Taiwanese-based company in energy category.
17. Top Producer Systems	Medium size firm in software category.
18. Honeywell	Subsidiary of US-based giant in energy technology category.
19. Motorola	Subsidiary of US-based giant in telecommunications and wireless communications catagory.
20. Glentel	Medium sized firm in telecommunications and wireless communications category.

Note: List based on employment rankings (Table 1). Categories based on Calynuik (2003).

The diversity and fragmentation of Vancouver's high tech sector is reflected in the composition and behaviour of these largest 20 high tech companies. These firms are highly varied in terms of product or activity focus. For both rankings by sales and employment, eight of the nine categories identified by Calynuik (2003) are represented (there is no large 'new media' firm). Even those classified in the same category are different. MD, EA and Crystal Decisions, for example, are software companies. Yet MD provides services for the aerospace and real estate industries, EA designs games and Crystal Decisions provides business development software. Similarly, while Ballard and Xantrex are both power-generation companies, Ballard focuses on developing hydrogen fuel cells for vehicles, while Zantrex focuses on solar energy products. Indeed, there are no examples of direct competition among the firms listed in the top 20, a feature that has probably limited the potential for local linkages and collaboration within Vancouver metro.

Moreover, the largest 20 high tech companies in Vancouver metro are not part of rich localised networks, especially within the private sector. The subsidiary operations, for example, are important employers of skilled labour and/or scientists and engineers and indeed part of their rationale is to tap into local expertise. Yet mandates of these subsidiaries are prescribed closely by parents based elsewhere, intra-corporate ties dominate over external local ties, and future growth depends on parental discretion. In this respect, EA is an unusual (US-based) subsidiary. Its competitive advantages are largely based on a North Vancouver-based company it acquired in 1991 and whose local founders are EA's key decision makers. In addition, EA's largest and most significant design and development studios are in Burnaby, where the games are created and are globally distributed from. Although ownership resides in California, EA is a virtual (Vancouver metro) LF and continues to expand locally.

Indeed, Creo, MD and EA are run by locally born entrepreneurs, each on the leading edge of highly sophisticated products and services. They serve global markets in which they have significant market shares, they have offices and operations beyond BC, and they have established distinctive forms of flexible work organisation designed to facilitate employee participation and commitment. They are all big firms locally and are well connected to local labour markets, yet they have few links to local supply systems.

Emergent or potential LFs behave in similar ways. QLT is a case in point. Like MD, QLT is a classic university spin-off, created in 1984 by a scientist at UBC. Among biotechnology companies (globally as well as in Vancouver metro) it is an unusual success story and its first pioneering drug to combat blindness continues to sell well even as QLT has commercialised other products. It sells world-wide, has forged strategic alliances with European and American partners, and frequently ranks as one of the best companies in which to work within BC. However, while it has strong links with UBC and the BC Cancer Research Unit its R&D connections are mostly non-local and its manufacturing occurs elsewhere.

Manufacturing is extremely limited among Vancouver's latest high tech companies. Avcorp Industries is the only firm Calynuik classifies as an 'advanced manufacturer', specializing in tail stabilizers and related components for commercial aircraft. Both Creo and Avcorp emphasize high quality in their production process but neither relies on local subcontracting, claiming that high quality local suppliers are not available. Similarly, Ballard Energy builds and tests its fuel cells in vehicles and portable power equipment in Burnaby, but should manufacturing become large-scale production would shift out of the province. Glenayre, a leading global supplier of pagers, was the last major high tech volume manufacturer in Vancouver metro, until the relocation of production in 1992 and its complete closure in 1999. As a one-time classic LF, Glenayre's restructuring and the deeply felt loss of over 500 jobs following its take-over by a US-based giant indicates the vulnerability of the region's high tech base. Paradoxically, it may also be concluded that the very diversity of LFs and emergent LFs hints at the growing maturity of Vancouver metro's high tech sector.

Vancouver Metro's High Tech Space as a Congregation of Talent

Across Canada, and elsewhere, there is much enthusiasm for the idea and potential of high tech clusters in Vancouver metro. Based on work in the USA, Florida (2002) claims that high tech activities are especially attracted to urban areas that offer both diverse location conditions, including multiple forms of amenity, and high levels of social tolerance and diversity that help contribute towards creativity. This argument has been well received in Canada and would indeed seem to be especially relevant to Vancouver with its multi-cultural population, embrace of different life styles and Pacific Rim as well as continental and European connections. Clusters, however, imply a localized social division of labour among a population of interacting firms in which rivalry and close inter-firm relations are key characteristics. Such social divisions of labour suggest clear sectoral specialisms.

In Vancouver metro, a distinctive sectoral 'high specialism' existed in the 1960s and 1970s in the form of a group of firms that specialized in the manufacture of various types of machinery for the resource sector. This 'cluster' is now much reduced. In its place, new types of high tech activities have emerged in a surprisingly wide range of sectors or categories. Among this apparently vibrant, emerging high tech sector, there is no single dominant or leading cluster that defines a distinctive localized social division of labour. The five case studies that we have noted in this paper as actual or potential 'LFs' are big firms locally but are different from one another. They therefore do not compete with other local firms, nor have they generated strong local supply systems. Rather, they have developed strong linkages outside of BC, typically globally characteristic of the fragmented, differentiated structure of Vancouver's high tech structure.

We suggest that Vancouver's high tech firms form a congregation rather than a cluster, all praising the virtues of free enterprise in general and the high tech culture in particular. As a congregation, they draw upon and contribute towards Vancouver as a high tech space yet retain their independence and differences. Despite its local usage, clusters of high tech activities are not apparent in the sense of a closely related, locally networked community. Moreover, such clusters are not likely to emerge. Vancouver metro in global terms is a relatively small market and a considerable distance from major centres of consumption. Government support for high tech in Vancouver is limited. Quebec has high tech priority in Canadian federal government circles while BC's provincial government policies have been ad hoc and unsuccessful or indirect. Further, high tech manufacturing in Vancouver metro is unlikely even on a modest scale as costs are relatively high for manufacturing, exports are vital and a strong anti-manufacturing culture has emerged in BC.

In contrast to the 'Japanese' model, LFs in Vancouver metro have therefore not stimulated a learning-based localised social division of labour. Rather, Vancouver metro's LFs have favoured greater local self-reliance similar to

Simon's (1992) claims for hidden champions in Germany. Yet, unlike the benefits enjoyed by the latter from their location in remote places, Vancouver metro's peripheral location has not protected LFs from technology loss and labour turnover.

Nevertheless, there are strong reasons to suppose that Vancouver metro will sustain a diversified high tech base and generate a range of LFs, highly innovative firms that are big locally. The quality of regional amenities is consistently recognized by various international organizations, typically ranking Vancouver in the top three cities in the world as a place to live. Vancouver metro is a diverse place with strong European, Pacific and continental connections and traditions. Already, a plethora of firms have demonstrated the viability of high tech in Vancouver metro by simultaneously exploiting global linkages of one kind or another. As for public policy, given the public sector's difficulties in identifying high tech priorities, let alone clusters, a continued emphasis on educational investment is probably the wisest emphasis.

Indeed there are many reasons why Vancouver may be an alternative model of high tech congregation in the early part of this century. As much manufacturing is 'offshored' to countries such as China and India that offer high tech skills *and* low wages, the windows for new clustering activities are rapidly closing. The continuance of clustering in old manufacturing bases may be vestigial and relatively short-lived. Outlying centres such as Vancouver are especially unlikely to develop a broad manufacturing base. The high tech future of these centres may well depend on their capacity to produce entrepreneurs who can turn innovation into LFs. These LFs may be isolated in their region but are integrated into the global economy.

Acknowledgements

The authors are grateful for the comments of Tim Reiffenstein and for the information provided by respondents at our case study firms.

References

BC Stats (nd), The British Columbia High Technology Sector 1988–1995, British Columbia: Information, Science and Technology Agency.

Brearton, S. and Daly, J. (2003), '50 best employers in Canada', *Globe and Mail*, 29 December, 2003. http://globeandmail.com/servlet/ArticleNews/TPStory/LAC/20031229/RO1BEST/TPBusiness/ROBM.

Calyniuk, M. (2003), *British Columbia's Techmap*, Vancouver: Pricewaterhouse Coopers.

Chancellor Partners. (1997), The Economic Impact of the Forest Industry on British Columbia and Metropolitan Vancouver, Vancouver: Commissioned by the Vancouver Board of Trade and Forest Alliance of BC.

Florida, R. (2002), 'The Economic Geography of Talent, *Annals of the Association of American Geographers*, 92: pp. 743-756.

Hanson, C. (2001), 'Walkie-Talkie Inventor Receives Order of Canada, *Vancouver Sun*, August 17: B1 and B7.

Hayter, R., Patchell, J. and Rees, K. G. (1999), 'Business Segmentation and Location Revisited: Innovation and the Terra Incognita of Large Firms', *Regional Studies*, 33: pp. 425-42.

Kuhn, R. L. (1992), Mid-sized Firms: Success Strategies and Methodologies, New York: Praeger.

Ley, D. F. (1980), 'Liberal Idealogy and the Post-Industrial City', *Annals of the Association of American Geographers*, 83: pp. 272-302.

Nakamura, H. (1990), *New Mid-Sized Firm Theory*, Tokyo: Keizai Shinpansha (In Japanese).

Patchell, J. R. (1993), 'Composing Robot Production Systems: Japan as a Flexible Manufacturing System', *Environment and Planning A* 25: pp. 923-44.

Patchell, J., Hayter, R. and Rees, K. G. (1999), 'Innovation and Local Development: The Neglected Role of Large Firms', in E. J. Malecki and P. Oinas (eds), *Making Connections: Technological Learning and Regional Economic Change*, Aldershot: Ashgate.

Rees, K. G. (1999), Innovation in the Periphery: Networks or Fragments in the High Technology Industry of Greater Vancouver. PhD thesis, Department of Geography, Simon Fraser University.

Rees, K. G. (2004), 'Collaboration, Innovation and Regional Networks: Evidence from the Medical Biotechnology Industry of Greater Vancouver', in A. Lagendijk and P. Oinas (eds), *Proximity, Distance and Diversity: Issues on Economic Interaction and Local Development*, London: Ashgate, in press.

Rees, K. G. and Hayter, R. (1996), 'Flexible Specialization, Uncertainty, and The Firm: Enterprise Strategies in the Wood Remanufacturing Industry of the Vancouver Metropolitan Area British Columbia', *The Canadian Geographer*, 40: pp. 203-219.

Simon, H. (1992), 'Lessons from Germany's Midsized Giants', *Harvard Business Review*, March-April: pp. 115-23.

Steed, G. P. F. (1982), 'Threshold Firms: Backing Canada's Winners', *Science Council of Canada*, Ottawa, Ministry of Supply and Services.

Withers, P. (2002), 'The Best Companies to Work For in B.C.', *BC Business Magazine*. http://www.bcbusinessmagazine.com/displayArticle.php?artId=256.

Chapter 4

Geographic Context and Radical Innovation: The Formation of Knowledge in the American and Japanese Electronic Musical Instrument Industries

Tim Reiffenstein

Introduction

Much of the literature of economic geography is concerned with understanding processes of incremental innovation (Asheim, 1999; Hudson, 1999). I reflect here on how episodes of *radical technological change* spawn new economic spaces. This lacuna in the economic geography literature on innovation needs investigation because these technological discontinuities destablize existing economic spaces while also creating new ones. Such episodes unseat entrenched advantages held by industrial cores. Indeed, entire foundations of regional advantage, which are underpinned by what Freeman (1982) terms a prevailing 'engineering common sense', are rendered obsolete as radical innovations illustrate the efficacy of applying entirely new approaches to solve old problems. In this manner, radical innovations simultaneously provide a platform from which other regions can leapfrog these cores. I examine this dynamic of creative destruction, by considering the mechanisms that draw spatially disparate *constellations of practice* (Coe and Bunnel, 2003) into alignment. Empirically, I illustrate these locational dynamics via a case study of knowledge transfer from the US to Japan in the electronic musical instrument industry.

Conceptually, I approach the problem of radical innovation through a critique and extension of the emerging literature on spatial innovation systems, which are problem solving networks transcending bounded scales of analysis (Amin and Cohendet, 1999; Gertler, 2001; Bunnel and Coe, 2001; Oinas and Malecki, 2002; Coe and Bunnel, 2003). This work debates the degree to which communities of practice (Wenger, 1998), defined by relational proximities, are able to mobilize knowledge over geographic space. Gertler (2001), in particular, questions Amin and Cohendet's (1999) assertion that the disciplinary and organizational relations underpinning such communities may be more important than geographical proximity for transferring 'best practices' amongst actors. Here I will highlight that in the contexts in which episodes of radical change emerge, there is little consensus as to what constitutes best practice. Consequently, actors scanning the horizon of these emerging technical landscapes are afforded only highly speculative and partial glimpses of their constitution. What unfolds is a situation in which different constellations of actors bring diverse practices to bear on a common problem. At this stage the transfer of knowledge over space is almost entirely discursive (as opposed to practical) in nature, and hinges on the rate of diffusion of codified knowledge. It is only when one constellation musters the resources to inscribe technological space in a proprietary manner that precludes the competition, that the dynamics of industrial advantage become decisive for establishing winners and losers.

Such a situation exists in the highly diverse community of engineers and inventors that create digital musical instruments. Unlike the preceding generation of instruments which relied on electro-mechanical knowledge foundations, these new instruments were grounded in the digital logic of the information and communications techno-economic prototype. So while engineers in the US and Japan could predict early-on that that micro-processors would have a profound impact on instrument design, the institutional mechanisms for realizing this objective still needed to be determined. My investigation of statements made by US engineers at the Audio Engineering Society conventions in the late 1960s and early 1970s is juxtaposed with perspectives derived from interviews with their Japanese counterparts working for Yamaha who reflect on the way in which that firm negotiated the transition to the digital age. I then analyze the patenting practices of Yamaha, in particular its strategies to appropriate key technologies developed in the US. It is this latter set of actions which proved decisive for *locking-in* the ascendancy of Japanese firms while simultaneously *locking-out* their American counterparts.

Radical Innovation

Innovation has received considerable attention in economic geography. At least implicitly, distinctions between incremental and radical innovations are widely recognized. Incremental innovations are minor improvements to existing technologies embodied in products and processes that occur almost constantly through everyday work practices, such as those that take place on the shopfloor. Radical innovations, in contrast, are discontinuities which appear infrequently, precipitating entirely new products, markets and ensuing capital investments. Innovations are radical if they could not have evolved through incremental improvements in the technology that they challenge in some particular use. For instance, the printing press could not have evolved out of the pen and quill. Radical innovations profoundly alter the production possibility frontier in a particular industry and offer the potential to redraw the economic landscape of a given sector.

Hudson (1999, p. 346) claims 'the issue of how radically new knowledge is produced and redefines "best practice" as radical innovations are created, is left largely unexplored'. Why this lacuna? I contend that radical innovation has been overlooked for two reasons. First, the adoption of the important Schumpeterian economic distinction between invention and innovation draws our focus towards the culmination of a process. So while it is important to recognize those breakthrough moments in which new markets are unmistakably spawned, it is necessary also to unravel the complex sequence of practices and instances (Lee, 2002) underlying the advance. Latour (1987) believed that to look only to the economic ends is to be content to view science as unproblematic and 'ready made'. Consequently, to understand radical innovation, geographers must deploy a set of tools to open technology's black box to reveal its geography. As geographers, we have failed to take advantage of our position to lend insight into the very radical spaces that take shape during these episodes which redefin the economic landscape in more than one place. Geographers have highlighted the ways in which place shapes technological innovation – viewing it as governed by practices that are embedded in a socio-cultural milieu. However, there has been little effort to broaden our horizon to accommodate various scales of analysis.

Innovation Systems as Constellations of Communities of Practice

Much of the geographical literature on industrial learning adopts a place-based perspective on innovation. The literature on national innovation systems (Lundvall, 1992), learning regions (Morgan, 1997) and regional innovation systems (Bracyk et al., 1998) assist understanding of the institutional basis of innovation. A recent strand reflects on how processes of innovation and industrial learning unfold amongst these scales over space (Gertler, 2001; Bunnel and Coe, 2001; Oinas and Malecki, 2002; Coe and Bunnel, 2003).

A debate between Amin and Gertler over the efficacy with which communities of practice can transfer knowledge between sites is especially germane. Amin and Cohendet (1999) assert that the organizational and relational proximity defining communities of practice can substitute and even supercede physically proximate relations, although Gertler (2001, p. 18), is skeptical that 'the idea that organizational or relational proximity is sufficient to transcend the effects of distance (even when assisted by telecommunications and frequent travel) seems improbable'. Coe and Bunnel (2003, p. 446) attempt a resolution, advocating a view of innovation systems as being 'constituted by constellations of communities of practice'. This perspective is dynamic and sensitive to the mechanisms that negotiate the boundaries between communities of practice, for 'while such communities will originally almost certainly be local configurations, sustained and repeated interaction facilitated by "boundary crossers" may create new spatially extensive constellations'.

These insights complement Oinas and Malecki's (2002) notion of spatial innovation systems (SIS) comprised of overlapping and interlinked national, regional and sectoral systems of innovations. SIS emphasizes the ex-local relations of actors as well as the variability of the relative weights of different places or regions as centre points of particular technological paths in time. Moreover 'spatial discontinuities may relate to specific phases of technological cycles' (Oinas and Malecki 2002, p. 110).

I seek to extend these perspectives in three ways. First, I direct my focus onto processes of radical innovation which involve the adoption of entirely new engineering mind-sets. I am interested in how communities emerge, with a view to understanding the dynamics that underlie their formation in different places. Second, I illustrate the mechanisms through which knowledge is transferred between spatially disparate constellations in an emerging technology system. It is through the juxtaposition of *mobile* tacit and codified forms of knowledge that I provide an explanation for how different places or regions establish the *potential* to become 'centre points of particular technological paths in time'. Third, I detail one example of how constellations within spatially extensive communities of practice assert their advantage over other constellations. I emphasise the tactics actors employ to codify knowledge by inscribing technological space in a proprietary manner; namely through the securing of key patents. My argument is that these tactics decisively alter the hitherto flexible constitution of a community of practice because they serve to *lock-in* advantage in one constellation while simultaneously *locking-out* rival constellations from whole swaths of technological space.

The Audio Engineering Society (AES): A Community of Engineers Looks Forward to the Digital Age

From the mid-1960s through the early 1970s, the Audio Engineering Society (AES), with its journal and conventions, was the key institutional forum for dialogue on the direction of electronic musical instrument design. The *Journal of the Audio Engineering Society* (*JAES*) and convention programs from 1964 through 1972 illuminate this community's assemblage, which included corporate engineers, entrepreneurs, lone inventors, researchers and academics (Table 4.1). These individuals were affiliated with a reasonably narrow list of leading institutions – large corporate electronics laboratories (RCA, Bell), leading organ manufacturers (Conn, Hammond), upstart synthesizer makers (Moog, ARP, Buchla) and universities (Princeton, U. of Illinois, Stanford). Occasionally, some participants appeared unexpectedly – Motorola, NA Rockwell – and it is these trans-sectorial sources of knowledge which would later prove to be catalytic.

The AES data suggests something of the shifting engineering mind-set at the threshold of the digital age. With each successive year, practitioners engaged with the problem of electronic music, joined together as session participants. How the community defined itself is revealed in the session titles, which early on shifted back and forth from 'Music and Electronics' to 'Speech and Music', even if the presenters were often the same. By the 1970s, participants had settled on the title of 'Electronic Music'. Constants, such as the virtually assured participation of Bob Moog, served to maintain the community. Also around this period, Harold Olson, the inventor of the first musical synthesizer at RCA labs and author of the disciplinary bible, *Music and Physics* (1952) served as the Society's president.

Table 4.1   Session Participant Affiliations at the AES Conventions 1964–1972

Date and Location	Session Title	Presenter's Affiliation	Location of Presenter's Affiliation
10/1964 (New York)	Music and Electronics	Bell Aerospace Co. Electronic Music Studio, BrandeisU. Research Lab of Electronics, MIT R.A. Moog Company School of Music, U. of Illinois (2) National Research Council of Canada	N. Tonawanda, N.Y. Waltham, Mass. Cambridge, Mass. Trumansburg, N.Y. Urbana, Ill. Ottawa, Ont.
	Speech Processing	Bell Telephone Laboratories Inc. (2) Bolt Beranek and Newman, Inc. Philco, Corp. Air Force Research Laboratories CRBS RCA Laboratories Nippon Electric Co. IBM Sperry Gyroscope Company	Murray Hill, N.J. Cambridge, Mass. Blue Bell, Pa. Bedford, Mass. Princeton, N.J. Tokyo, Japan Yorktown Heights, N.Y. Carle Place, N.Y.
10/1965 (New York)	Music and Electronics	Hammond Organ Company Astrosonics Incorporated R.A. Moog Co. Hofstra U. Argonne National Laboratory (2) Bell Aerospace Co. Contact Associates, Inc.	Chicago, Ill. Syosset N.Y. Trumansburg, N.Y. Hempstead, N.Y. Argonne, Ill. N. Tonawanda, N.Y. New York, N.Y.
10/1966 (New York)	Music and Electronics	C.G. Conn (Organs), Ltd. Catgut Acoustical Society Perma-Power Co. General Radio Company Motorola Semiconductors R.A. Moog Co. School of Music, U. of Illinois (2) Bell Telephone Laboratories Inc. Princeton U.	Elkhart, Ind. Montclair, N.J. Chicago Ill. W. Concord, Mass. Phoenix Arizona Trumansburg, N.Y. Urbana, Ill. Murray Hill, N.J. Princeton, N.J.
10/1967 (New York)	Speech and Music	R.A. Moog Co. Wayne State University RCA Laboratories National Research Council of Canada Identitones Inc. Dept. of Computer Science, University of Toronto Cunningham Dance Foundation The Wurlitzer (Organ) Company	Trumansburg, N.Y. Detroit, Mich. Princeton, N.J. Ottawa, Ont. New York, N.Y. Toronto, Ont. New York, N.Y. N. Tonawanda, N.Y.

5/1968 (Los Angeles)	Music and Speech	Bell Telephone Laboratories Inc. School of Music, U. of Illinois University of Southern California Department of Music, Stanford University (2) University of Massachusetts UCLA Independent	Murray Hill, N.J. Urbana, Ill. Los Angeles, CA Stanford, CA Amherst, Mass. Los Angeles, CA Washington, D.C.
10/1969 (New York)	Developments in Electronic Music System	C.G. Conn (Organs), Ltd. (2) Electronic Music Studio, University of Toronto National Research Council of Canada R.A. Moog Inc. Radatron Inc.	Elkhart, Ind. Toronto, Ont. Ottawa, Ont. Trumansburg, N.Y. Tonawanda, N.Y.
10/1970 (New York)	Electronic Music	CBS Musical Instruments Hammond Organ Co. Dept. of Music, Queen's College ARP – Division of Tonus Inc. Dept. of Electrical Engineering, Ohio University Alfred Mayer Ionic Corp. Norm Milliard Electronic Music Laboratories R.A. Moog Inc.	Fullerton, CA Chicago Ill. New York, N.Y. Newton Heights, Mass Athens, OH Cambridge, Mass Hartford, Conn. Trumansburg, N.Y.
10/1971 (New York)	Electronic Music	ARP – Division of Tonus Inc. (2) Hammond Organ Co. (2) New England Conservatory of Music Moog Musonics Co. Autonetics Division, North American Rockwell Inc.	Newton Heights, Mass Chicago, Ill. Boston, Mass. Willamsville, N.Y. Anaheim, CA
5/1972 (Los Angeles)	Electronic Music	Department of Music, Stanford U. (2) Independent Different Fur Trading Company Buchla and Associates National Research Council of Canada Moog Music Inc.	Stanford, CA New York, N.Y. San Fancisco, CA Berkeley, CA Ottawa, Ont. Williamsville, N.Y.

Source: Journal of the Audio Engineering Society, various issues 1964–1972.

Geographically, participant lists point to a limited number of core centres – New York and New Jersey, Upstate New York, Chicago and Greater Boston. Until the late 1960s, conventions were almost exclusively held in New York hotels and these ephemeral forums attracted participants only from a catchment area of limited range. The 1968 convention held in Los Angeles included Californians breaking the regional dominance, shifting the community's composition and outlook.

Both culturally and technologically a sense of transition pervaded professional discourse. A review of the 1969 conference proceedings noted that,

'As serious and creative as before, the 1970 audio engineer doesn't look much like one any more. Beards, bell bottoms, "hair" and granny glasses made the scene in appropriate numbers'.

This cultural change also disrupted the conventions of the convention. Don Buchla's participation in the 1969 convention in Los Angeles was one such occasion. 'By refusing to rent a booth and instead playing a concert, and thus gaining lot's of free publicity, [Buchla] broke most of the rules for such conventions' (Pinch and Trocco, 2002, p. 51). Apart from the contingent of young Turks, it is worth commenting on the older, first generation engineers, for their career paths indicate where this cohort learned their trade (Table 4.2). These careers steeped in the aerospace and consumer electronics sectors suggest a pattern of transectorial boundary-crossing migration as the origin of this population's way of thinking. This thinking was quickly brought up to date, especially in instances when it was forced to confront the radically unfamiliar. Bob Moog's presentation in 1968 entitled 'Recent trends in electronic music studio design' featured a recording of Wendy Carlos' soon to be released landmark album 'Switched on Bach' – the first album to demonstrate that synthesized sound could be used to make music the general public could appreciate.

Table 4.2   Sample Career Path Profiles of Authors Publishing Papers on Electronic Musical Instruments in the *JAES* (1969–1972)

Engineer	Firm(s)	Career profile
Daniel Martin	Baldwin Piano and Organ Co.	MSc (1939) and PhD (1941) in physics from the University of Illinois. Worked for RCA between 1941 and 1949 developing microphones and headsets before joining Baldwin in 1949 where he rose to the position of director of engineering and research.
Victor J. Blong	Conn Organs	BSc 1956, MSc 1957 in electrical engineering from Notre Dame. Prior to completion of his degrees he worked in automotive engine research and as a project engineer in a jet engine division of Studebaker Corp. After graduation joined Conn, as research engineer in Electronic Organ Division. Later work fell in area of New Organ Model Department Since 1961 was the Department Section Head for organ section etc.
David Luce	Melville Clark Associates – Moog-Norlin	BSc 1958 in physics from the Case Institute of Technology. PhD in physics from MIT in 1963. From 1963–64 research associate in Cooperative Computing Laboratory of MIT working on development of computer controlled printing methods. Currently consultant for Melville Clark.

Melville Clark Jr.	Melville Clark Associates – Moog-Norlin	BSc from MIT in 1943, PhD Harvard 1949 in physics. Worked for MIT Radiation Laboratory on microwave radar, on the Manhattan Project at Brookhaven National Laboratory specializing in reactors, at Radiation Lab UC on atomic and hydrogen bombs, for Sylvania Electric Inc. on ionospheric propagation, auditory perception and speech research, for Avco on electrical propulsion, orbit calculations and gamma ray transport, and for NASA on plasma physics and solid state physics. For a number of years he has also had his own business concerned with the development of musical instruments and devices as well as research in musical acoustics. Was also faculty member of Dept of Nuclear Engineering at MIT.
Richard Schaefer	Rodgers Organs	Graduate of Georgia Institute of Tech. in Electrical Engineering (1951). After graduation he specialized in aerospace flight control system design with the Martin-Marietta Corp. Was responsible for the Mace missile system and for various new space-craft altitude control systems. He later joined Radiation Inc. in Melbourne Fla. Worked on design and analysis of advanced digital data and communications systems before moving to the technical staff at MITRE corp. Now organ designer with Rodgers.
David Friend	ARP	Degrees in music and electrical engineering from Yale followed by graduate studies in industrial and management engineering at Princeton. Before joining ARP in 1969 he worked for RCA labs in Princeton, NJ. Currently marketing manager for ARP.
Harald Bode	Bell Aerospace Moog	Graduated from Hamburg University and Heinrich Hertz Institute of Berlin. Afterwards specialized in the field of electronic music, creating the Bode-Melochord and pioneering the industrial production of electronic organs (Polychord) in Germany. Came to US in 1954, held several positions before joining the Bell Aerospace Company in Niagara Falls NY where he is currently specializing in the field of micro-electronics while remaining active in the field of instrument design.
Ray Schrecongost	Hammond	BSRE degree from Indiana Tech College 1949. Joined Sylvania TV and Radio Division, Buffalo, NY where he engaged in television design. In 1954 he was employed at Admiral Corp., Chicago doing design work on military and consumer television systems. Joined Hammond in 1960.
Warren Brunsting	Hammond Hammond-Suzuki (Hamamatsu)	Wilson College and Illinois Institute of Tech. Worked for seven years on the design of military communication equipment for ITT Kellogg and also was employed in recording and instrumentation section of Illinois Inst. Of Tech Research Institute. Joined Hammond in 1967 team leader of Phoenix Hammond's first MDD tone-generation instrument. [Currently Vice-President Manufacturing Hammond Suzuki Inc.]

Source: Author profiles compiled from articles in the *JAES*.

Technologically, the implications of the ICT paradigm were beginning to be reflected in discourse. So, for instance, in 1969, David Martin, chief engineer at Baldwin, the large Cincinnati piano and organ manufacturer, wrote a piece for the *JAES* that earnestly prophesized the trajectory of his discipline. In an article titled 'Electronic Music: Audio 1988', Martin (1969, p. 387) presciently observed that:

> In the circuitry, the adoption of IC is expected, *but who knows what other discontinuities in the state of the art* might be equally important or more so, not only for electronic organs but also for other instruments and for their tonal accessories (emphasis added).

Two years later in the *JAES*, Richard Shaefer (1971, p. 570) of Rodgers Organ Co. also commented on the fusing of electronic and musical technologies:

> In the last decade ... some very significant advances have been made. The best of the modern electronic organs are a study in cost effective sophistication. Their development has been guided by more rigorous theoretical and analytic studies of the nature of pipe tone, supplemented with relatively comprehensive test programs and coordinated with the limitations imposed by practical semiconductor circuits ... the problem facing the electronics engineer in this field are considerable.

By 1972, the trajectory had been refined yet again. In a session at the 42nd AES convention organized by Stanford University's John Chowning, Hammond Organ engineer Ray Schrecongost (1972, p. 602) proclaimed that:

> Now the solid state era is here, with adaptations that greatly expand the whole art of musical instrument design. ... The computer industry has been providing the impetus to this rapid development, and now it appears that other industries will be requiring answers in the linear applications as well as in the digital areas. With such universal interest in MOSFET LSI [Metal Oxide Semiconductor Field-Effect Transistor Large-Scale Integrated Circuit], the musical instrument industry, which is small compared to other industries can only benefit by adapting to this technology.

Academics sensed the wider import of what was happening. Hubert Howe, Professor of Music, Queens College, NY stated during his presentation at the Audio Society's 39th conference in October 1970:

> The most important musical result of the revolution of the electronic method of sound generation has been a reevaluation of the fundamental ways in which music has been thought about.

In summary, between 1969 and 1972, conventional wisdom within the EMI section of the AES proclaimed that radical technological change, derived from exogenous sources, was afoot. Yet amidst this transition, much uncertainty prevailed and despite the public pronouncement that the instrument industry would reap the benefits of the space age, hesitancy would characterize the response of American firms when they confronted the specific technologies that actually moved instrument design into the digital era. It is worth mentioning briefly, and in specific reference to Schrecongost's comments about MOSFET LSI, that in 1972, Yamaha was already producing its own application specific LSI, a fact that was entirely overlooked by the US industry. We consider why this was so in the next section.

The Formation of Knowledge in Japan

Today Japanese firms dominate the global market for EMI, an industry that is highly concentrated both in ownership and control as well as in its territoriality. The two largest manufacturers in the sector, Yamaha and Roland are both headquartered in the city of Hamamatsu, while the third largest Korg, which is 51 per cent owned by Yamaha, is based in Tokyo. However, 40 years ago, the sector was in its infancy and was technologically almost entirely dependent on the pace of innovation in the US. At that time, two communities of practice confronted the new field of electronic musical instrument design, both deriving their inspiration from the transfer of technology from the US. The first was a community of amateurs, tinkering away outside the corporate context, using what resources could be obtained in an ad hoc manner. The second community was comprised of engineers working in the corporate context for large firms such as Yamaha who possessed sufficient capital to invest in a dedicated R&D infrastructure.

The amateur enthusiasts who took apart foreign organs to gain a working understanding of their underlying technology was a community that derived much of its basic knowledge from the import of textbooks and other literature. These sources provided the stock recipes that flavoured subsequent efforts to cultivate a tacit knowledge of instrument design via the reverse engineering of foreign organs. With regards to the transfer of textual knowledge, cultural and physical distance severely checked a process that today would be rapidly subject to ubiquification (Maskell and Malmberg, 1999). Roland's founder Kakehashi (2002, pp. 159-160) recalls this sticky quality of codified knowledge:

> When I learned of a relevant book having been published, I would immediately place an order and then would have to wait as long as five months for delivery. It was only in 1962 that I was able to obtain *Electrical Musical Instruments*, which was published in the US in 1958. To say there was a technology and information 'gap' between Japan and the US would be a major understatement ... In those early days the only [other] way we could pursue our development efforts was by examining imported instruments and adapting their technology.

Since Kakehashi could not afford to purchase new imported instruments he had to engineer opportunities to get a look at them. So Kakehashi Musen, his electronic appliance repair shop, started accepting jobs to repair organs. His second, more cavalier tactic was to invite himself to the homes of new organ buyers (Kakehashi, 2002).Unlike the situation for amateurs, large firms like Yamaha could afford to importforeign organs. However, once in their possession, these instruments were similarly deconstructed. Through much of the 1950s and 1960s this amateur-tinkerer mindset defined the engineering common sense at that firm. While conventional wisdom holds that such strategies amounted to little more than mimicry, I would counter this argument by pointing out the value this practice serves in producing a culture of learning that keeps the sights trained on the state of the art.

Also contrary to the experience of Kakehashi and his kind, Yamaha could afford to dispatch its engineers on *shisatsu ryoko*, or overseas study trips, which enabled the firm to tap directly into the emerging constellation of practice in the US. Yamaha funded its most gifted young engineers to do graduate work at leading US universities, while also sending out teams of technicians and managers to tour not only US organ makers like Baldwin, but also the laboratories of RCA and Bell. As a Yamaha engineer reflected:

> The first lessons that were learned came from the engineers who were sent overseas. Olson's textbook especially, dominated our discussions around the time the D-1 came out [in 1960]. Even until maybe 1985, the Olson book greatly contributed to our thinking about technology, not in a narrow sense, but in a general way (Interview with Yamaha engineer 21/7/02).

While this knowledge was being absorbed, Yamaha massively increased its electronic engineering workforce by providing scholarships to university students who agreed to commit to the firm upon graduation. As this labour force took shape, the organization of R&D became more formalized with a view to linking the tacit and codified domains of knowledge.

> This way of doing things changed into a system, especially for electronic instruments where we started to work from diagrams ... President Kawakami called up Mr. Kondo, head of the laboratory and told him to, 'work off of the documents'. In fact there was a system in place for learning from documents, for instance – 'getting the specifications by inspection' – 'copying the circuit diagram for the unit' ... Many general things can be learned, if the structure of a transistor is known (Interview with Yamaha engineer 21/7/02).

Beyond the firm, the regulatory environment governing intellectual property rights served to further the advantages of large firms in accessing and applying foreign knowledge. Kakehashi recalls how until the mid 1960s Japanese importers of foreign instruments were granted the right to patent these technologies 'as is' thereby preventing amateurs, smaller firms and other bottom feeders from using this knowledge. This system amounted to a particular social construction of the novel, since foreign prior art was deliberately not recognized. In response to this bizarre situation, Kakehashi and peers (2002) immediately published their own ad hoc textbook *Everything about Electronic Instruments* in order to establish domestic prior art – a tactic that freed this knowledge from falling into the proprietary orbit of Yamaha.

So until the late 1960s the formation of a new engineering common sense in Japan rested on the transfer of codified knowledge from the US and the accumulation of tacit knowledge via the reverse engineering of imported instruments. Large firms possessed or were granted a number of structural advantages in this capacity although amateurs and smaller firms like Roland developed novel strategies for mitigating these constraints. Yet, Japanese firms could not hope to overcome their American rivals if they were continually playing catch-up. There was clearly a need to develop a home-grown approach to radical innovation.

By the late 1960s it was apparent to Yamaha's chief engineer Mochida Yasonori that the transistor, as the core technology of the electronic organ, was not powerful enough to perform real time synthesis (Johnstone, 1999). Indeed, in the electronics field in general, the transistor was rapidly being eclipsed by the integrated circuit which contained thousands of transistors on one chip. Moreover, it was apparent to Mochida that for sound generation, generic chips would not pass muster application specific integrated circuits (ASICs) were necessary. However, when Mochida approached suppliers like NEC and Hitachi about making such chips, 'they told us to stop thinking about something so difficult' (quoted in Johnstone, 1994, p. 3). Against strenuous opposition from the company's board of directors, Mochida proposed to the firm's mercurial president Kawakami Gen'ichi that Yamaha would probably have to spend ¥2 billion – an amount equal to Yamaha's entire capital at the time (Yamaha, 1987, p. 52) – in order to become a chip maker in its own right. Kawakami agreed, saying (according to Mochida), 'if we can make the best musical instruments in the world, then no matter how difficult it is, no matter how much money it costs – we'll do it'. (quoted in Johnstone, 1994, p. 3).

Yamaha's quest to develop the capability to produce LSI and the central role that this decision played in the firm's subsequent evolution has been discussed by Nakagawa (1984). Such a grand endeavor made it imperative that Yamaha cultivate the knowledge and expertise necessary to make its own chips. Once again, in 1969 a team of young engineers was dispatched, this time to Tohoku University and the labs of Professor J. Nishizawa. Today, he is known in Japanese engineering circles as the 'father of optical communication' and the 'DaVinci of semiconductors', but at that time, he was virtually the only person in Japan in possession of the knowledge which Yamaha sought. Under the rigorous tutelage of Nishizawa, these engineers acquired the fundamental and applied skills that would enable Yamaha to voyage along a path, the trajectory of which was a radical departure from its basis in electro-mechanical engineering and instrument manufacture. By 1971 Yamaha's Toyooka plant began producing MOS/LSI at a rate of 50,000/month.

Lock-in and Lock-out

By the early 1970s, engineers in the US and Japan viewed the future of the technological frontier lay in the transectorial impacts of the micro-chip. Yamaha alone possessed the capability to make its own chips, yet it still did not possess a platform technology to apply this advantage for digital tone synthesis. Very quickly however, it took steps to secure the two fundamental technologies to mass produce and commercialize a digital instrument. The first technology it sought to capture was for digital organ technology, originally patented by the Anaheim aerospace firm Rockwell but transferred to Allen Organ. The second technology was a method of tone synthesis using frequency modulation (FM), developed by a Stanford composer and graduate student named John Chowning. How did Yamaha access these technologies?

The answer is partly by default, for both of these technologies were developed at the turn of the 1970s in California, in contexts far removed from the locus of instrument manufacturers in the north-east and mid-west. With the digital organ patent, Rockwell went through a series of trials attempting to prove its worth to the large US organ makers. Only Allen Organ of Macungie, PA was interested, and he eventually took out a license of first refusal. This agreement proved problematic, for even though Allen took control of the digital organ technology, cultural and personal differences between the two firms terminated any possibility for subsequent collaboration. Rockwell's team leader on the project soon left the firm and entered into a three-year contract with Yamaha, and subsequently that firm's neighbour and rival Kawai. The technologies that this individual developed for Yamaha eventually drew the attention of Allen who sued for infringement. Yamaha settled for $1.5 million and licensed the technology from Allen (Markowitz, 1989). More importantly, Yamaha inventors, including the former Rockwell engineer published a battery of ancillary and dependent patents that laid claim to the technological space surrounding the digital organ patent, circumscribing its efficacy. In the case of the FM synthesis patent, Stanford and Chowning similarly failed to convince any US firm of its worth. To Chowning, the algorithmic logic on which it was based was simply 'not part of their world' (Johnstone, 1994, p. 3). Soon thereafter, Yamaha took out an *exclusive* license for FM synthesis, again, barring rival firms from accessing this very critical threshold in technological space.

Once Yamaha absorbed these keystone patents into its technological orbit it spent just over ten years developing their potential for the market. In 1983 Yamaha released the DX7 synthesizer, the first mass-market all-digital synthesizer, an instrument that Pinch and Trocco (2002, p. 317) refer to as the, 'breakthrough digital instrument, the first one to achieve commercial success'. This event signaled the ascendance of Yamaha and other Japanese firms in the digital age, sounding the death knell for US industry. In short, the landscape had changed, which is precisely the sort of spatial discontinuity one might expect from radical innovation.

Conclusion

This chapter's case study looked at the way innovation systems unfold in space during episodes of radical technological change. It began by pointing to the tentative origins of a community of practice in the USA that congregated under the institutional umbrella of the AES. This constellation evolved to include 'boundary-crossing' actors from highly diverse circumstances, and the infusion of trans-sectorial knowledge defined the sector of electronic music as one that would be dependent on the pace of technological change in electronics. It is curious that none of these actors, especially the large organ manufacturers endeavoured to make their firm independent in the way that Yamaha did by developing a capability to produce micro-chips. Even more damning is that US industry failed to recognize the platform technologies of the digital era – an opportunity that was not overlooked by Yamaha.

For the constellation of practitioners in Japan, knowledge transfer from the US involved various forms of spatial 'boundary-crossing' including *shisatsu ryoko*, the import of texts and instruments, and at the most critical time, the licensing of key technologies. Long before the moment of radical innovation represented by the release of the DX7, the technological pivot of history in this sector's evolution, the Japanese engineering mind-set was committed to catching-up by literally deconstructing the state of the art. This informal and systematic monitoring likely gave this constellation an advantage when it came to realizing the import of technologies such as FM synthesis.

What lessons can be extracted from the study? To begin, it suggests that much more work needs to be done in understanding the ways in which communities of practice jump scale. While processes of knowledge transfer are implicated in this mobility, it appears as though research has been overly fixated on the efficacy of tacit knowledge transfer, while neglecting the codified dimension. Indeed, as the case study demonstrated, Yamaha's cultivation of tacit knowledge (via tinkering and reverse engineering) rested on a knowledge base derived from the diffusion of US textbooks. Geographers interested in innovation have often cited Nonaka and Takeuchi's (1995) observation that it is the cycling between tacit and codified knowledge that is important, yet in too many cases there is a failure to complete the loop.

References

Amin, A. and Cohendet, P. (1999), 'Learning and Adaptation in Decentralized Business Networks', *Environment and Planning D: Society and Space*, 17: pp. 87-104.

Asheim, B. (1999), 'Interactive Learning and Localized Knowledge in Globalizing Learning Economies', *Geojournal*, 49: pp. 345-52.

Braczyk, H., Cooke, P. and Heidenreich, M. (eds) (1998), *Regional Innovation Systems: The Role of Governances in a Globalized World*, London: UCL Press.

Bunnell, T. and Coe, N. (2001), 'Spaces and Scales of Innovation', *Progress in Human Geography*, 25(4): pp. 569-589.

Carlsson, B. and Stankiewicz, R. (1991), 'On the Nature, Function and Composition of Technological Systems', *Journal of Evolutionary Economics*, 1: pp. 93-118.

Coe, N. and Bunnell, T. (2003) 'Spatializing Knowledge Communities: Towards a Conceptualization of Transnational Innovation Networks', *Global Networks*, 3(4): pp. 437-456.

Freeman, C. (1982), *The Economics of Industrial Innovation*, London: Frances Pinter Publishers.

Freeman, C. and Perez, C. (1988), 'Structural Crisis of Adjustment, Business Cycles and Investment Behavior', In G. Dosi, C. Freeman, R. Belsoy and G. Silverberg (eds), *Technological Change and Economic Theory*, London: Pinter, pp. 38-66.

Gertler, M. (2001), 'Best Practice? Geography, Learning and the Institutional Limits to Strong Convergence', *Journal of Economic Geography*, 1: pp. 5-26.

Hudson, R. (1999), 'The Learning Economy, The Learning Firm and The Learning Region: A Sympathetic Critique of the Limits to Learning', *European Urban and Regional Studies*, 6: pp. 59-72.

Johnstone, B. (1994), 'Wave of the Future', *Wired*, 2(3): pp. 1-7. http://www.wired.com/wired/archive/2.03/waveguides.html?pg=2&topic.

Johnstone, B. (1999), *We Were Burning: Japanese Entrepreneurs and the Forging of the Electronic Age*, New York: Basic Books.

Kakehashi, I. (2002), *I Believe in Music: Life Experiences and Thoughts on the Future of Electronic Music by the Founder of the Roland Corporation*, Milwaukee, WI: Hal Leonard.

Latour, B. (1987), *Science in Action: How to Follow Scientists and Engineers Through Society*, Cambridge, MA: Harvard University Press.

Lee, R. (2002), 'Nice Maps, Shame About the Theory? Thinking Geographically About the Economic', *Progress in Human Geography*, 26(3): pp. 333-355.

Lundvall, B-A. (1992), *National Systems of Innovation: Towards a Theory of Innovation and Interactive Learning*, London: Pinter Publishers.

Maskell, P. and Malmberg, A. (1999), 'The Competitiveness of Firms and Regions, "Ubiquification" and the Importance of Localized Learning', *European Urban and Regional Studies*, 6(1): pp. 9-25.

Markowitz, J. (1989), *Triumphs and Trials of an Organ Builder*, Macungie, PA: Allen Organ Company.

Morgan, K. (1997), 'The Learning Region: Institutions, Innovation and Regional Renewal', *Regional Studies* (31): pp. 491-503.

Nakagawa, Y. (1984), *Nihon Gakki no LSI Kaihatsu Senryaku*, Tokyo: Diamond.

Nonaka, I. and Takeuchi, H. (1995), *The Knowledge Creating Company: How Japanese Companies Create the Dynamics of Innovation*, New York: Oxford University Press.

Oinas, P. and Malecki, E. (2002), 'The Evolution of Technologies in Time and Space: From National and Regional to Spatial Innovation Systems', *International Regional Science Review*, 25(1): pp. 102-131.

Pinch, T. and Trocco, F. (2002), *Analog days: The Invention and Impact of the Moog Synthesizer*, Cambridge, MA: Harvard University Press.

Takahashi, Y. (2000), 'A Network of Tinkerers: The Advent of the Radio and Television Receiver Industry in Japan', *Technology and Culture*, 41: pp. 460-484.

Wenger, E. (1998), *Communities of Practice: Learning, Meaning and Identity*. Cambridge: Cambridge University Press.

Yamaha (1987), *Yamaha 100 Nenshi*, Hamamatsu: Yamaha.

Chapter 5

Governing by 'Certifying': International Standards Organization and Capability Maturity Models as Regulatory Practices in Offshore Software Outsourcing, St. Petersburg, Russia

Melanie Feakins

Introduction

In the mid 1990s, the rapidly globalizing computer software industry began expanding its production, marketing and distribution activities to sites located in the transforming economies of post-soviet sphere. This latest extension is one of several within the past decade to have developed software production firms and networks in locales outside of the established software cores of Western Europe and North America. Indeed, from the 1990s to the present the growth of the software industry in India, Israel, Russia, Ireland, Chile and the Philippines, among others, has been substantial in real terms and is an identified dynamic within the industry. The growth of the industry in these places reflects an increasing inclination for the production milieu of the software industry to develop outside of conventional western/northern contexts.

This emerging pattern of geographic expansion can be analyzed in predictable terms of 'push-pull' factors. While developed world sites are described in terms of high labour costs, skill shortages in relevant technical fields, and inflexible labour practices for hiring and firing that 'push', second and third world (or underdeveloped and post-soviet/post-socialist) sites offer lower wages and an abundance of skills and educated labour pools in technical and mathematical areas that 'pull'. This description proposes a rationale for the industry to expand to these different locales, suggesting that wage levels, skills availability and flexibilities in employment practices are causal factors in the globalization of production in the software industry. This explanation offers a macro-oriented account of reasons for the software production industry's globalisation and the 'economic' factors associated. It does not however attempt to examine the procedures and mechanisms that enable the intensely complex practices associated with organization and execution of software production to become multi-sited in this way.

The geographic dispersal of the production activities involved in the software industry entails the expansion and intensification of network relations between and among firms. Offshore outsourcing in particular, as it is only one of several organizing types, requires the development of relations between entities across national and organizational borders. The terminology 'offshore outsourcing' highlights the external-ness of contexts that are defining features in this sub-area of the industry. 'Offshore' designates a space that is not only 'beyond the shore' of expensive and tightly regulated Western countries; it also implies the existence of alternative contexts where it may be possible to make use of advantageous differences (i.e. the availability of specific labour resources, different wage structures, provision of access to restricted but opening markets, etc), in this case Russia. The classification 'outsourcing' also designates an external socio-economic space, but of a more micro-scale. It describes the realm of activities and contracts for 'work' (in this case ranging from software production, system maintenance, platform conversion, database design and implementation, system maintenance, etc.) that occur *outside* the hiring firm, with the implied possibilities for limiting commitments, hiring specialized human resources for specific periods/projects, and benefiting from the past experiences of the contracted firm. These portrayals of the 'external' through the linguistic metaphors 'off' and 'out' intimate an emergence of economic space where new governance processes and structures are developing.

With the aim of contributing to a growing literature in economic geography that investigates the practices and discourses which 'are constitutive of new governmental forms' (Larner and Le Heron, 2002, p. 754), this chapter analyses the role of industrial certification in the offshore software outsourcing industry. By adopting an approach to governance that acknowledges a focus on 'micro economic spaces and subjects' as a means to study emergent governmental forms, we can focus on how governance emerges at the level of the firm through certification related experiences and interactions (Larner and Le Heron, 2002, p. 754). Certification introduces the means to connect to networks of third parties (consultants and advisors), non-human actants (pamphlets and guidelines) and industry talk sessions (by providing the international 'lingo'), all of which furnish the information and communicative means for offshore firms to become subjects and sites of the international software industry. This chapter proposes that the discourses and practices of certification operate within the 'offshore' as devices to imagine and participate in the globalization of the industry (Larner and Le Heron, 2002). Rather than exploring the causes of globalization in the industry, this chapter examines *how* this globalization is enabled and made comprehensible through the guidelines and structures of certification.

As the title of this chapter suggests, the processes and procedures involved in International Standards Organization (ISO) and Capability Maturity Models (CMM) certifying regimes are conceived of as regulatory practices that form an emerging form of governance. Recognizing these certifications as an emergent form of governance requires the review of spatial/scalar imaginations in economic geography and of Foucault's work on governmentality. Certification operates outside of the standard, ordered categories of scale that depict international, national, regional and local. Instead, certification has influence precisely because of its bridging and linking possibilities, by making the international possible in the micro world of the small firm, and in this case at the micro level of the post-soviet Russian offshore software firm. Using highly structured and citational methods for managing 'complex international flows of knowledge', certification provides the means for firms located in 'offshores' to become part of the industry's globalization (Storper, 2000, pp. 49-50). Certification in offshore outsourcing derives its influence from imagined and real recognitions within the international industry and is able to effect practices at the very micro-level of the small firm where the ISO and CMM certification can be earned.

In developing the case for employing a relational framework in economic geography, Dickens et al. (2001) suggest that we acknowledge and explore the difficulties of conceptual categories, multiple scales of analysis and multiple sites of organizational influence. Their relational framework provides scope for analyzing certification plans and procedures as a process of governance, linking the non-analogous scales of 'international' and 'firm-level', and querying how the western-based 'international' certifications have exceptionally strong influence in non-western offshore locations. This approach allows us to move 'outside of fixed national, regional and local scale orientations towards conceptions of scale that account for shifting levels and multiple influences that allow "jumping scales" in both directions' and provide new accounts for changing economic spaces and scales (Bunnell and Coe, 2001).

Certification is beginning to reveal itself as a form of governance through its representation and reproduction in the experiences of Russian firms. The certification which operates in the offshore outsourcing software sector uses its international recognition to advise offshore outsourcing firms in developing recognizable and certifiable forms of work, organisation, production flows, role formalization and internal checking mechanisms for quality assurance. From the Foucauldian perspective of governmentality, these certification practices are introducing particular logics, categories, languages and controls that condition how possibilities become conceivable or inconceivable. This chapter illustrates how in specific cases the processes of certification instantiate a form of governance by examining categorization and preparation for the 'open market', the creation of western management practices and the forms of value that certification enables all of which are tangible expressions of such categories, languages and logics.

This chapter draws on field research and interviews conducted with owner/managers of firms, project managers, employees and industrial groups that are active in the offshore outsourcing industry in St Petersburg, Russia. Plans to engage with certification, as well as relevant experiences and impressions of its use were discussed in 'close dialogue' interviews forming this chapter's basis of analysis (Clark, 1998). The chapter presents this research in four sections. First, the history and contents of International Standards Organisation (ISO) and CMM certifications are described and presented. The following sections examine the circulations and meanings of certification offshore St. Petersburg. The latter three sections address certification and the open market, the creation of western management style and certification as worthy in its own right.

Certification Regimes: CMM and ISO

The ISO and CMM guidelines for the structuring of quality production processes have established specified sets of principles and norms that imply quality assurance if employed. In the research and arguments presented here, these two certification regimes function similarly, albeit there are significant differences would be of interest to those examining certification regimes in different industries (Paulk 1994, 1995). Officially labeled ISO 9000, ISO is a series of standards for quality management systems. The ISO 9000 series was published and is maintained by the European based International Standards Organisation, which began as a federation of engineers after the Second World War. The first version of ISO 9000 was published in 1987 with a significant upgrading of the certification guidelines in 1994 (Arora and Asundi, 2000). In the year 2000, ISO established the series ISO 9001-2000. This was a revision/update to the 1994 version that took into account 'previous experience of the organization with and emerging insights into generic management systems' (http://www.iso.ch/iso/en/iso9000-14000/iso9000/faqs.html).

CMM is a software development model created by the Software Engineering Institute at Carnegie Mellon University in the US. The CMM is intended to help software organizations 'improve their software processes in terms of an evolutionary process from ad hoc, chaotic processes to mature, disciplined software processes'. The structured and staged model for software development proposes specific procedural, informational, and technical flows in combination with reporting, management, and work project structures to organize software development and production work. The CMM model specifies five levels of compliance that help firms achieve specified forms of process maturity and ranges from the 'Initial' Level 1 to the 'Optimizing' Level 5 (Paulk, 1994, p. 3). The CMM for software has been described as a roadmap for software process improvement that has had a major influence on the software community around the world (Paulk, 1995).

These 'rational unified process'/'best practice' (CMM) and defined/documented processes for external quality assurance (ISO 9000 series) guidelines offer established principles for how to organise processes within firms. Within the offshore industry, CMM and ISO have become symbolic reference points that are used to indicate specific awareness and knowledge regarding 'Western' organization styles and 'professional' practices. The presence of these international standards and certifications within offshore outsourcing has influence precisely because they 'translate' across borders – political, industrial, sectoral, linguistic and cultural. This translate-ability is a dynamic and multi-sited process with different actors proposing contents, meanings, uses, and interpretations. How the certification meanings are translated varies significantly according to different firms and people who are affected by, and in turn affect, certification regimes. The next sections dissect and interpret the meanings that are attributed to these guidelines. The aim is not to discover *what* translates, but rather to reveal the complex circulation of certification categories and logics in order to understand how forms of reception, knowledge and practices form a mode of governance in the offshore.

Certification as an Entrée to the 'Open Market'

The complexity of what 'the market' is and how it is assumed to coordinate offshore software outsourcing is revealed by examining how certification interacts with, and constitutes, ideas of the market from the view of Russian software firms. The market, though rarely defined colloquially in the industry, is activated in a series of discourses that are associated by the common reference to what the 'market' is said to possess and create. These casual discourses portray 'the market' as: creating and articulating demands, fostering and enabling opportunities for success, experiencing downturns, becoming increasingly tight or competitive and as a space where contracts are to be won on a competitive basis. The discourse creates images of the market as something 'out there' with its own existence, knowable mainly through what is said about it. At the same time, the market is portrayed in terms that codify legal, managerial and economic information such as: American, European, Scandinavian and British; offshore and domestic; public and private. This bifurcation of discourse and description (i.e. portrayals of market principles and effects versus named cultural, political, and economic market identities) is a significant colloquial response to the incomprehensible 'global market', providing analysis and articulation about the 'types' of markets and market experiences that one can encounter. In addition to these now pervasive descriptions, the idea of the 'open market' has emerged as another market discourse. The 'open market' is a concept that is often brought up during discussions of ISO and CMM certifications, suggesting that the open market is connected to certification plans or experiences.

Russian offshore sector software firms are constantly creating and interpreting both what the market is and how market boundaries are experienced in ways that are antithetical to portrayals of the market as openly and fairly competitive. These complexities were articulated in many ways throughout the field study. The idea of boundaried markets and in particular the open market as a boundaried market was, however, a persistent theme. This concept was articulated by many firms, and in an interview with several owner/partners of a software firm in Petersburg we began to discuss the possibilities of certification. Addressing the idea of potentially seeking certification of ISO or CMM, one of the outsourcing firm partners of an owner/management team said:

> Most of our customers are not asking us to provide some certificate for management. Of course when we are working in the open market it is highly desirable to have such kinds of certification. I think that it's a lot of additional work to provide all these documents, but that may be paid with new contacts ... So we are considering this, but not immediately. We are rather thinking of just establishing our own process and getting a certificate for it. We have a good coding standard, much more developed, for example, than one of our customers. One of our customers first demanded that all of development should be according to their internal coding standards. At the same moment, when we had just got acquainted with them, we provided our own coding standard to them. Their requirement remained in the statement of work. And a few weeks ago we asked 'Will you give your coding standards so that we can follow it?' and they answered, 'We'd rather you follow your own one! (laughter) We are happy with your version.'

The active separation of current client relationships from the realm of the 'open market' suggests two significant ideas. First, active client relationships are understood to take place outside of the 'open market', as the open market is conceived as a sphere where contacts and contracts are *established*, not where work is conducted. Second, and perhaps more important, when working in the open market and when clearly trying to make contacts and contracts, '*it is highly desirable to have such kinds of certification*'. The portrayal of the 'open market' as a sphere where possessing certification creates particular advantages is accompanied by the sense of being 'outside' the experience and space of that open market. The implied temporality and segmentation of the open market, noticeable from the quote 'when we are working in the open market', suggests that open market is a bound space that can be entered and exited. The open market is clearly shaped and governed differently than other spheres, with certification as a particularly telling point. For example, in this firm's recent experience with a foreign client, the internal non-certified standards for software production exceeded the quality expectations of the foreign client and the work was eventually conducted according to the 'non-certified' standards. And yet this firm perceives that, regardless of the strength of the internal coding standards used with current clients, certification would be a more useful confirmation of quality processes for the open market. The open market is clearly a space where the certification of a firm's quality standards has particular influence for allowing a firm to recognized, and in turn, providing it a means to enter the open market.

In explaining the importance of certification for the 'open market', the idea of 'signaling' is often summoned as a description of how certification works. Using signaling as an explanation of how certification works in the open market suggests that webs of sent and received signals containing information about the abilities of firms are established, and that new contacts are sought on these bases. In the above quote, this view is expressed by the suggestion that the hassles of certification might 'be paid with new contacts'. As a strategy to signal a particular preparedness, certification may be thought of as a means for firms to advertise their familiarity with, and uptake of, standards in the industry. In research with Indian software firms, Arora and Asundi (2000) explored certification as a strategy used by firms to signal knowledge of industry norms and create reputation. They found that it was a strategy used by some, but certainly not all the firms interviewed. But from the perspective of governance, it may be more interesting to explore how the signals that encourage firms to pursue certification circulate. Examining the beliefs about the necessity of certification reveals that it is far more deeply inscribed than a simple act of signaling or as a marketing procedure. Certification has become part of the imagined trajectory of successful offshore software firms.

In the same interview as quoted above, when the topic of quality and standards of the firm's processes and 'open market' requirements for certification were raised, another owner/manager spoke on the topic stating that:

> This is an issue. This is a small company and because of this we need strong and formalized rules for checking the quality of our products. Of course if, I hope, if our company will grow, in this case, as we will be big, I think we will provide more

formalized steps in testing and development. Now we use the preferences of a small firm, but it's the situation at the present moment. When we change our status, our size, of course the situation will change. We completely understand, if we want to go with, the open market – we will have to get CMM or ISO or so on. We know this very well.

Here again, the 'open market' figures as a sphere with different practices of recognition that commands a change from this firm's current lack of certification. Certification seems to be a necessary part of successful market participation because gossip and talk around the market portray certification as almost a prerequisite for participating. Beyond the notions of what the open market requires, it is unambiguous that the development and growth of the firm, in particular the formalization of its processes, should be guided by one, or both, of these certifications. Certification is not necessarily relegated to a scripted performance of getting ready for the market. It is regarded as worthwhile because of the formality and structure it would encourage in different software development processes within the firm.

Certification and the Crafting of Management Practice

There is a continuous flow of statements about the improvement and development of management and project leadership skills within the offshore community in Russia generally and St Petersburg is not an exception to this. Nearly all of the firms interviewed were new 'private' firms, meaning they were established independently and are not privatized departments of state enterprises. The owner/managers of these firms had previous professional lives in research institutes, universities, and teaching institutions as faculty, employees and students. There is a clear collective self-perception of having learned management, and continuing to learn management skills and practices 'on the job' 'through trial and error' and with little or no specialized training. The experiences of these once very small firms that now number twenty to one hundred employees, is not unusual within the software industry. However, the perception of weak 'ancillary capabilities' including management and organization, which are often portrayed in the literature about post-socialist economic transformation, seems to be particularly strong in this industry where there is little legacy of soviet management experience (Radosevic, 1998; 1999; 1999b).

Concern for developing management practices that fit with the industry and to the projected demands of western clients created a specific expectation of certification. Within this specific situation of craving management, ISO and CMM operate as markers that acknowledge awareness of western management practice, and of equal importance, recognizing the preferences for western management styles. These recognitions play on a certain outsidedness to dominant western practices which allows ISO and CMM to be construed as western, meaningful and useful in the crafting of management for offshore firms. Both certifying regimes have explicit ideas about internal organisation of the firm that propose defining roles, responsibilities, structures of reporting and divisions of tasks. In addition, they make explicit how 'work' (be it projects or longer more stable production routines) should be structured in phases, with finished pieces passing from one phase to another and potentially one group of people in the firm to another. The specific guidelines offered by ISO and CMM for creating structures, flows of work, transparencies and defined responsibilities offer a framework of what is regarded as western, and in the case of offshore outsourcing, desirable practice.

While discussing ISO and CMM certifications with an owner/manager of a firm in Petersburg, the interviewee told me they had been preparing for a CMM evaluation. His response to my question regarding whether the preparations for CMM had been helpful in terms of internal structuring was:

> Yes yes. That's right. Because ... *because it's very important for us, especially as we don't have education in management area. For us, it's very important for us to have a milestone. Some described paths we have to follow.* It's really helpful for us, very helpful. Contacts with foreign experts, with assessors, people who have been working in foreign companies, and who have real experience. At least who can tell us, you have chosen the right way. It's very important. (Emphasis added.)

Here certification is not only education in management practice, but is also extended to gaining international knowledge, expertise of people in the industry, and evaluations of current practices in comparison with successful companies elsewhere. As inferred in italics, certification and its proposed guidelines for structuring the firm are seen as an externally defined pathway where a satisfactory evaluation signals 'correct' developments within the firm. The interviewee also mentions the spaces of evaluation as not only external to the firm, but as spaces with particular international knowledge. The interviewee finally mentions that he seeks an exposure through certification that has consultants and assessors who are able to provide comparative forms of judgment with specific knowledge of the foreign practices, of certified firms operating in international markets.

The formalizing of acquired knowledge and capability is part of the certification desire, but is also clear in discussion of education and degrees. The parallels between educational degrees and certifications are quite clear even though ISO and CMM, unlike university degrees, leaving certificates and finishing statements of technical courses earned by individuals, reside with the collective body of a firm. ISO and CMM certifications confer evaluations of how a firm, rather than an individual, conforms to, or reaches the standards and stipulations of particular procedural guidelines. Importantly, the firm can continue to hold the certification even if the employees change.

The Worthiness of Certification

CMM and ISO certifications are invoked as milestones in the development of offshore outsourcing firms because they offer a means for firms to compare themselves against industry standards and other firms that have or are seeking certification. But aside from the possibilities of measuring and signaling the presence of quality assured processes in the firm, many firms expressed certainty that the CMM in particular, offered valuable ideas and designs for software development firms. In an interview with another firm in St. Petersburg that has a long history and is relatively large with nearly one hundred employees, the owner/manger spoke about certification at length, stating that:

> CMM is one of our goals. We have passed, or gone through a pre-assessment in April this year. We take CMM very seriously. We believe that they are offering a very good model of how to improve our process, so we are not implementing CMM for marketing purposes only. That could probably be faster maybe and even easier, if we just decided that we are going to produce a bunch of documentation and train three people who we could show to the assessors. But we really take it seriously and we would like the CMM to become, or the processes of CMM to become, a part of company culture. We would like to really instantiate it here. So, the current situation, after this pre-assessment, we've been told that we are between levels four and five. Which means that we are almost done with level two, but there are also things that we are doing on level three and level four and even on level five. Like preventive testing and things like that, quality controls and things like that. So our decision was that we will not go through assessment on level two in September; That was an option. But rather, we will go through assessment on level three in March.

Here again, though in a somewhat different way, the model or proven path of how to improve the firm's processes is a stimulus for certification. But it is not blind trust that makes industry gossip about certification for marketing as its rationale. Rather, CMM is evaluated as a model that also offers something for internal processes and company culture. The above statement illustrates how certification is more than a marketing instrument or a pre-condition for access to the open market, but rather, is embraced because of the opportunities for upgrading internal process and structure. The owner/manager of this firm however, also alludes to how receiving particular grades can also be achieved through selecting 'what' represents the firm to the assessors. This knowledge of how certifications can also 'mis-represent' capabilities of a firm were widespread and remarked on throughout the fieldwork. It adds complexity to the meaningful aspects of improvement to process what owner/managers desire because it suggests that the certification tags are potentially misleading.

Conclusion

This chapter has proposed that examining certification as a form of governance in the offshore software outsourcing sector in St. Petersburg, Russia allows us to recognize how CMM and ISO certifications encourage a coherent assemblage of logics, categories, languages and defined paths for industry success. It is, however, important to realize that these certifications have powers of governance in 'offshore' places, making the intersection of the international and the firm a critical site of analysis. This implicit international/firm/certification juncture is adopted in the portrayals of the 'open market', learning western management, having access to foreign assessors and advisors, and the worthiness of implementing the CMM model. The jumping of scales in this analysis, where the micro practices of the firm in the offshore intersect with international certifications and industrial, addresses how governance through certification is predicated on particular 'externals' (offshores, outsourcing) that require particular 'insider' knowledges. By using a concept of governance that embraces more subtle expressions of categories and development paths, it is possible to examine and understand the connectivity and economic structuring taking place in the offshore as governed through the presence and promotion of certification regimes.

References

Arora, A. and Asundi, J. (2000), 'Quality Certification and the Economics of Contract Software Development: A study of the Indian Software Industry'. Working paper, Carnegie Mellon University – H. John Heinz III School of Public Policy and Management and Carnegie Mellon University – H. John Heinz III School of Public Policy and Management.

Arora, A. and Athreye, S. (2001), 'The Software Industry and India's Economic Development'. Working paper, Carnegie Mellon University – H. John Heinz III School of Public Policy and Management and Carnegie Mellon University – H. John Heinz III School of Public Policy and Management.

Arora, A., Arunachalam, V. S., Asundi, J. and Fernandes, R. (2001), 'The Indian Software Services Industry', *Research Policy*, 30: pp. 1267-1287.

Bunnell, T.G. and Coe, N. M. (2001), 'Spaces and Scales of Innovation', *Progress in Human Geography*, 25(4), pp. 569-589.

Burchell, G., Gordon, C., Miller, P. (eds) (1991), *The Foucault Effect: Studies in Governmentality*, Chicago University Press.

Clark, G. (1998), 'Stylized Facts and Close Dialogue: Methodology in Economic Geography', *Annals of the Association of American Geographers*, 88(1): pp. 73-87.

Correa, C. M. (1996). 'Strategies for Software Exports from Developing Countries', *World Development*, 24(1): pp. 171-182.

Dicken, P., Kelly, P. F., Olds, K., and Yeung, H. W. (2001), 'Chains and Networks, Territories and Scales: Towards a Relational Framework for Analysing the Global Economy', *Global Networks*, 1(2): pp. 89-112.

Gerrefi, G., Korzeniewicz, M. and Korzeniewicz, R. P. (eds) (1994), *Commodity Chains and Global Capitalism*, Westport, Conn: Praeger.

Grabher, G. and Stark, D. (1997), *Post-socialist Pathways: Restructuring Networks in Post-Socialism*, Oxford: Oxford University Press.

Heeks, R. (1998), 'The Uneven Profile of Indian Software Exports' Working Paper No 3 from Development Informatics Series, Institute for Development Policy and Management, University of Manchester.

Katkalo, V. and Mowery, D. (1996), 'Institutional Structure and Innovation in the Emerging Russian Software Industry' in Mowery, D. (ed.), *The International Computer Software Industry: A Comparative Study Industry Evolution and Structure*, Oxford: Oxford University Press.

Larner, W. and Le Heron, R. (2002), 'The Spaces and Subjects of a Globalising Economy: A Situated Exploration of Method', *Environment and Planning D: Society and Space*, 20: pp. 753-774.

Meske, W. 'Restructuring and Reintegration of S&T Systems in Economies in Transition' available at http://www.sussex.ac.uk/spru/cce/d-summar.html.

Murdoch, J. (1995), 'Actor-Networks and the Evolution of Economic Forms: Combining Description and Explanation in Theories of Regulation, Flexible Specialization, and Networks', *Environment and Planning A*, 27: pp. 731-757.

O'Riain, S. (1997), 'An Offshore Silicon Valley?', *Competition and Change*, 2: pp. 175-212.

Paulk, M. (1994), 'A Comparison of ISO 9001 and the Capability Maturity Model for Software', Software Engineering Institute, CMU/SEI-94-TR-12.

Paulk, M. (1995), 'How ISO 9000 Compares with CMM', IEEE Software.

Paulk, M. (1999), 'Practices of High Maturity Organizations', The 11th Software Engineering Process Group (SEPG) Conference, Atlanta, Georgia, 8-11 March 1999.

Radosevic, S. (1998), 'The Transformation of National Systems of Innovation in Eastern Europe: Between Restructuring and Erosion', *Industrial and Corporate Change* 7 (1): pp. 77-108.

Radosevic, S. (1999), 'Alliances and Emerging Patters of Technological Integration and Marginalization of Central and Eastern Europe with the Global Economy' in Dyker, D. and Elgar, E. (eds) *Foreign Direct Investment in the Former Soviet Union.*

Radosevic, S. (1999b), 'International Technology Transfer Policy: From "Contract Bargaining" to "Sourcing"' *Technovation*, 19: pp. 433-444.

Storper, M. (2000), 'Globalisation and Knowledge Flows: An Industrial Geographer's Perspective', In J. Dunning (ed.), *Regions, Globalisation and the Knowledge Based Economy.* Oxford: Oxford University Press.

Torrisi, S. (1998), Industrial Organisation and Innovation: An International Study of the Software Industry, Cheltenham: Edward Elgar.

Chapter 6

Geopolitical Economy of Global Syndicated Credit Markets

Bongman Seo

Introduction

Since the mid-1980s two important developments in global finance have failed to attract much interest from economic geographers or scholars in related disciplines. First, although private financial firms are now widely recognised as the primary decision makers of global financial flows replacing nation-states or international financial institutions (including the IMF and the World Bank), no research has examined ways in which inter-organizational dynamics among private financial firms, especially power dynamics, are connected to financial flows. Second, while experts in the early 1990s anticipated that the position of commercial banks and their syndicated credit markets would weaken, global syndicated credit markets remain the main funding vehicle in capital markets. Commercial banks remain the key players in global financial markets.

Global syndicated credit markets have been an integral part of global financial markets since 1960s. Their market potential was not realized, however, until the second half of the 1990s. We can gauge the nature of these markets by looking at international bank loans. These loans are syndicated in order to diversify risk exposure among lenders. In the early 1990s, experts anticipated the demise of global syndicated credit markets in competition against debt securities such as Euronotes and Eurobonds, which were thought to be main beneficiaries of financial innovations, especially securitization (Armitage, 1998). However, global economic growth in the second half of the 1990s was spurred by the revitalization of the U.S. economy. This resulted in the growth of both global syndicated credit markets and bond markets, rather than a race to zero-sum competition between them. In fact, global syndicated credit markets have become increasingly integrated with global bond markets. This is due in part because corporations started using syndicated credits mainly as standby facilities to back up their bond issuance (Armitage, 1998).

The rise of global syndicated credit markets in the latter half of the 1990s was accompanied by a modest amount of research on the market. Management scholars and market practitioners primarily conduct the current research (Rhodes et al., 2000; Zaheer and Mosakowski, 1997). This is supplemented by analyses in such journals as *International Financing Review* and *Euroweek*, as well as focuses on either analyses of market trends (e.g. liquidity, pricing of fees and interest rates, and league tables of lenders) and borrowers, or practical guides to market mechanisms which illustrate how to construct the deals (e.g. selection of participants, decisions on terms of deals, fees and interest margins). In other words, analyses of the syndicated credit markets are done in order to provide market practitioners with proficiencies for better investment decisions. Generally, the information provided concerns global market trends such as the total number of deals with changes in fees and rates, supplemented by regional league tables with some episodic explanations about specific deals and general economic trends. This practical knowledge, however, offers little information about the inter-organizational dynamics among lenders in global syndicated credit market, or of geographical dimensions of this fastest growing market (beyond the regional league tables).

This chapter examines the political economy of global syndicated credit markets through a geo-relational framework that stresses specific geographies of financial flows, as well as the inter-organization dynamics among financial firms behind these financial flows. Here I explore the emerging global geo-political economic structure of global syndicated credit markets as a geo-historical product since the mid-1980s. This chapter will focus primarily on spatial linkages between lenders and borrowers with different geographical origins, as well as power relationships among lenders prescribed by divisions of labour in credit syndication. This analysis of financial relationships in regional markets reveals the ways in which lenders and borrowers have interacted and positioned themselves at the regional scale, and furthermore, the ways in which their relationships in regional markets have constituted the global financial market. I will first examine the historical geographies of the lenders and the borrowers, which show the overall spatial flows of global syndicated credits. Second, I analyze changes in inter-organizational dynamics embedded in the syndicated credit networks among lenders in three core regional markets: Industrialized Asia, North America, and Western Europe. This chapter looks in particularly at the power structures, or divisions of labor, among lenders in the regional markets, examining whether there have been significant changes in the positions they occupy.

Geographies of Lenders and Borrowers in Syndicated Credit Markets

Data and Measurement

Syndicated credit markets are one of the most well documented markets as most syndicated credit facilities are publicly announced in a tombstone in financial journals. The data used in this analysis are from Loan Pricing Company's DealScan database, one of the most comprehensive sources of syndicated credit markets, along with Euromoney's Loanware. I have excluded purely domestic syndicated credit facilities because the analysis focuses on cross-border financial flows. A total of 32,917 facilities are identified as 'international', meaning that at least one syndicate partner's nationality is different from the borrower's.

Two different measures of syndicated credit flows are used: the actual commitment and the lead share. The actual commitment is the actual amount that each lender commits to a syndicated credit facility, usually represented in a percentage of total facility amount. The lead share is the estimated amount that each lead lender controls out of total facility amount. The lead share is obtained by dividing the total facility amount by the number of lead lenders in the credit syndicates. In DealScan, there are 21 different roles, which can generally be divided into three larger functional groups: arrangers (agents), managers, and participants. Due to their critical roles in organizing the credit syndicates, arrangers/agents are identified as 'lead lender' while other lenders are classified as 'subordinate lender'.

Along with descriptive statistics, I use two indexes to measure geographical diversification, the Hirschman-Herfindahal Index (HHI), and the Financial Leverage Index (FLI). HHI measures the extent to which lenders' operations are concentrated on certain regional borrowers and syndicate partners. Higher HHIs means less regional diversification.

$$HHI = \sum_{1}^{n} S_i^2 \quad \text{where } S_i \text{ is the regional share.}$$

FLI is measured by dividing the lead share by the actual commitment. FLI estimates the amount of money that each lead lender controls compared to the actual amount of money that they commit to the market. If one lender's FLI is over 1, then the lender controls more money than it commits to the market and is considered to have a leverage power in the market.

FLI = Lead Share/Actual Commitment

The temporal division is set during critical moments in global finance, especially with regard to Asian (Japanese) finance. An example is the evolution of Japan's financial history: the Japanese bubble period (1986–1989), the burst of the Japanese bubble and the pre-BIS capital adequacy (1990–1992), and the pre- and post-Asian financial crisis (1993–1997 and 1998–2000). The pre-Asian financial crisis period is split into two periods comparable to other periods.

Spatial Distribution of Borrowers

Since the mid-1980s, global syndicated credit markets have only experienced two setbacks, resulting from the Gulf War (1990–1991) and from the Asian financial crisis (1997). Overall, global syndicated markets have expanded their geographical reach from 22 countries to over 100 countries since the second half of the 1980s, channelling approximately US$ 1.8 trillion over 5000 facilities in the year 2000 (Table 6.1, Panel A). The HHI decreased over time, except during the two brief periods of crisis, indicating diversified access to the markets by borrowers outside

Table 6.1   Regional Distribution of Borrowers

Panel A: Regional Distribution of Borrowers

Region	Total over 15-yr period**	1986	1988	1990	1992	1994	1996	1998	2000
Caribbean	39.13	0.00	0.29	1.15	0.36	1.92	1.50	9.10	6.02
Central America	62.61	0.00	0.00	0.13	2.32	3.87	7.41	9.20	9.78
North America	6847.33	46.15	271.94	177.33	219.40	501.45	698.70	763.78	996.79
South America	124.26	0.00	0.00	0.47	0.48	2.99	9.54	26.47	31.08
Industrialized Asia	219.47	0.00	0.00	1.38	1.80	6.07	21.97	5.72	90.69
Oceania	106.84	0.00	0.41	0.84	6.01	5.84	9.31	7.29	25.34
Socialist Asia	30.45	0.00	0.00	0.92	0.68	1.64	5.05	3.36	6.12
South Asia	19.57	0.00	0.00	0.00	0.15	1.82	3.47	1.27	2.33
Southeast Asia	81.55	0.00	0.00	0.01	1.80	5.88	10.45	4.03	14.79
Eastern Europe	43.93	0.00	0.00	0.00	0.00	1.12	7.37	8.57	5.64
Former USSR	25.67	0.00	0.00	1.32	0.00	0.10	0.92	4.92	3.49
Western Europe	2122.82	0.00	30.92	57.86	39.96	89.54	164.28	224.72	576.52
Middle East and Northern Africa	122.01	0.00	0.00	0.83	1.59	2.80	14.36	22.65	21.44
Sub-Sahara Africa	25.55	0.00	0.00	0.00	0.18	0.78	3.60	2.22	6.35
Unknown	2.68	0.00	0.00	0.00	0.00	0.22	0.35	0.18	0.00
Grand Total	9873.88	46.15	303.56	242.22	274.75	626.03	958.26	1093.47	1796.38
HHI	5282	10000	8129	5932	6596	6624	5623	5315	4142

Table 6.1 (continued)

Panel B: Regional Distribution of Lenders

Region	Total over 15-yr period**	1986	1988	1990	1992	1994	1996	1998	2000
Caribbean	2.09	0.00	0.00	0.04	0.04	0.04	0.16	0.27	0.34
Central America	5.03	0.00	0.00	0.00	0.01	0.45	0.26	0.87	1.03
North America	5026.90	31.33	171.21	114.65	143.66	332.13	489.54	599.73	850.31
South America	16.29	0.00	0.00	0.15	0.18	1.45	1.41	2.27	2.83
Industrialized Asia	1151.00	5.04	49.41	41.93	33.88	96.25	146.80	71.07	160.53
Oceania	106.59	0.27	5.13	3.45	4.50	2.53	6.79	9.16	31.05
Socialist Asia	21.31	0.00	0.00	0.06	0.13	0.36	1.22	0.93	13.22
South Asia	1.94	0.00	0.00	0.00	0.01	0.09	0.17	0.21	0.81
Southeast Asia	9.98	0.00	0.00	0.04	0.09	0.62	1.03	0.04	4.09
Eastern Europe	5.24	0.00	0.00	0.11	0.02	0.07	0.61	1.32	0.94
Former USSR	4.77	0.00	0.00	0.40	0.01	0.07	0.51	0.76	0.98
Western Europe	3124.46	7.06	60.52	72.85	78.28	168.57	270.26	373.48	680.26
Middle East and Northern Africa	63.53	0.24	1.40	1.47	1.60	2.19	4.87	9.59	11.34
Sub-Sahara Africa	2.10	0.00	0.00	0.00	0.00	0.05	0.20	0.35	0.70
Unknown	1.34	0.00	0.07	0.45	0.00	0.08	0.07	0.03	0.05
Grand Total	9542.57	43.93	287.74	235.60	262.41	604.94	923.90	1070.09	1758.47
HHI	3994	5474	4281	3644	4057	4044	3917	4405	3922

* Discrepancies between total lending and total borrowing are present due to over- or under-subscription of syndicated credits.
** Totals are drawn from all years 1986 to 2000 inclusive, but for reasons of space only even years are displayed in table.
Source: DealScan (2001) Loan Pricing Corporation. Calculation by Author.

of the developed economies of North America and Western Europe. Interestingly, the demand of syndicated credits in Industrialized Asia increased dramatically and resulted in the lowest HHI since the mid-1980s. However, whereas syndicated credits available to borrowers in developing countries have largely grown in absolute terms, their relative shares have stagnated as the main regional shift has been from North America to Europe rather than from North to South. Within the southern hemisphere, borrowers in Southeast Asia and South America are heavily favoured over those in Sub-Saharan Africa and Eastern Europe. It is also notable that the impact of the two crises tended to be larger outside of North America and Europe, as banks largely curtailed their commitment in developing countries, indicating the ongoing marginality of these markets compared to those of developed economies.

Spatial Distribution of Lenders

Compared to the distribution of regional borrowers, regional lenders show higher diversification, as lenders from Industrialized Asia and Western Europe account for much higher market shares than borrowers from the regions (Table 6.1, Panel B). Lenders from Industrial Asia committed more than 80 per cent of their money to borrowers outside their home/regional markets while Western European lenders committed around 32 per cent to non-regional borrowers. Despite their dominant market shares, North American lenders' commitment fell short of the syndicated credit demand from home/regional borrowers.

1986–1992

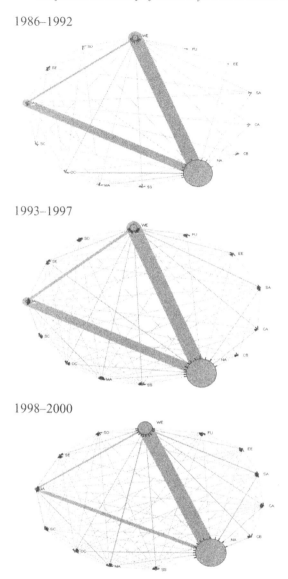

1993–1997

1998–2000

Figure 6.1   Inter-Regional Flows of Syndicated Credits, 1986–2000

The size of nodes represents the relative size of intra-regional syndicated credit flows, scaled 3 to 50 (the largest). The thickness of the line represents the relative ties strength measured by total inter-regional flows (including both outflows and inflows), scaled 1 to 50 (the strongest). It is not possible to tell the relative strength of inflows and outflows, while possible to tell whether the flows are bi-directional or one-directional.
Source: Author's Calculation using Loan Pricing Company's DealScan (2001). Graphics are done by Borgatti's Netdraw (2002).

Appendix 6.1 Regional Classification for Figure 6.1

Regions	Sub-Regions	Countries
America	Caribbean (CB)	Bahamas, Barbados, Bermuda, British Virgin Islands, Cayman Islands, Dominican Republic, Haiti, Jamaica, Netherlands Antilles, Puerto Rico, Republic of Trinidad and Tobago
	Central America (CA)	Belize, Costa Rica, El Salvador, Guatemala, Honduras, Mexico, Panama
	North America (NA)	Canada, USA
	South America (SA)	Argentina, Bolivia, Brazil, Chile, Colombia, Ecuador, Paraguay, Peru, Uruguay, Venezuela
Europe	Eastern Europe (EE)	Bulgaria, Croatia, Czech Republic, Hungary Macedonia, Poland, Romania, Slovakia, Slovenia
	Former USSR (FU)	Estonia, Kazakhstan, Latvia, Lithuania, Russia, Tajikistan, Turkmenistan, Ukraine, Uzbekistan
	Western Europe (WE)	Austria, Belgium, Denmark, Finland, France, Germany, Greece, Iceland, Ireland, Italy, Luxembourg, Malta, Monaco, Netherlands, Norway, Portugal, Spain, Sweden, Switzerland, United Kingdom
Asia-Pacific	Industrialized Asia (IA)	Hong Kong, Japan, Singapore, South Korea, Taiwan
	Oceania (OC)	Australia, New Guinea, New Zealand
	Socialist Asia (SC)	China (PRC), Vietnam
	South Asia (SA)	Bangladesh, India, Pakistan, Sri Lanka
	Southeast Asia (SE)	Indonesia, Malaysia, Philippines, Thailand
Middle East/ Africa	Middle East and Northern Africa (MA)	Algeria, Bahrain, Cyprus, Egypt, Iran, Israel, Jordan, Kuwait, Lebanon, Morocco, Oman, Qatar, Saudi Arabia, Turkey, United Arab Emirates
	Sub-Sahara Africa (SS)	Angola, Burkina Faso, Cameroon, Congo, Ghana, Guinea, Ivory Coast, Kenya, Lesotho, Liberia, Mali, Mauritius, Namibia, Nigeria, Senegal, Seychelles, South Africa, Tanzania, Tunisia, Uganda, Zambia, Zimbabwe

Discrepancies between regional lenders' commitment and borrowers' demand only reveal the net-flow of syndicated credits. This chapter, therefore, examines the overall geographies of syndicated credit flows and how regional flows of syndicated credits are organized through inter-organizational dynamics among lenders.

Changing Patterns of Inter-Regional Syndicated Credit Flows

In the late 1980s and the early 1990s, major syndicated credit flows existed between North America, Western Europe and Industrialized Asia, with secondary flows between these cores and Oceania (Figure 6.1). During the rapid growth period of the mid-1990s, spatial flow patterns among three core regions were strengthened and many secondary flows emerged between three core regions and emerging economies in South America, Southeast Asia, Middle East/Northern Africa, Eastern Europe, and Oceania. Global syndicated credit markets thus significantly extended and diversified their geographical reach beyond the three core regions. Western Europe established new secondary connections with South and Central America, Eastern Europe, former USSR countries, Middle East/Africa, and Southeast Asia. North America strengthened its connection with South and Central America and Southeast Asia.

The burst of the Asian financial crisis in 1997 together with a rush of mergers and acquisitions in Europe during the late 1990s re-organized spatial flows of syndicated credits. Although more minor financial connections emerged, major and secondary financial flows changed little except for connections with Southeast Asia and Asia. Most countries affected by the Asian financial crisis recovered their pre-crisis financial inflows except for Indonesia. Indonesia's syndicated credit inflow was the sixth largest (US$ 13.64 billion) in 1997 and collapsed to US$ 0.10 billion in 2000. Syndicated credit flows between North America, and Southeast and Industrialized Asia significantly decreased between 1998 and 2000, while Europe sustained its financial linkages to other regions except Industrialized Asia. Additionally, for regions outside the triad, the strongest linkage was to Europe, indicating the rising importance of both European lenders and borrowers in global syndicated credit flows.

Since the mid-1980s, syndicated credit markets have increased their geographical reach. Their linkages have emerged among peripheral sub-regional economies, in addition to dominant flows among three core regions and secondary flows between core regions and periphery sub-regions. By the late 1990s, every sub-region had developed financial linkages with at least eight other sub-regions, with the three core sub-regions connected to all the other sub-regions. Unlike the emerging tri-polar structure found in international trade patterns, however, global syndicated credit markets have become increasingly bi-polarized with little market development in Asia. This tendency toward a bi-polarized financial flow structure may represent another dimension of uneven global syndicated credit market development between East and West. This is particularly evident as Asian financial firms, especially Japanese financial firms, failed to sustain their competitiveness against North American and Western European financial firms with major home/regional markets integrated with strong spatial linkages to borrowers.

Despite their relatively important status in global syndicated credit flows, intra-regional syndicated credit flows (represented by the size of node circles in Figure 6.1) of Industrialized Asia remained much smaller than those present in North America and West Europe. The relatively limited opportunities in their home/regional markets pushed lenders from Industrialized Asia to search for opportunities in foreign regional markets. Financial firms from Industrialized Asia, including Japanese financial firms, are therefore more likely to be burdened with a *liability of foreignness* than their counterparts from North America and Western Europe. Over time, deregulation and improved information availability may have reduced the impact of liability of foreignness.

Changing Geopolitics in Regional Syndicated Credit Markets

Syndicated credits depend on lead lenders' monitoring powers rather than public credit ratings. Because they also require significant information flows between lead role banks and borrowers, they resemble relation-based financing more than transaction-based financing. Due to the relational financing nature, especially between lead lenders and borrowers, syndicated credit markets are likely to pose liabilities of foreignness for global financial firms outside their home/regional market, and to favor home/regional lenders over foreign ones in syndicated credit markets.

Inter-Organizational Dynamics in North America

North American lenders were dominant in their home/regional market, accounting for more than 60 per cent of total actual commitment to borrowers (Table 6.2, Panel A) and their dominance as lead lender was even greater, accounting for more than 75 per cent of total lead share amount (Table 6.2, Panel B). The North American market has always been one of net-borrowers and their capital needs were met by financial in-flows mainly from Industrialized Asia and Western Europe, as well as minimal contributions from other periphery regions. During the 1990s, lenders from Western Europe and Industrialized Asia took opposite strategic paths in North America. Western Europe sustained its share in total commitment at around 20 per cent and became the only regional lenders to increase their lead share from less than 5 per cent in the 1980s to 18 per cent in the late 1990s. In contrast, Industrialized Asia decreased their actual commitment share in North America from some 15 per cent in the late 1980s to 6 per cent a decade later. Although Industrial Asia never accounted for more than 5 per cent of the total lead share, their actual commitment was always higher than 13 per cent except during the last period (1998–2000). As a result, while actual absolute amount financial in-flows to North America from the other regions increased, North American borrowers had a less diversified group of lenders in the late 1990s than in the late 1980s. This occurred as (primarily) Japanese Industrialized Asia lenders withdrew from the market and facilitated further concentration of market share in the hands of North American lenders and Western European lenders.

   While collaborating with other lenders as both lead-role and subordinate partners in credit syndication, North American lenders were the only group with FLIs over 1, arranging a greater amount than their actual commitment in facilities. Most regional lenders in North America had FLIs below 0.5 (Table 6.2, Panel C), although they improved their financial leverage power throughout the 1990s as North American lenders' FLIs decreased (1.59 to 1.19). Much lower financial leverage indexes of non-North American lenders indirectly suggest their large burden of foreign liabilities against North American lenders, as well as their resulting role as subordinate participants in credit syndicates arranged by North American lenders. Even though Southeast Asia showed a very high financial leverage index in the late 1990s, it was too premature and too small to attach any meaningful explanation.

Table 6.2   Profile of Regional Lenders in North America (US$m)

Panel A: Actual Commitment

Lender's Regional Origin	1986–1989		1993–1995		1998–2000	
Caribbean	13.04	0.00%	127.74	0.01%	857.20	0.03%
Central America	0.00	0.00%	0.00	0.00%	182.47	0.01%
North America	393266.30	62.75%	818274.28	59.75%	1651481.79	64.46%
South America	40.00	0.01%	398.76	0.03%	240.89	0.01%
Industrialized Asia	98934.27	15.79%	203659.10	14.87%	156856.27	6.12%
Oceania	9225.97	1.47%	4240.82	0.31%	20137.63	0.79%
Socialist Asia	0.00	0.00%	94.12	0.01%	1332.93	0.05%
South Asia	0.00	0.00%	0.00	0.00%	439.84	0.02%
Southeast Asia	0.00	0.00%	195.53	0.01%	11.96	0.00%
Eastern Europe	0.00	0.00%	50.63	0.00%	560.04	0.02%
Former USSR	22.50	0.00%	20.23	0.00%	560.89	0.02%
Western Europe	122093.52	19.48%	338775.79	24.74%	718757.27	28.05%
Middle East and Northern Africa	2957.92	0.47%	3652.94	0.27%	10344.65	0.40%
Sub-Sahara Africa	4.30	0.00%	48.65	0.00%	121.06	0.00%
Unknown	134.45	0.02%	62.50	0.00%	87.52	0.00%
Grand Total	626692.27	100.00%	1369601.09	100.00%	2561972.41	100.00%
HHI	4569		4403		4981	

Panel B: Lead Share

Lender's Regional Origin	1986–1989		1993–1995		1998–2000	
Caribbean	0.00	0.00%	0.00	0.00%	222.25	0.01%
Central America	0.00	0.00%	0.00	0.00%	126.70	0.00%
North America	625649.18	94.09%	1231200.07	85.71%	1970551.53	75.68%
South America	0.00	0.00%	0.00	0.00%	25.00	0.00%
Industrialized Asia	10282.47	1.55%	49733.83	3.46%	75445.09	2.90%
Oceania	1613.65	0.24%	496.67	0.03%	8758.23	0.34%
Socialist Asia	0.00	0.00%	0.00	0.00%	65.24	0.00%
South Asia	0.00	0.00%	0.00	0.00%	0.00	0.00%
Southeast Asia	0.00	0.00%	135.00	0.01%	17.31	0.00%
Eastern Europe	0.00	0.00%	0.00	0.00%	0.00	0.00%
Former USSR	0.00	0.00%	0.00	0.00%	0.00	0.00%
Western Europe	27351.37	4.11%	154914.02	10.78%	547441.56	21.03%
Middle East and Northern Africa	37.00	0.01%	0.00	0.00%	975.99	0.04%
Sub-Sahara Africa	0.00	0.00%	15.00	0.00%	14.17	0.00%
Unknown	0.00	0.00%	0.00	0.00%	0.00	0.00%
Grand Total	664933.67	100.00%	1436494.59	100.00%	2603643.07	100.00%
HHI	8873		7474		6179	

Panel C: Financial Leverage Index

Lender's Regional Origin	1986–1989	1993–1995	1998–2000
Caribbean	0.00	0.00	0.26
Central America	NA	NA	0.69
North America	1.59	1.50	1.19
South America	0.00	0.00	0.10
Industrialized Asia	0.10	0.24	0.48
Oceania	0.17	0.12	0.43
Socialist Asia	NA	0.00	0.05
South Asia	NA	NA	0.00
Southeast Asia	NA	0.69	1.45
Eastern Europe	NA	0.00	0.00
Former USSR	0.00	0.00	0.00
Western Europe	0.22	0.46	0.76
Middle East and Northern Africa	0.01	0.00	0.09
Sub-Sahara Africa	0.00	0.31	0.12
Unknown	0.00	0.00	0.00
Grand Total	1.06	1.05	1.02

Source: Loan Pricing Company (2001) DealScan. Author's Calculation.

Inter-Organizational Dynamics in Industrialised Asia

Industrialized Asian lenders dominated their home/regional markets in terms of both the actual commitment and the lead share, accounting for some 40 per cent and 35 per cent, respectively (Table 6.3). Despite aggressive penetration by Western European lenders, Industrialized Asian lenders maintained their dominance in the actual commitment throughout the 1990s. Penetration of foreign lenders stalled in the late 1990s, however, when Industrialized Asia suffered from a series of post-financial crisis problems. In particular, North American lenders' actual commitment share dropped from 23 per cent to 13 per cent. Industrialized Asian lenders' dominance in the lead share was undermined rapidly in the early 1990s as Western European lenders became the main market makers (arrangers), edging out the home/regional lenders. As withdrawal of U.S. banks created credit gaps in the market in the late 1990s, Industrialized Asian lenders had to double the value of their commitment in terms of both actual commitment and lead share to meet the almost tripled credit demands from home/regional borrowers during the crisis recovery. In the late 1990s, Industrialized Asian lenders became the major market makers again, and Chinese lenders aggressively penetrated this booming market, as Hong Kong, Taiwanese and Japanese borrowers became active.

Despite the presence of prominent regional lenders, Industrialized Asian borrowers drew more funds from North American and Western European lenders than their home/regional lenders, becoming the most diversified core market. However, the relatively smaller home/regional market size and the relatively higher penetration of foreign competitors have placed Industrialized Asian lenders in a situation where they were forced to explore new opportunities in foreign markets, and were potentially burdened with higher 'liabilities of foreignness' than their counterparts.

Despite their declining market share in both actual commitment and lead share, North American lenders are the only group that consistently kept their financial leverage index over 1, exceeding 2 in the late 1990s (Table 6.3, Panel C). Western European lenders maintained their financial leverage index slightly over 1 during the 1993–1997 period, while falling to 0.92 in the late 1990s. Industrialized Asia lenders consistently improved their financial leverage indexes, but only reaching near 1 (0.98) in the late 1990s. Oceania lenders seemed to strengthen their financial leverage power in the second half of the 1990s, reaching 1.16 in the late 1990s. In short, while lenders from Western Europe and Industrialized Asia dominated the market in terms of market shares, North American lenders were much more effective in utilizing their money (actual commitment) owing to their relatively frequent participation as arrangers.

Table 6.3   Profile of Regional Lenders in Industrialised Asia (US$m)

Panel A: Actual Commitment

Lender's Regional Origin	1986–1989		1993–1995		1998–2000	
Caribbean	0.00	0.00%	20.87	0.09%	15.47	0.01%
Central America	0.00	0.00%	0.00	0.00%	0.00	0.00%
North America	634.02	14.74%	4414.50	19.92%	14314.45	12.00%
South America	0.00	0.00%	14.00	0.06%	63.16	0.05%
Industrialized Asia	3526.60	81.98%	9075.79	40.95%	49215.02	41.27%
Oceania	4.20	0.10%	122.89	0.55%	2185.92	1.83%
Socialist Asia	0.00	0.00%	290.56	1.31%	12234.88	10.26%
South Asia	0.00	0.00%	0.00	0.00%	61.32	0.05%
Southeast Asia	0.00	0.00%	83.27	0.38%	817.60	0.69%
Eastern Europe	0.00	0.00%	31.45	0.14%	5.47	0.00%
Former USSR	0.00	0.00%	0.00	0.00%	23.04	0.02%
Western Europe	97.65	2.27%	8032.87	36.24%	39546.86	33.16%
Middle East and Northern Africa	8.40	0.20%	60.98	0.28%	723.82	0.61%
Sub-Sahara Africa	0.00	0.00%	0.00	0.00%	54.17	0.05%
Unknown	31.15	0.72%	16.91	0.08%	2.00	0.00%
Grand Total	4302.02	100.00%	22164.09	100.00%	119263.18	100.00%
HHI	6943		3389		3056	

Panel B: Lead Share

Lender's Regional Origin	1986–1989		1993–1995		1998–2000	
Caribbean	0.00	0.00%	0.00	0.00%	0.00	0.00%
Central America	0.00	0.00%	0.00	0.00%	0.00	0.00%
North America	0.00	0.00%	6160.20	27.75%	30196.10	23.48%
South America	0.00	0.00%	0.00	0.00%	0.00	0.00%
Industrialized Asia	3550.00	93.54%	7106.64	32.01%	48297.79	37.56%
Oceania	0.00	0.00%	57.00	0.26%	2533.21	1.97%
Socialist Asia	0.00	0.00%	171.67	0.77%	10710.33	8.33%
South Asia	0.00	0.00%	0.00	0.00%	0.00	0.00%
Southeast Asia	0.00	0.00%	0.00	0.00%	302.00	0.23%
Eastern Europe	0.00	0.00%	0.00	0.00%	0.00	0.00%
Former USSR	0.00	0.00%	0.00	0.00%	0.00	0.00%
Western Europe	105.00	2.77%	8420.83	37.93%	36206.69	28.15%
Middle East and Northern Africa	0.00	0.00%	168.00	0.76%	299.38	0.23%
Sub-Sahara Africa	0.00	0.00%	0.00	0.00%	56.25	0.04%
Unknown	140.00	3.69%	118.40	0.53%	0.00	0.00%
Grand Total	3795.00	100.00%	22202.74	100.00%	128601.75	100.00%
HHI	8772		3234		2828	

Panel C: Financial Leverage Index

Lender's Regional Origin	1986–1989	1993–1995	1998–2000
Caribbean	NA	0.00	0.00
Central America	NA	NA	NA
North America	0.00	1.40	2.11
South America	NA	0.00	0.00
Industrialized Asia	1.01	0.78	0.98
Oceania	0.00	0.46	1.16
Socialist Asia	NA	0.59	0.88
South Asia	NA	NA	0.00
Southeast Asia	NA	0.00	0.37
Eastern Europe	NA	0.00	0.00
Former USSR	NA	NA	0.00
Western Europe	1.08	1.05	0.92
Middle East and Northern Africa	0.00	2.76	0.41
Sub-Sahara Africa	NA	NA	1.04
Unknown	4.49	7.00	0.00
Grand Total	0.88	1.00	1.08

Source: Loan Pricing Company (2001) DealScan. Author's Calculation.

Western Europe

Western European lenders were the major market makers as well as market participants in their home/regional markets, while North American lenders followed behind with widening gaps (Table 6.4). Western European lenders increased their market share from 45 per cent to nearly 68 per cent in actual commitment, and from 48 per cent to 65 per cent in the lead share, indicating their sustained focus on their home/regional markets throughout the 1990s. Especially in the late 1990s, Western European lenders drastically increased their home/regional market shares, exceeding North American lenders' home/regional share in actual commitment. Meanwhile, North American lenders maintained their shares in Western Europe in both actual commitment and lead share. Industrialized Asian lenders struggled to sustain their market shares in both their actual commitment and lead share in the mid-1990s, only to drop to the single digit level in the late 1990s.

Although they maintained their dominant market shares, Western European lenders had FLI values slightly less than 1, compared to those of North American lenders at around 1.5. North American lenders may have been lead lender partners of Western European lenders rather than their subordinate partners. Industrialized Asian lenders' shares continuously decreased in both actual commitment and lead share amount, reflecting increasing competitive pressures from European lenders and North American counterparts. Their FLIs remained at around 0.5, suggesting that their main role in the market was as subordinate partners. Like North America, Western European markets became increasingly controlled by two core regional lenders – North America and Western Europe, while Industrialized Asian lenders failed to keep up with market growth.

Emerging Patterns and Conclusions

Since the mid-1980s, global syndicated credit markets expanded their geographical reach, supporting the pro-globalization view of freer access to credits and investment opportunities for borrowers and lenders of developing countries. Detailed analyses at the regional level revealed that in all three regional markets, home/regional lenders largely maintain their dominance in both the actual commitment and lead share. Particularly Western European lenders, as well as North American lenders, have consistently challenged the dominance of Industrialized Asian lenders in their home/regional market. Meanwhile, North American lenders sustained their dominant lead share in home/regional markets at some 75 per cent (the highest regional lead share) and West European lenders reinforced their dominance in both actual commitment and lead share. As a result, Industrialized Asia was the most diversified market with HHI (lead share) ranging from 4060 to 2828 in the 1990s, compared to North America's HHI from 7807 to 6176, and Western Europe's HHI from 4310 to 5223.

Table 6.4   Profile of Regional Lenders in Western Europe (US$m)

Panel A: Actual Commitment

Lender's Regional Origin	1986–1989		1993–1995		1998–2000	
Caribbean	0.00	0.00%	0.00	0.00%	12.15	0.00%
Central America	0.00	0.00%	9.12	0.00%	0.00	0.00%
North America	28649.43	32.94%	76865.27	24.97%	276111.74	23.73%
South America	28.57	0.03%	1936.85	0.63%	3248.60	0.28%
Industrialized Asia	16603.74	19.09%	54967.05	17.86%	71014.59	6.10%
Oceania	1772.34	2.04%	1006.41	0.33%	15825.30	1.36%
Socialist Asia	0.00	0.00%	40.35	0.01%	213.49	0.02%
South Asia	50.00	0.06%	9.44	0.00%	45.11	0.00%
Southeast Asia	25.86	0.03%	42.12	0.01%	49.18	0.00%
Eastern Europe	0.00	0.00%	187.03	0.06%	132.56	0.01%
Former USSR	0.00	0.00%	342.73	0.11%	1300.62	0.11%
Western Europe	39141.11	45.01%	171518.45	55.73%	789663.91	67.87%
Middle East and Northern Africa	696.89	0.80%	782.90	0.25%	5580.41	0.48%
Sub-Sahara Africa	0.00	0.00%	0.00	0.00%	211.45	0.02%
Unknown	0.00	0.00%	81.82	0.03%	23.51	0.00%
Grand Total	86967.94	100.00%	307789.54	100.00%	1163432.62	100.00%
HHI	3480		4049		5209	

Panel B: Lead Share

Lender's Regional Origin	1986–1989		1993–1995		1998–2000	
Caribbean	0.00	0.00%	0.00	0.00%	0.00	0.00%
Central America	0.00	0.00%	9.12	0.00%	0.00	0.00%
North America	36118.80	42.80%	118073.50	38.01%	379690.87	31.40%
South America	0.00	0.00%	1733.61	0.56%	1537.55	0.13%
Industrialized Asia	7652.77	9.07%	25842.94	8.32%	33177.00	2.74%
Oceania	0.00	0.00%	71.17	0.02%	6932.51	0.57%
Socialist Asia	0.00	0.00%	64.90	0.02%	0.00	0.00%
South Asia	0.00	0.00%	0.00	0.00%	0.00	0.00%
Southeast Asia	0.00	0.00%	0.00	0.00%	20.48	0.00%
Eastern Europe	0.00	0.00%	6.71	0.00%	49.13	0.00%
Former USSR	0.00	0.00%	83.33	0.03%	1001.51	0.08%
Western Europe	40614.62	48.13%	164709.39	53.02%	786335.67	65.03%
Middle East and Northern Africa	0.00	0.00%	32.16	0.01%	361.29	0.03%
Sub-Sahara Africa	0.00	0.00%	0.00	0.00%	0.00	0.00%
Unknown	0.00	0.00%	0.00	0.00%	0.00	0.00%
Grand Total	84386.19	100.00%	310626.83	100.00%	1209106.01	100.00%
HHI	4231		4326		5223	

Panel C: Financial Leverage Index

Lender's Regional Origin	1986–1989	1993–1995	1998–2000
Caribbean	NA	NA	0.00
Central America	NA	1.00	NA
North America	1.26	1.54	1.38
South America	0.00	0.90	0.47
Industrialized Asia	0.46	0.47	0.47
Oceania	0.00	0.07	0.44
Socialist Asia	NA	1.61	0.00
South Asia	0.00	0.00	0.00
Southeast Asia	0.00	0.00	0.42
Eastern Europe	NA	0.04	0.37
Former USSR	NA	0.24	0.77
Western Europe	1.04	0.96	1.00
Middle East and Northern Africa	0.00	0.04	0.06
Sub-Sahara Africa	NA	NA	0.00
Unknown	NA	0.00	0.00
Grand Total	0.97	1.01	1.04

Source: Loan Pricing Company (2001) DealScan. Author's Calculation.

While both the North American and Industrialized Asia markets became increasingly diversified, Western Europe's market became less diversified. However, further diversification in North America is mainly done by infiltration by Western European lenders without simultaneous by Industrialized Asian lenders. Consequently in both North America and Western Europe, financial market globalization took the form of trans-Atlanticization as North American and Western European lenders increased their collaboration, and Industrialized Asian lenders' share continued to shrink. There may be two possible explanations for this trans-Atlanticization. First, major booms in these two core markets were driven by a wave of mergers and acquisitions, which are supposedly riskier and require more information to arrange deals in comparison with general purpose syndicated facilities. Second, the market share of Industrialized Asian lenders decreased as financial turmoil and reforms followed the 1997 crisis, especially in Japan. This forced Industrialized Asian lenders, especially Japanese, to reduce their market activities in the late 1990s when the market was growing at accelerating rates. Meanwhile, Industrialized Asia had a more diversified cross-regional participation of lenders, indicating their home/regional lenders' relatively weak competitiveness and higher competitive pressure from North American and Western European lenders.

The patterns of FLIs across regional markets suggest another story. While North American lenders were the only group that consistently showed FLIs over 1 across regional markets, their FLIs in foreign markets were higher than those in home/regional markets. The lower FLIs of North American lenders in home/regional markets indicate high competitive pressures among home/regional lenders in North

America as well as competitive pressures from foreign lenders. While FLIs are lower for North American lenders even in their home/regional markets, Industrial Asian and Western European lenders' FLIs are higher in their respective home/regional markets than those in foreign markets. This indicates their relative competitiveness in home/regional markets. Although Industrial Asian and Western European lenders were able to raise their financial leverage indexes throughout the 1990s, although it is not clear whether this was due to adjustment to incorporate regional lenders co-arranging syndicate partners to exploit further information, or to increased competitiveness of these regional lenders. In short, North American lenders are the only ones that achieved globally expansive circuits of financial flows along with globally competitive performances. European lenders successfully expanded their circuit of syndicated credits while defending their regional markets, while failing to improve their leverage power in their expanded financial circuits. Although Industrialized Asia became the most diversified and competitive market, Industrialized Asian lenders grew increasingly marginal in the other two markets.

References

Armitage, S. (1998), *Syndicated Lending in Europe*. London: Stationery Office.

Borgatti, S. (2002), *NetDraw*. Network Visualization Software.

Loan Pricing Company (2001), *DealScan*, New York: Loan Pricing Company.

Rhodes, T. Clark, K. and Campbell, M. (2000), *Syndicated Lending: Practice and Documentation*. London: Euromoney Books.

Zaheer, S. and Mosakowski, E. (1997), 'The Dynamics of Liabilities of Foreignness: A Global Study of Survival of Financial Services', *Strategic Management Journal*. 18: pp. 439-464.

Chapter 7

State Governance, Regulatory Processes and Entrepreneurship: Singapore's Concentrating Banking Sector

Shuang-Yann Wong

Introduction

This chapter argues that the spatial integrity of key metropolitan financial centres is upheld due to the continued importance of their services to place, economy and people (Corbridge et al., 1994; Massey, 1993; Sassen, 1998; Martin, 1999). The continuous innovations, flows of information within and between networks, and the maturation of skilled finance labour markets further enhance the competitive advantages of these localities. Such social and local embeddedness enables financial firms such as retail or commercial banks to play an intermediary role. The important questions are why some banks fail while others get stronger. To what extent does social and locational embeddedness explain such differential outcomes? Do the star performers tend to exhibit higher levels of accountancy, accountability, flexibility and reflexivity (Dodd, 1995; Leyshon, 2000; Thrift, 1994) and effectively capitalize on established network relations to overcome adversities and multiply resources? Some actors thrive on the basis of politico-economic support. Hence relationships between firms, between states, between firms and states, and socialization are important, depending on where the banks are located and the governance regime. Singapore's experience is used to illustrate the impact of such globalizing tendencies on its banking sector, entrepreneurship development and the contested banking space (Hamilton-hart, 2003; Tan, 1985; Toh and Tan, 1998).

The chapter uses the constructivist approach to integrate the socio-economic and political in a study of local banking enterprise experience in the contest of an increasingly competitive economic space under globalization and liberalization pressures. The experience of one of the strongest local banks is used to reveal the sector/enterprise's trajectory path under different governance regimes. Success and survival appears to depend on maintaining the trust and information flows that social networks provide, while developing regulatory structures that facilitate openness and transparency.

State Governance and Singapore: Options and Strategies

A statist concept of economic governance emphasizes the way in which state uses its authority and power to structure market exchange in various ways through regulatory practices and rules. In East Asia, Singapore together with Taiwan and South Korea achieved their economic success in the 1970s using such statist developmental policy (Lim, 188, 1991; Low, 1998, 1999). Recent evidence shows, however, that market-driven forces have compelled many states, including Singapore, to become more active in playing the supervisory and regulatory roles as they strive to sustain national competitiveness. In some countries, there may be some weakening of the state's role, a partial shift from top-down forms of governance. In general, the state remains the central institution that alone can allocate rights, regulations, sanctions, incentives and resources, as well as penalties.

State governance involves the use of authority and institutions to mobilize and allocate resources, to coordinate and control activities in a country. The state via the government can command its supporting networks to get involved in governance functions with the aims of achieving desired collective outcomes. Effective governance can only take place, however, when there are proper systems of evaluation, transparent communication, and accountability through some form of public-private partnership.

In Singapore state governance has taken two paths. First, more market-conformance has occurred by opening up protected sectors such as finance, banking, telecommunication and transportation to greater foreign participation. Second, more regulations and policies are enforced to manage and coordinate the financial sector as new products and instruments are introduced. Thus, the trajectory of the economy continues to be shaped by the state but is based on a broader neo-liberal governance regime. The state stays vigilant regarding the investment process and activities of key actors such as transnational corporations. State governance has shifted from the protectionism of the last three decades to forceful competition and external-orientation. The realization is that national competitiveness no longer rests on traditional factor endowments only, but also specific institutional capacities for market and non-market forms of economic coordination. The greater risks and uncertainties for the resource-scarce city-states inevitably demand such regulatory governance. In the aftermath of the 1997 regional crisis, the state has vigorously pursued cluster specialization, privatization, mergers and acquisitions, skills upgrading and innovations.

Research on 'network' approaches to governance emphasizes collaboration and cooperation. This implies devolution of authority, joint policy-making and implementation pacts between government and organized interests. The preference of such strategy stems from the rejection of dichotomies such as markets versus state, or public versus private. Such networks, embedded within markets, societies and hierarchies, are governed by goal-directed, collaborative and associative activity involving interdependent networks of actors and organizations. Effective governance requires such embedded social capital and the ability to govern. The National Wage Council and cost-cutting measures such as wage restraint and tax rebates are some examples of governmentalities that have been contested in the recent moves of the government to sustain Singapore's competitiveness. The state and citizens need to act in unison in constructing economic reality for the nation-state.

Additionally, effective state governance is reflected in its empowered institutions such as the Economic Development Board (EDB) and the Monetary Authority of Singapore (MAS), which will shape the behaviour of actors and policy possibilities. The effective functioning of these institutions in turn depends on the organizational and bureaucratic capacity of the state to choose and implement policy strategies or state autonomy. A degree of insulation from societal pressures and political opponents is crucial. Additionally, the same political party has governed Singapore since independence with a lack of any strong opposition parties, giving the state the capacity to push through policy reforms. Being a city-state with no other local or provincial governments to challenge, the state's capacity is enhanced greatly by having a relatively hierarchical and centralized bureaucratic structure that gives its policy-makers the institutional means for purposeful and coordinated action. Singapore's bureaucracy is staffed with expert and dedicated policy advisers that ensure the supply of adequate resources, especially taxation revenue, further augment the state's capacity.

After many years of economic restructuring, Singapore has evolved from its former status as an *entrepot* of the British Empire into a modern global city. Despite lacking natural resources, it succeeded in diversifying into manufacturing industries that have earned it the highest per capita income in Southeast Asia. The country's weaknesses in small size and resource scarcity have been turned into strengths, as early on it began to globally source the requisite capital, labor, technology and markets to create wealth. The accountability of the banking system and management efficiency has enabled Singapore to become the region's financial hub. Singapore's economy is relatively unscathed by the 1997 regional crisis and was able to donate funds to poverty stricken larger-sized and resourceful neighbours. The 1970s oil crises, the mid-1980s recessions, the 1997 crisis, the terrorism fear and SARs have alerted the government to the need for close safeguarding, monitoring and managing its valuable resources.

It is increasingly evident that the city-state becoming less competitive in major manufacturing sectors, especially electronics and electrical goods, which has been its key growth engine. The uphill task is to intensify the development of this sector, which will require tremendous amount of skills re-training, research and technology development. While making the adjustments, efforts are made to revitalize the banking and finance sector through deepening and diversification as the manufacturing sector is expected to stabilize at about a quarter of the GDP. The lack of entrepreneurship is listed as one of the obstacles in future development. The existing literature takes either an economic or cultural-political perspective in reviewing Singapore's development outlook.

The remainder of the chapter comprises three sections. First is the general background of local banking sector. This is followed by an account of the United Overseas Bank's formation, territorial expansion, and social and cultural relations, highlighting the bank's resource mobilization strategy. The second part examines state regulatory measures and the impact they have exerted on local banks. Finally, the implications of the changes and contemporary outcomes are discussed. It is argued that the early stage of the bank's success is largely an outcome of cooperation based on closely-knit ethnic-based socio-economic working relations. However, the bank's subsequent consolidation and entrepreneurship are derived not only from the founding members' economic inertia or socialization, but more importantly, from the state's institutional support and protection in different periods of governance regimes. The chapter tries to show that the relations between enterprises and the state could be mutually reinforcing especially in a small city-state like Singapore.

The Local Banking Sector: General Background

Local banks of the early period were born out of the needs of the colonial state's mercantilist capitalism. The booming commodity trading businesses, mainly rubber and tin and other tropical produce, encouraged the birth of such banks to cater to the varied needs of merchants (Wong, 2002). These banks flourished and diversified into other enterprises. The dependence on commodity trade eventually led to the demise of some of the banks while others were bought by the stronger ones.

The post-independence economic restructuring period ushered in many changes to the financial and banking landscape. The reforms of the 1970s culminated in local sector expansion as the number of local banks increased to 13 and remained so until the 1990s. The pressures of competition led to more regulatory measures and the government's emphatic call for consolidation and the number of local banks had dwindled to only 3 by 2002: Overseas Chinese Banking Corporation (OCBC), United Overseas Bank (UOB), and Development Bank of Singapore (DBS). Unlike the first two local banks, DBS is a government-linked company (GLC) that has evolved from its previous function as a local enterprise developmental bank to a commercial/investment bank today.

The question is how these three banks have managed to thrive while the others have not. OCBC was established much earlier than UOB and has gone through many changes, making it one of the strongest local banks. UOB is a latecomer in comparison and has become the largest local bank, overshadowing even DBS, which was ranked the largest in Southeast Asia. UOB is still owned and managed by a family, yet continues earning profitable returns and diversifying into many other financial and non-financial businesses. It is important to learn how UOB has risen to today's enviable position, in what ways social, cultural and economic ties have been instrumental, and what kind of institutional support and state governance have facilitated the bank's expansion and consolidation. We will explore these questions by unfolding the development processes that the bank has traversed over the years.

UOB's Organizational Formation and Expansion: The State and Networks

The founding of UOB in 1935 grew out of Wee Kheng Chiang's own vested interest to control his business of transshipping goods and overcoming the long distance and infrequent transport services between Kuching and Singapore. Singapore was chosen partly because of its strategic location and *entrepot* status. More importantly, it is the place where his good social relations and strong ties with people of the same community and ethnicity could provide the requisite capital, knowledge, expertise and reliability to help run the bank. There he could entrust his business to partners who could tolerate his frequent absence as he plied between the two places for his own business activities. The bank confined its activities to business transactions with Chinese merchants engaged in the region's trading of primary commodities, mainly rubber, rice, pepper and tin. It also offered remittance services to China, business loans to small businesses, and deposits taking. Capable and experienced personnel were sourced to provide the stewardship that contributed to the bank's robust development in the early stage.

In 1960, Wee Cho Yaw joined to help manage the bank in Singapore. His working experience at Kheng Leong was an asset as UOB is a commercial bank dealing mainly with merchants in Southeast Asia commodity trades. Similarly, Wee depended on community and business networks to expand the bank's business and draw able and influential professionals into the Board of Directors. The subsequent economic and political turmoil, however, compelled him to take a more diversified and organizational approach often in compliance with the country's development objectives. Wee and his family control the bank's ownership as substantial shareholders and his eldest son, who is groomed to succeed him, is now the bank's deputy chairman.

Wee's dexterity in turning crisis into opportunities has persisted over the years. The Hong Kong branch was set up to avert the Indonesia confrontation crisis in the 1960s. When the currency interchangeability with Malaysia was terminated in 1973, UOB issued US Dollar Convertible Bonds while the government floated the Singapore dollar and encouraged the Asian Dollar Market. He has co-managed syndicated loans with the Industrial Bank of Japan, DBS and European Investment Bank, gradually promoting the bank's internationalization. During the mid-1980s' recession, loans repayment problems were resolved by acquiring debtors' associated companies or property, thereby amassing profitable returns from industries, property and real estates including The Plaza Building, New Park Hotel, Plaza Hotel, UOL Building and UIC. The bank continued to invest in property with the construction of hotels, resorts and condominium both at home and abroad.

Under Wee, UOB has flexibly used its close networks to internationalize its business sphere while seizing opportunities offered by the state, continuing to grow as Wee suggested. The 1971 takeover of Chung Khiaw Bank from Slater Walker Securities was facilitated by the state's regulation of forbidding foreign ownership of local banks as well as MAS's intervention to disapprove the resale to the founding family. The 1972 acquisition of Li Hwa Bank was due to the latter's loan default and employees' embezzlement. In 1986, fearing that family disputes of the Industrial and Commercial Bank (ICB) may blemish local banks' accountability, MAS recommended a public offer and UOB won the deal (Wong, 2002).

The 1990s was marked by an unprecedented amount of mergers and acquisitions in developed economies. Foreseeing the imminent threat, local banks were urged to consolidate, but the response was slow. The government-linked bank

DBS initiated the move by first acquiring POSB in 1998. In 2002 OCBC followed suite, merging with KTLB. UOB then outbid DBS for OUB to become UOB-OUB group, now the biggest lender in the city-state with assets of US$115 billion. The merger has helped broaden the bank's scope in SME loan services, wireless internet banking service, as well as China's connections (Wong, 2002).

UOB's banking business at home currently comprises 85 branches and service centres. However, the bank's businesses outside Singapore tend to cluster in Southeast Asia with a 37-branch network in Malaysia, a 68-branch network in the Philippines, and a 75 per cent stake in Thailand's Radanasin Bank. UOB is expanding into Northeast Asia covering Hong Kong, China, Taiwan, Australia, Brunei, Vietnam and South Korea. Its branches or subsidiaries are located in key metropolitan centres including New York, Los Angeles, London, Sydney, Paris and Tokyo and has recently set a goal to derive 40 per cent of its income from overseas in eight years' time. By 2003, UOB had gained approval to offer foreign currency services to Chinese citizens and companies in Beijing.

Reconfiguration of Local Banks' Economic Space – Liberalization, Regulation and State Governance

The UOB experience has illustrated the trajectory path taken by local banks in reaching today's strength and stability. The free trade regime and absence of foreign exchange controls have enabled these banks to flourish. The few quantitative restrictions such as controls on the internationalization of the Singapore dollar are meant to meet international obligations and ensure public safety of their funds. Despite the liberal regime, Singapore was still criticized for its protectionist stance in banking and financial services at WTO meetings. Recently, major unilateral financial reforms were launched and bilateral free trade agreements (FTAs) were signed with New Zealand, Japan, Australia, EFTA and USA. This begs the question whether the remaining local banks can continue to rely on strong state governance to reinforce their performance as the dynamics of globalization, liberalization and innovations in ICT give rise to changing economic space.

The fact that Singapore was not hit as hard by the 1997 crisis compared to its regional counterparts is a demonstration of its relatively developed economy. The marginal growth of its financial sector in the post-crisis period (1.1 per cent between 1998 and 2001) testifies to its strength and accountability. The stunted growth is primarily related to close association with regional economies that expose the city-state to greater vulnerability than Hong Kong or Sydney, for example. The 1997 lesson informs a need for market and product diversification as well as continued vigilance and facilitation by the state. To sustain the reputable standard in a liberal environment, the next stage of governance would involve high prudential supervision and more rules-based regulation that aim at sustaining local banks' competitiveness, complementing their deficiencies and methodically erasing the perceived protectionist stance. Supervision of risk/asset management, corporate governance and market discipline will be emphasised. Entry barriers and limits on ownership and branching will diminish in time. Local banks' market territories are likely to be safeguarded, as they constitute a kind of oligopoly that is central to the stability of domestic financial, economic and political system.

The unilateral financial reforms implemented since 1999 aim to inject greater dynamism and innovation under MAS's risk-focused supervision. With liberalization local banks are expected to become more enterprising and proactive in their business ventures. On the other hand, the state acts to effect changes in the monetary policy that will facilitate free intensive capital flows and complex derivative products while allowing for progressive internationalization of the Singapore dollar. There will be more and new scope for banks to tap into as the state cautiously guards the position of Singapore as the hub of financial services.

MAS will commence prudential regulation and supervision involving liberalizing commercial banking, promoting a more open banking environment and upgrading local banks. A 2-tier bank-licensing regime (full and wholesale) will replace the 3-tier regime for foreign banks (full, restricted, offshore). Foreign banks will be granted new privileges usually enjoyed by local banks. These include the status of Qualifying Full Bank (QFB), up to 10 locations of operations, free re-location of existing branches and sharing of ATMs with other QFBs. Restricted banks are renamed Wholesale Banks (WB) and could engage in the whole range of banking business with the conditions of having only one operating office in Singapore, accepting Singapore fixed deposits of at least S$250,000 per deposit and operating savings accounts only in Singapore dollars. Offshore Banks once upgraded to WB status will deal mainly in the Asian Dollar Market, foreign exchange transactions and wholesale banking business with non-residents. They may then engage in Singapore dollar financing to resident borrowers, but are subject to a ceiling of S$200 million per bank. Offshore banks with QOB privileges would have their Singapore dollar-lending limit raised to S$1 billion from the current S$300 million and could accept Singapore dollar funds from non-bank customers through swap transactions. Such measures should enlarge the pools of funds for financing businesses, and reinforce Singapore's position as the region's business hub.

To enlarge capital markets, the Stock Exchange of Singapore and SIMEX have merged to form the Singapore Exchange (SGX). SGX has now expanded its product offerings to include single stock and bond futures and exchange-traded funds, as well as encouraging foreign companies to list in SGX alongside existing domestic firms. With the liberalization of fees and access to stock-broking, brokers may now transact shares on behalf of clients and advise them on financial investments. Since borrowing Singapore dollars to speculate is forbidden, investors could either swap or convert the Singapore dollars.

The island state is set to upgrade itself into a centre of wealth management, universal processing and Asia risk exchange. The banks have moved vigorously into wealth management in private equity and hedge funds. To be a universal processing centre would entail the attraction of unimpeded massive business and capital flows, which may be aided by TNCs' use of Singapore as their regional headquarters. The Asia Risk Exchange will combine Singapore's existing insurance and capital market expertise into a new vehicle for the transfer of large and sophisticated risks. It will complement Singapore's risk transfer capabilities and fill a market gap for risk transfer in the Asian time zone. How local banks will carve their niche in this new banking and financial space will require extensive investigation.

Local and foreign banks are thus encouraged to diversify and create more specialized services such as wealth or asset management, or offer services formerly not widely available such as housing loans to HDB flat buyers and insurance. These reforms will reconfigure the economic space of local banks as the business scope and products expand. Banks will become multi-tiered, specialized and multi-faceted as their clients become increasingly varied in taste, preferences and sophistication. The mandate for banks to concentrate on financial activities is a signal to move into the supply of highly value-added financial services to preempt the encroachment of foreign counterparts. The same tendencies are found in the USA and the UK.

In Singapore, the two local private banks are still owned substantially by the founding families who have accumulated enormous resources by diversifying into non-banking businesses such as property and real estate development. The banks have developed significant cross-shareholdings without running into serious problems largely due to stringent regulations. They do not optimize returns from their significant property holdings, which are used to cushion against uncertainties. These local banks have become the three largest banks in Southeast Asia, but remain small on a global scale. DBS, the largest, is only ranked 86th by assets in the world (*The Banker*, July 2002). The unwinding of the cross-shareholdings and re-organization of banks' activities may diminish resources that they can maneuver to sustain market territories. To stimulate greater spin-offs and to keep banks resourceful, banks could hold properties solely for investment purposes within MAS's prudential limits. Banks, however, are not allowed to develop or manage hotels or other properties directly or indirectly. Before the end of 2004, banks must divest all properties held for development and shareholdings in property development companies that are beyond the portfolio investment limits.

For local banks, carving new niches would require extra or new entrepreneurial skills. Transnational banks possess highly skilled knowledge, information and management expertise necessary to realize new sets of sophisticated, specialized and global-oriented services such as venture capital or equity portfolio investments. To sustain local banks' competitiveness, Nominating Committees chaired by independent directors must be set up to ensure the appointment of competent individuals to the banks' Board and key management positions. Banks' auditors will be rotated every five years to update disclosure standards in line with industry developments and international best practice.

Local banks have responded readily to these regulatory measures with little dissent except for the request to extend the divestment deadline of non-core activities. UOB, for example, has reduced its Haw Par shares and is rationalizing its financial shareholdings in United Overseas Land (UOL), Hotel Negara and Overseas Union Enterprise (OUE). Its OUB Centre branch will specialize in upper-end wealth management services while its UOB Plaza branch will target customers with lower income levels. The first generation of local banks has succeeded by benefiting from ethnic-based socio-cultural networks and effective state governance. The next generation will not tread the same path, as the new banking space is increasingly dominated by trans-nationals that can exert power beyond the controls of sovereign states.

Beyond the Socio-Cultural Networks?

These rules-based reforms seem to have weakened the role of socio-cultural networks in Singapore's banking business. Local banks have even been told to reduce reliance on family networks or *guanxi*. The emphasis is now on credit risks assessment, management and rigorous investments based on arms-length and commercial considerations within the politico-economic framework. The domestic banking landscape has become concentrated and local banks have responded to the new regulatory measures with few grudges. State governance, social capital and embeddedness have generated an effective win-win economic and political interaction and cooperation. These governance networks based on close state vigilance are significant for a small, natural resource-scarce city-state that is given the unchallenged autonomy to do so.

The weakening of socio-cultural significance to local banks is reflected in UOB's third generation caretaker. Wee Ee Chung, the founder's grandson, is now the bank's Vice-Chairman. Graduated from Harvard with a business degree, his western education has equipped him with professional knowledge and expertise in modern banking and finance. He is the first Singaporean elected to represent in the VISA RHQ, and holds directorship in several subsidiaries of the UOB group and local schools, yet is visibly less active in community activities than were his father and grandfather. The Senior Wee has stated his wish to see the successor participate more actively in local social, cultural and community activities.

The founders of other local banks such as Lee Kong Chien, Aw Boon Haw and Tan Lark Sze are often recognized as exemplary Singapore entrepreneurs. Wee Cho Yaw never considered himself exemplary, recognizing that unlike the others, his achievements were not attained through personal hard work and perseverance. Wee considered himself lucky to have worked in a rich family's business, with everything arranged for him to learn, manage and develop. As Wee said, UOB is actually a company that is run by well-trained administrators and a political environment that gave the bank the opportunity to grow and prosper. To thrive in the openly contested banking space in the new global economy, neither socio-cultural relations nor institutional support *per se* suffices. What is required is effective state governance that could marshal the essential resources at the critical time, and the actors/banks will have to respond flexibly, reflexively, and demonstrate the knowledge and accountability to succeed and persevere.

References

Corbridge, S., Thrift, N. and R. Martin (eds) (1994), *Money, Power and Space*, Oxford: Blackwell.

Dodd, N. (1995), 'Money and the Nation-State: Contested Boundaries of Monetary Sovereignty in Geopolitics', *International Sociology*, 10, pp. 139-54.

East Asian Analytical Unit (1995), *Overseas Chinese Business Networks in Asia*, Canberra: Department of Foreign Affairs, East Asia Analytical Unit.

Hamilton-Hart, N. (2003), *Asian States, Asian Bankers: Central Banking in Southeast Asia*. Singapore: Singapore University Press; Talisman Publisher, Pte Ltd.

Lee T. Y. and Low, L. (1990), *Local Entrepreneurship in Singapore: Private and State*, Institute of Policy Studies (Singapore). Singapore: Times Academic Press.

Leyshon, A. (2000), 'Money and Finance', in F. Sheppard and T. J. Barnes (eds), *A Comparison to Economic Geography*, Oxford: Blackwell Publishers, pp. 432-449.

Lim, C. Y. (1988), *Policy Options for the Singapore Economy*, Singapore: McGraw-Hill.

Lim, C. Y. (1991), *Development and Underdevelopment*, Singapore: Longman.

Low, L. (1998), *The Political Economy of a City-State: Government-Made Singapore*, Singapore: Oxford University Press.

Low, L. (1999), *Singapore: Towards a Developed Status*, National University of Singapore, Centre for Advanced Studies. Oxford: Oxford University Press.

Martin, R. (1999), 'The New Economic Geography of Money', in R. Martin (ed.), *Money and the Space Economy*, Chichester; John Wiley and Sons, pp. 3-27.

Massey, D. (1993), 'Power-Geometry and a Progressive Sense of Place', in J. Bird et al. (eds). *Mapping the Futures*, Oxford; Routledge.

Monetary Authority of Singapore. *MAS Annual Report*; MAS, Singapore. Various years.

Sassen, S. (1998).*Globalization and Its Discontents*, New York; The New Press.

Straits Times, Singapore.

Tan, C.H. (1985), *Financial Markets and Institutions in Singapore*, Singapore: Singapore University Press.

Thrift, N. (1994), 'On the Social and Cultural Determinants of International Financial Centers: The Case of the City of London', in S. Corbridge, N. Thrift and R. Martin (eds), *Money, Power and Space*. Oxford: Blackwell, pp. 327-355.

UOB (1985), *Growing with Singapore*, Singapore, UOB Group.

UOB. UOB Annual Report. Various years. Singapore.

Toh Mun Heng and Tan Kong Yam.(eds) (1998), *Competitiveness of the Singapore Economy: A Strategic Perspective*. Singapore University Press. World Scientific.

Wong, S.Y. (2002), 'Cross-National Ethnic Networks in Financial Services: The Case Study of Local Banks of Singapore', Paper presented at the IGU Commission on 'The Dynamics of Economic Space Conference', Johannesburg, South Africa, paper available from author.

Chapter 8

Foreign Direct Investment and Economic Change in the Yangtze Valley, China: Opening up a New Economic Space

Yufang Shen

Introduction

The Yangtze is 6,300 kilometers long and is the largest river in China and the third largest in the world. It flows across China's middle mainland from southwest to the east before emptying into the East China Sea. The Yangtze valley includes in total 11 provinces and autonomous regions and 2 municipalities and is currently the most highly developed region apart from China's East Coast. It contains nearly half of China's total population, more than one third of the total cultivated land and half of China's total economic capacity in terms of GDP.

The Yangtze valley region linked into the outside world after the Opium War treaty and was a cradle area in Chinese modern times industrial civilization. After liberation in 1949, however, because of the cold war between the eastern and western worlds, it was isolated for nearly 30 years from western countries. Now, the region is opening again to the outside world following an open-door policy issued by the China's central government in 1978. This has seen vitality of the economy of the region with rapid growth of the GDP and constant increase of FDI (foreign direct investment) for many years particularly since the 1990s. In 2000, the GDP growth rate was 9.6 per cent in the Yangtze valley region and 9.8 per cent in the Yangtze Economic Zone (YEZ) (Hu, 1999). These growth rates were respectively 1.3 and 1.5 points above the national average level. The 'Yangtze Strategy' policy has helped the Yangtze valley, particularly the YEZ, become China's core economic development zone, connecting the east and the west with great potential.

In terms of regional development thinking in China, the fundamental pattern that the coastal areas should develop first, following the opening up policy to the outside world in the 1980s, changed at the end of 1990s into a new pattern that laid emphasis on sustainable and balanced development of all regions, particularly balanced development between the west and the east. In this regional development vision, the Yangtze valley, particularly the YEZ, is expected to play an important role in transmitting the growth from east to west and making contributions to the national targets. Given that FDI has exerted and will certainly exert more and more important effects on the overall growth of the Yangtze valley after China's accession to the WTO, it is useful to analyze the region's relationship with FDI against the background of changing situations.

General Trend of Economic Growth in the Yangtze Valley

Trend and Features of Economic Growth of Individual Province, Autonomous Region and Municipality in the Yangtze Valley (1996–2000)

Following the implementation of the 'Yangtze Strategy' development policy in the mid-1990s, the economy of the Yangtze valley, particularly the YEZ, has grown rapidly. Between 1996 and 2000, the GDP increased continuously in almost all of the provinces, autonomous regions and municipalities in the Yangtze valley. In total, the Yangtze valley region GDP increased from 2,920.11 billion yuan in 1996 to 4,110.90 billion yuan in 2000. The country's total GDP increased from 42.5 per cent in 1996 to nearly 46 per cent in 2000. The total YEZ GDP accounted for over 42 per cent of the country's total GDP in 2000. This growth was felt very widely in the valley; most areas were above the national average growth rate except for a few provinces of Jiangxi, Yunnan and Qinghai (in exceptional years, the growth rates of the GDP of even these provinces nearly reached the average level).

This general regional growth trend was accompanied by changes in the region's economic structure. Between 1996 and 2000, the total GDP output value of the secondary and tertiary sectors increased annually. In contrast, the output value of the primary sector remained fairly constant. Secondary production grew modestly. Most importantly, the tertiary sector grew rapidly and continuously, a trend that echoed throughout the Yangtze valley. This pattern of regional growth has produced a distinctive economic structure. In 2000, the sectoral ratios in the Yangtze valley and the YEZ were respectively, 15.7 : 46.5 : 37.8 and 15.0 : 46.9 : 38.1. When compared with that of the whole country (15.9 : 50.9 : 33.2), the overall level of the economic structure of the Yangtze valley, especially the YEZ, featured a larger service sector level.

Main Features of Economic Growth in Different Areas of the Yangtze Valley

A more disaggregated view shows other dimensions. In Shanghai, Jiangsu and Zhejiang at the lower reach of the Yangtze, local economies grew at high speed, where growth rates were higher than the national average level and the Yangtze valley as a whole. While the national average growth rate was 8.3 per cent and the Yangtze valley's 9.6 per cent, Shanghai's 10.8 per cent, Jiangsu's 10.6 per cent, and Zhejiang's 11.0 per cent were markedly higher. Compared with the lower areas, the upper and middle reaches of the Yangtze were below the average level of the Yangtze valley. Growth rates of Jiangxi and Yunnan provinces in 2000 were below even the national average level.

This intra-regional unevenness becomes even sharper in terms of per capita GDP. By this measure economic growth was seriously unbalanced between the upper, middle and lower reaches of the Yangtze. In 2000, Shanghai's per capita

GDP of accounted for 488.1 per cent of the national average level, while Jiangsu's was 166.3 per cent and Zhejiang's 190.2 per cent. In contrast, areas at the upper and middle reaches of the Yangtze were far below the per capita GDP national average, with exception of Hubei Province, in which the per capita GDP was above the average level. A comparison of development levels between areas at the upper and the middle reaches of the Yangtze, shows that the overall economic level of areas at the middle reach (including four provinces of Hubei, Hunan, Anhui and Jiangxi) was higher than that of areas at the upper reaches, particularly Hunan and Hubei provinces. In the upper reaches, economic levels of Chongqing and Sichuan were higher than that of others.

Based on analysis of the economic structure's evolution, differences of economic development in different areas become apparent. The primary sector's total GDP in comparison to that of Shanghai, Jiangsu and Zhejiang were lower than the average level of the Yangtze valley, while the secondary sector's amount was above the average level of the Yangtze valley, and far above that of the primary industry. The tertiary sector's amount is sometimes dramatic, particularly in Shanghai, which has a strong tertiary base. In 2000 Shanghai's economic structure was 1.8, 47.5 and 50.6 per cent, respectively. Although, the relative importance of the primary and secondary sectors has diminished in recent years, the output value of these activities has increased. In the case of tertiary activities, both absolute and relative values have increased greatly. The relative contribution increased from 43.0 per cent in 1996 to 50.6 per cent in 2000, and the output value increased from 124.81 billion yuan in 1996 to 230.43 billion yuan in 2000. In the upper and middle reaches of the Yangtze, Hubei was the only province with an economic structure similar to that of the lower reach areas. The amount of primary industry in other areas was often excessively high, with the exception of Qinghai Province in 2000. Secondary industry activities in these areas were lower than the average level of the Yangtze valley although those of the tertiary industry were high generally. This economic structure poses a problem for these areas. Based on their existing structure, without powerful support of the secondary sector, prospects of real and sustainable economic growth are low.

In general, economies of the Jiangsu and Zhejiang provinces and Shanghai municipality at the lower reach of the Yangtze are relatively advanced, and their development levels are high. In these areas, the secondary and tertiary sectors dwarf the primary sector. At the beginning of the 21st century the regions sought to upgrade their industries by promoting new and high-tech industries with low energy costs, less pollution and high value-added products. They also sought to develop finance, trade, commerce, information and other modern service industries. Many policy makers believe that labour-intensive and resource-intensive industries should be moved to other areas like middle and west China where there are plentiful natural resources and great market potential. Areas at the upper and middle reaches of the Yangtze, with the exception of Jiangxi, are still in the process of industrialization, but with secondary and tertiary industries exceeding primary activities. For these areas, then, it is possible to speed up further development of the secondary and tertiary industries using their existing foundations. Additionally, by improving manufacturing capabilities in processing materials and the quality of some high value-added products, they will accomplish their goal of having resource-based economies.

Influence of FDI on the Overall Economic Growth of the Yangtze Valley

General Situation of FDI in Different Areas of the Yangtze Valley

In 2000, the total foreign direct investment (contracted) in the Yangtze valley was 23.65 billion US dollars and the total realized foreign direct investment was 14.24 billion US dollars. These figures accounted for 37.9 per cent and 34.9 per cent of the country's total. That same year, the total FDI (contracted) in the YEZ amounted to 23.11 billion US dollars and the total realized FDI was 14.10 billion US dollars, accounting for 37.0 per cent and 34.5 per cent of the country's total.

Actual Influence of FDI on the Overall Economic Growth of the Yangtze Valley

Using foreign capital to promote the Chinese economy followed from the reforms and the open-door policy. This strategy has helped make up for funding shortages, as well as bringing advanced technologies and managerial experience to China. Importantly, it has resulted in the transformation of the overall organizing system of Chinese industries, strengthening their capabilities in adapting to the outside market and international competitiveness.

According to Chinese statistics, foreign capital includes FDI, foreign loans and other sources. In recent years, the ratio of FDI compared to total realized foreign capital has been increasing dramatically. Data show that between 1994 and 1998 the percentage of FDI compared to the total realized foreign capital reached nearly 80 per cent for four successive years in China. It is therefore important to analyze the actual influence of FDI on the overall economic growth of the Yangtze valley.

Since the reforms, the Yangtze valley, especially the YEZ, has become a 'hot' region attracting foreign investor attention. From a development point of view, when transnational companies pursue profits, they simultaneously promote the movement and relocation of the resource factors including capital, technology, manpower and so on. This facilitates developing the export-oriented economy and inevitably the overall growth of the Yangtze valley, particularly the YEZ.

Through analysis of FDI in the individual provinces, autonomous regions and municipalities in the Yangtze valley, a clear picture emerges. FDI in almost all areas of the Yangtze valley kept increasing at a high level between 1990 and 2000. The figures were much above the national average level of 27.9 per cent, with the exception of Guizhou Province. Meanwhile, FDI growth rates far exceeded that of the GDP in many areas (see Table 8.1). Spatially, however, there was a sizeable disparity between different areas of the Yangtze valley and the YEZ in terms of total sum of FDI. In general, the total FDI absorbed in areas at the lower valley was much higher than that of other areas. The highest was in Jiangsu at 43.38 billion US dollars, accounting for 13.0 per cent of the country's total. Total FDI absorbed in areas at the upper reaches was much lower than elsewhere, with the exception of Sichuan.

Table 8.1 Analysis of the Relationships between FDI and the Growth of GDP (1990–2000)

	FDI			Elasticity rate of the FDI			Regression analysis between FDI and GDP		
	Total value (100 million USD)	% of the country's	FDI/GDP (%)	FDI (%)	GDP (%)	Elasticity rate of the FDI	R^2	Contribution rate of FDI to GDP	Constant
Country's total	3324.48	100.00	0.56	27.9	10.1	0.363	0.8573	0.56	2293.9
Shanghai	271.04	8.15	1.00	33.6	12.2	0.362	0.7679	0.44	624.6
Jiangsu	433.84	13.05	0.81	48.4	14.0	0.290	0.8498	0.43	1057.0
Zhejiang	110.09	3.31	0.30	42.0	15.0	0.356	0.8209	0.49	1093.9
Anhui	29.82	0.90	0.15	41.9	12.2	0.291	0.7060	0.35	1369.4
Jiangxi	26.76	0.80	0.21	43.3	9.9	0.228	0.7006	0.34	893.7
Hubei	63.49	1.91	0.24	41.7	11.9	0.285	0.7860	0.44	1161.2
Hunan	52.62	1.58	0.23	50.9	10.1	0.199	0.7809	0.35	1290.8
Sichuan	53.89	1.62	0.15	45.5	10.0	0.220	0.6689	0.37	1907.2
Guizhou	3.94	0.12	0.06	18.2	8.8	0.484	0.4516	0.42	928.6
Yunnan	9.54	0.29	0.07	47.6	9.3	0.195	0.7601	0.32	1334.1
Tibet (Xizang)	0.00	0.00	0.00	—	11.9	—	—	—	—
Qinghai	0.56	0.02	0.03	66.2	8.7	0.131	0.4305	0.20	335.8
Yangtze valley	1055.19	31.74	0.41	—	—	—	0.8007	0.41	3706.7
YEZ	1041.12	31.32	0.44	—	—	—	0.8020	0.42	3323.6

Source: National Bureau of Statistics of China 2001 *China Statistical Yearbook 2001*, China Statistics Press.

New Economic Spaces: New Economic Geographies

The per cent of FDI to total GDP is also geographically uneven. FDI was high in areas at the lower reach, particularly Shanghai, lower in areas at the middle reach, and least in areas at the upper reaches (with no FDI at all in Tibet). Table 8.2 illustrates elasticity coefficients for the actual influence of FDI on the overall economic growth of different areas. The elasticity coefficients, however, only illustrate the average situation of the FDI to total GDP and are therefore only guides to the relationship between FDI and the growth of GDP. A regression analysis goes further.

Table 8.2   Analysis of the Elasticity Coefficients of the FDI to Imports and Exports (1992–2000)

	Growth rate of FDI (%)	FDI and imports and exports		FDI and exports		FDI and imports	
		Growth rate of imports and exports (%)	Elasticity rate of the FDI to imp. and exp.	Growth rate of exports (%)	Elasticity rate of the FDI to exp.	Growth rate of imports (%)	Elasticity rate of the FDI to imp.
	A	B	C	D	E	F	G
Country's total	17.4	14.1	0.809	14.4	0.828	13.7	0.788
Shanghai	26.1	17.2	0.659	16.4	0.626	18.0	0.687
Jiangsu	20.3	23.2	1.141	24.8	1.220	21.5	1.060
Zhejiang	26.9	22.7	0.842	23.1	0.858	21.9	0.815
Anhui	24.6	9.6	0.390	15.2	0.619	4.7	0.190
Jiangxi	10.8	8.5	0.785	8.7	0.806	8.2	0.757
Hubei	21.2	6.3	0.297	5.8	0.276	6.8	0.319
Hunan	22.7	6.8	0.299	4.5	0.197	10.3	0.455
Sichuan	25.3	8.4	0.331	9.0	0.358	7.6	0.302
Guizhou	3.0	9.8	3.291	10.1	3.411	9.3	3.154
Yunnan	20.5	8.0	0.391	9.4	0.459	6.3	0.309
Tibet (Xizang)	—	—	—	—	—	—	—
Qinghai	66.2	6.7	0.102	6.9	0.105	6.6	0.099
Yangtze valley	22.3	17.8	0.800	18.3	0.822	17.3	0.775
YEZ	22.3	18.1	0.812	18.6	0.834	17.6	0.788

Note: (C) = (B) / (A), (E) = (D) / (A), (G) = (F) / (A); FDI in Guizhou Province initially increased and then decreased from 1992 to 2000, resulting in low annual growth rates of FDI. Hence, the elasticity rates of FDI in 3 indicators are unreasonably higher than normal ones. For this reason, Guizhou Province is not included in this analysis when comparing it with other provinces and municipalities.
Source: National Bureau of Statistics of China 2001 *China Statistical Yearbook 2001*, China Statistics Press.

Suppose there is an interrelationship between FDI and GDP as follows:

LN (GDP) = a $\times$ LN (FDI) + b

or,

LN (GDP) = a*LN (FDI) + b

Here, 'a' and 'b' present the regression coefficients, and 'LN' is the logarithm with base letter e. Then the above equation can be changed into:

GDP = $e^b \times FDI^a$

or,

GDP = $e^b * FDI^a$

This equation is equivalent in nature to the Cobb-Douglas production functional equation. Its economic meaning is that there is a logarithmic relationship between the input factor (FDI) and the output factor (GDP). In which, 'a' represents the contribution ratio referring to the growth rate the output (GDP) when the input factor FDI increases one unit; and 'e^b' is the constant indicating influence of other factors to the GDP besides FDI. In other words, extraneous factors including labor and technology factors will be reflected in the constant 'e^b'.

Associated with this, R^2 in Table 8.3 can be used to measure the fit of a linear regression line, and reflects the percentages of certainty of the dependent variable that can be explained by the regression model. According to the results, the average level of the Yangtze valley is 0.80, showing that 80.1 per cent of the Ln (GDP) variation is caused by Ln (FDI). In this, however, R^2 indices in Sichuan, Guizhou and Qinghai were lower than that in other areas, indicating a relatively weak interdependent relationship between increase of FDI and GDP growth in these areas.

An examination of the contribution ratio 'a' and constant 'e^b' indicates that in almost all of the areas the contribution of FDI and the constant are inversely related. This identifies the basic production relationship that where the contribution ratio of FDI was high, that of other factors (mostly labor and technology) would be low and vis-a-vis conversely. For example, in Shanghai and Anhui, the contribution ratios of the FDI to the total output (GDP) were 0.44 and 0.35, and their corresponding constants were 624.6 and 1,369.4. From the preceding discussion, we know that Anhui's overall economic development level was comparatively low and both the labor cost and technology level were lower than Shanghai's. So, in Anhui, the contribution ratio of the labor-intensive industry to the total output (GDP) was high. This analysis suggests a recent focus on labour-intensive industries in Anhui, and capital and technology-intensive industries in Shanghai, although the actual situation is more complicated.

Table 8.3   Regression Analysis between FDI and Total Investments in Fixed Assets (1990–2000)

	Total investments in fixed assets (100 million yuan)	Total investments as percentage of the country's (%)	FDI as percentage of the country's (%)	R^2	Contribution rate	Constant
Country's total	205753.8	100.00	100.00	0.9124	0.71	327.3
Shanghai	13838.2	6.73	8.15	0.8617	0.64	165.1
Jiangsu	17364.7	8.44	13.05	0.9298	0.48	285.2
Zhejiang	13675.6	6.65	3.31	0.8913	0.58	334.1
Anhui	5097.5	2.48	0.90	0.7764	0.41	320.2
Jiangxi	3019.8	1.47	0.80	0.7893	0.42	194.6
Hubei	7992.0	3.88	1.91	0.8762	0.63	240.9
Hunan	5825.5	2.83	1.58	0.8642	0.45	275.8
Sichuan	10936.6	5.32	1.62	0.7176	0.50	446.3
Guizhou	1964.2	0.95	0.12	0.4215	0.62	306.4
Yunnan	4311.4	2.10	0.29	0.8575	0.47	438.5
Tibet (Xizang)	335.4	0.16	0.00	—	—	—
Qinghai	765.0	0.37	0.02	0.5630	0.33	215.7
Yangtze valley	85125.8	41.37	31.74	0.8007	0.41	3706.7
YEZ	77749.8	37.79	31.32	0.8020	0.42	3323.6

Note: Because FDI were zero in Qinghai Province in 1990 and 1991, for Qinghai, data used in regression analysis were only from 1992–2000.
Source: National Bureau of Statistics of China 1997–2001 *China Statistical Yearbook 1997–2001*, China Statistics Press.

Four conclusions can be drawn from the above results. First, the increasing pace of FDI was clearly higher than that of the GDP in most of the areas of the Yangtze valley, particularly the YEZ with total FDI absorbed in the Yangtze valley and the YEZ accounting for 31.7 per cent and 31.3 per cent of the country's total. Second, in almost all of the areas, increasing FDI exerted a remarkable influence on the overall growth of GDP with average R^2 at 0.80 of the Yangtze valley as a whole and 0.80 of the YEZ as a whole. Third, the contribution ratios of FDI to the total output (GDP) were relatively high with average level at 0.41 per cent. Finally, differences amongst areas were noticeable.

In general, the total FDI absorbed in areas at the lower reach were high, while comparatively lower in areas at the middle reach and lowest in areas at the upper reaches except for Sichuan. In developed areas of Shanghai, Jiangsu, Zhejiang and Hubei, the total FDIs absorbed were higher than in other areas, which indicates that foreign capital is very important to their growth (refer to 'FDI/GDP' in Table 8.1). The positive interrelationship between an increase in FDI and the growth of GDP is evident because contribution ratios of FDI to GDP were also higher than those of other provinces (refer to 'R^2' in Table 8.1).

This relationship has undergone significant change over the past decade. Funding sources for fixed asset investment derive mainly from four outlets: i) the state budgetary appropriation; ii) bank loans and foreign investments; iii) independently funded enterprises; and iv) extraneous. Influenced by investment system reforms, fund sources of the total investments in fixed assets have since 1981 changed dramatically. It is important to note that the ratio of state budgetary appropriation to total investments in fixed assets has been decreasing for years and the state budgetary appropriation has now become a secondary source. As a result, FDI has played an increasingly important role in promoting the increase of the investments in fixed assets in the Yangtze valley, as well as and covering the overall shortages related funding sources. Comparatively, while total investments in fixed assets in areas at the lower reach were highest, they were lower in areas at the middle reach (with the exception of Hubei, accounting for 3.9 per cent of the country's total), and lowest in areas at the upper reaches (with the exception of Sichuan accounting for 5.3 per cent of the country's total). Comparing the distributional differences between FDI and the total investments in fixed assets in the Yangtze valley reveals that they followed a very similar pattern (Figure 8.1). This figure shows a strong interdependence between FDI and the total investments in fixed assets in the Yangtze valley, particularly the YEZ.

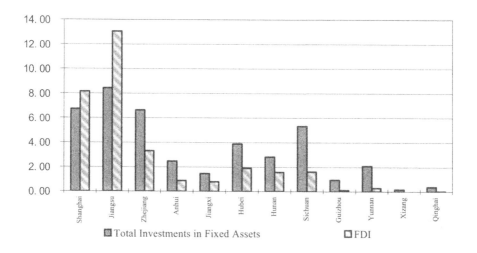

Figure 8.1   Map of Distribution of FDI and the Total Investments in Fixed Assets in the Yangtze Valley by Region (1990–2000)

Data between 1990 and 2000 have been used to regress FDI and the total investments in fixed assets. Most of the R^2 in Table 8.2 in the YEZ areas are above 0.7176. The positive relationship between FDI and the total investment in fixed assets mirrors the preceding finding for FDI and GDP. Little difference can be discerned between different areas of the Yangtze valley, indicating that the primary effect caused by FDI was widespread. The analysis shows that the average contribution ratio of FDI to the total investments in fixed assets was 0.41 per cent. Here the total FDI absorbed in Shanghai, Jiangsu, Zhejiang and Hubei was higher than that in other areas, with their contribution ratios slightly higher than that of others.

Figure 8.2 explores the relationships between FDI, the total value of imports and exports, and imports value and exports value in foreign trade by region. Figure 8.2 shows that the distributional patterns of FDI, the total value of imports and exports, and imports value and exports value were very similar in the Yangtze valley (except for Jiangsu Province where there were exceptional high levels of FDI in corresponding years). Additionally, it shows that overall, the interrelationship between FDI and the total investments in fixed assets was positive.

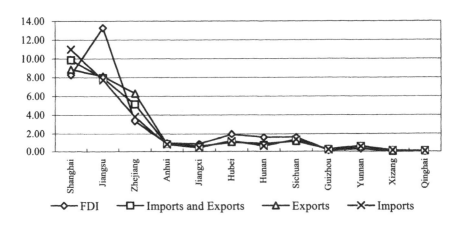

Figure 8.2   Map of Distribution of the Four Indicators in the Yangtze Valley as Percentages of the Country's Total by Region (1992–2000)

Note: Percentages of FDI of the country's total refers to percentages of the total FDI of the country's total between 1992 and 2000 (the same as other indicators).

Figure 8.3 shows a temporal analysis of the relationships between FDI and the total value of imports and exports, and imports value and exports value in foreign trade. From the data of FDI, the total value of imports and exports, and import value and exports value between 1992 and 2000, we find that, during this period, they all showed a steady increase. Although the FDI grew comparatively slowly, the main trend was upwards, with a slight decline in 1999, followed by a rise in 2000.

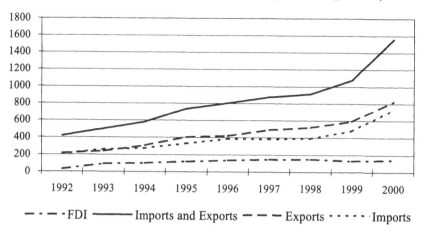

Figure 8.3   **Map of Distribution of the Four Indicators in the Yangtze Valley as Percentages of the Country's Total by Time (1992–2000)**

Rethinking of the Effects of FDI on Development of the Regional Economy of the Yangtze Valley: Further Networking of the Region with the Outside World

The analysis suggests a positive internal relationship between FDI and development of the regional economy of the Yangtze valley. Through growing investment and expansion of foreign trade, foreign capital has promoted, and will promote again, the overall growth of the Yangtze valley and the YEZ. By and large, sustainable and rapid growth of the Yangtze valley regional economy depends on FDI. In addition, main cities alongside the Yangtze will and should play a role in terms of absorbing FDI and stimulating the growth of the regional economy.

In their research regarding urbanization processes in Asia and Latin America, Armstrong and McGee (1986) explained the relationship between changes of urban function and structure, and transnational investments in developing countries. They argued that the urban system is not only the place for capital concentration, but also the centre of diffusing ideas and culture. Along with concentration of capital, culture, and ideas, urban cities in many developing countries now appear to have the character of agglomeration and diffusion functions. Other writers have noted the impact of the internationalization of capital on the world spatial economy and suggested development in two opposing directions. i) the controlling organizations in the world economy have the tendency to concentrate in a few world cities; and ii) on the other hand, the location of manufacturing activities will move to the periphery. The first spatial movement has formed world cities and the second has accelerated the transferring of manufacturing industries from developed countries to the third world. Therefore, how to take advantages of these influences and to improve the overall investment environment of the main cities alongside the

Yangtze remains an important issue in expansion and extension of foreign investment in the Yangtze valley in the long run.

However, admitting the influence of the international capital on changes of the nature and spatial structure of the Yangtze valley does not mean we can ignore the role that networks play. Thus, it is also very important for the Yangtze valley to use foreign funds sensibly and efficiently by ensuring that networking occurs amongst areas/cities within the region and, more importantly, with the outside world.

References

Armstrong, W. and McGee, T. (1986) Theatres of Accumulation: Studies in Asian and Latin American Urbanisation. London: Methuen.

Hu, D. (1999) 'An outline research on foreign investments and economic sustainable development in China', Journal of Zhangzhou Teachers University (2).

Chapter 9

Cooperating to Realign Supply Chains: Representations, Networks and Tacit Knowledge in New Zealand's Dairy and Sheep Meat Industries

Guy Penny

Introduction

According to Storper (1997, p. 31), 'a substantive goal of studying the dimensions of the new economic reflexivity should be to understand how relations of coordination between reflexive agents and organisations are established'. This chapter provides a social psychological window on the phenomena of supply chain realignment in a neo-liberalising context, examining the evolving relationship between farmers (suppliers/producers) and processing companies (buyers/processors) in New Zealand's export sheep meat and dairy industries throughout the late 1990s. Supply chain processes are examined at the micro-scale, focusing on the development of cooperation between farmers and processors in New Zealand's export dairy and meat industries. Cooperation is recognised as a key factor in the sustainability and 'success' of enterprises, as well as regions and nations, because it underpins social capital, knowledge creation processes and competitive advantage (Clemens and Row, 1992; Macleod, 2000). As such, cooperation is widely advocated as an economic strategy especially when operating in competitive and dynamic environments (Cooke, 1994), which is the case for New Zealand's pastoral industries (Pickford and Bollard, 1998).

New Pressures, New Economic Spaces, New Research Opportunities in New Zealand's Agri-food Supply Chains

New Zealand's agricultural reforms not only removed producer input subsidies and other supports but gradually dismantled the producer marketing boards and licensing authorities which, for the previous century, had arranged secure market access for low-value commodities. These arrangements, which tended to shelter producers and processors from autonomously negotiating international market relations, dissolved under neo-liberalising processes (Le Heron and Cloke, 1994). By the mid 1990s restructuring and rationalisation of processing and farming in both industries had resulted in productivity and efficiency gains, an increase in valued added activity and the development of more extensive global partnerships (Maughan, 1998; Nixon, 1998; see Tables 9.1 and 9.2 for summary statistics from each industry).

Table 9.1   Lamb Processing, Production and Value 1990–2000

	1990	1995	2000
Frozen Carcasses (% of total export lamb)	50	30	15
Bone-in cuts (% of total export lamb)	50	68	80
Boneless-cuts (% of total export lamb)	0	<2	5
Chilled Lamb (% of total export lamb)	5	10	15
Number of Sheep in NZ (million)	55	—	45
Average Lamb Carcass weight (kg)	13.5	15	16
Value NZ$ Billion (Fob)	0.9	1.2	1.6

Source: Meat Industry Associations, 2000.

Table 9.2   Summary of Dairy Farm Statistics 1992–2002

	Number of Dairy Farms	Herd size (average)	Stock rate (av. Cows/ha)	Milk solids/cow (av. kg/year)
1992	14500	170	2.3	259
2002	13600	271	2.7	307

	Milk solids %	Herd test (% cows nationally)	Somatic cell count** (kcells/ml/cow)	Payout* ($kg/milk solids)
1992	8.4	60	280	3.98
2002	8.3	80	210	5.00

* Inflation adjusted.
** Somatic cell count refers to the number of somatic cells in a millilitre of milk. This is used as milk quality indicator in the dairy industry and is regulated to < 400kSC/ml.
Source: Livestock Improvement Corporation, Dexcel, 2003.

The new structural arrangements had, however, left dairy and meat processing companies and their suppliers more directly affected by and responsible for establishing and maintaining international market arrangements. While the agricultural reforms had generated a suite of supply chain pressures, farmers and processors in both the dairy and sheep-meat industries were now subject to a range of new supply chain pressures. This was creating new economic spaces, generating common and exclusive problems and opportunities, and forcing farmers and processors into unfamiliar relational territory (Le Heron et al., 2001). This is consistent with developments elsewhere in the world which have identified the producer-processor relationship as one in which there is a need for increased cooperation and coordination, especially for domestic industries (Lazonick, 1993; Cooke, 1994).

These 'new' supply chain pressures were primarily market-led. They originated in the international arena, based on the World Trade Organisation's (WTO) establishment of specific volumetric quotas and tariffs on trade in agricultural/food products between nations, specific food health, handling and testing procedures and standards (Wilkinson, 1998), and a shift in economic power to the highly concentrated retail sector. These supply chain pressures manifest as heightened consumer and government concerns for 'food health and safety', raised expectations for the 'quality, diversity and availability' of food products and broader societal concerns over the equity and sustainability of industrialised agriculture were catalysed (Marsden and Arce, 1995; McMichael, 1996; Whatmore and Thorne, 1997; Morgan and Murdoch, 2000). For example, to satisfy rigid consumer and legal requirements, high value markets, have established systemic 'from farm to plate product traceability' as mandatory for access (Murdoch, et al., 2000). This requires products *and* production, processing, storage, handling, packaging and transport processes to be tightly monitored, controlled and *certified* to international standards throughout the agri-food supply chain (Hobbs and Young, 2000). Table 9.3 summarises supply chain (realignment) pressures and responses.

Table 9.3 **Summary of Supply Chain (Realignment) Pressures and Responses**

Supply Chain Realignment Pressures	Effect on New Zealand's Pastoral Industries
Access Minimum market access (quota) established.	• Guaranteed volumes/quota • Incentive to maximise value of quota • Develop new high value products/services
Food Safety Specific regulations, standards and monitoring procedures.	• Extends liability to downstream firms • Improved Traceability and monitoring of product throughout supply chain • Demonstrate quality assurance measures • Imposition of harsher penalties on substandard milk (Dairy)
Subsidisation Withdrawn in NZ Reducing in competitor nations – disadvantages New Zealand exporters	• Need to reduce production and processing costs to be competitive in global markets
Diversity of Markets Increasing	• Supply timing and product quality more complex. • Introduction of more precise specification contracts (lamb) and tighter milk quality specifications (i.e. SCC and prohibited substances)
Removal of Producer Marketing Boards	• Global and market forces directly acting on processors and farmers • Develop new capacities

In New Zealand, the farmer-processor interface is of considerable interest due to the central place of these actors in the agricultural sector, and because the agricultural sector is of great significance to New Zealand's economy, environment and culture (Pickford and Bollard, 1998). As key supply chain partners, farmers and processors are dependent on one another and bring complementary values to the supply chain. To a growing extent cooperation defines the new and evolving economic and relational spaces that farmers and processors operate in. Yet, how it develops and is constituted at the farmer-processor site in the New Zealand dairy and sheep meat industries remains largely un-researched. Furthermore, within the supply chain, business management and economic geography literature regarding the development and specific nature of cooperation at various sites in supply chains is rarely examined at the micro-scale, much less in an agricultural context.

Supply Chain Relations, Cooperation Unpacked and Social Representation Theory

A supply chain is conceived as an integrated system in which the geographically dispersed activities of production and consumption are connected by flows of raw and processed materials, finances, goods, services and information (Harland, 1996). While supply chain pressures privilege some actors more than others, they eventually lead to the alteration of supply arrangements, product characteristics and delivery conditions which often require supply chain actors to co-operate more fully and adjust their activities with respect to each other (Christopher and Juttner, 2000). This process of mutual adjustment, to manage risk, add-value and/or take advantage of market opportunities, is referred to as supply chain re-alignment (Trienkens, 1999). Conti (2000) considers this process to be *co-evolutive* whereby a company evolves in relation to other companies and to the external environment that constrains it or presents it with opportunities. A parallel process in which relations between companies also evolve, 'conferring a strategic-operational identity i.e. a capacity to relate to the external environment' further underpins this process (Conti, 2000, p. 30).

According to Storper (1997) and Hughes (2000), market-led requirements and the World Trade Organisation's (WTO) global regime of rules and standards governing and promoting 'free trade' between countries in agricultural products have initiated more secure, integrated and cooperative supply chain relations. These are becoming prominent features of globalising economic processes, appearing as 'new networks of interdependence' (Morgan and Murdoch, 2000). These networks are configured around closer vertical linkages between disparate producers, processors and retailers throughout the world and within national industries (Hughes, 1999; Hobbs and Young, 2000). Indeed, we are witnessing a proliferation in cooperation in the form of alliances, partnerships, joint ventures and the like (Spekman et al., 1998). As Loader and Hobbs (1999, p. 697) attest:

... this organisational strategy reduces information asymmetries along the supply chain, enabling retailers to offer quality guarantees to their customers with more confidence. It also creates the potential for the capture of additional rents from the customer market if the participants of a closely co-ordinated supply chain can offer greater security and more credible guarantees to consumers than can their competitors.

Despite growing recognition of cooperation as an economic strategy in its own right (Cooke, 1994), cooperation itself is not usually regarded as an ends, but as a means to an end. Nonetheless individuals and groups cooperate when they recognize the benefits of doing so and owing to the consequences of non-cooperation. Cooperative behaviour and competitive behaviour are not opposites nor are they mutually exclusive. They stand in contrast to a third category of behaviour – individualistic behaviour (Tuomela, 2000). Although acting cooperatively can carry extra costs (e.g. opportunistic behaviour, transaction costs), it is a strategy that can greatly influence the ability of actors to respond to supply chain pressures, coordinate functions more readily and develop and retain value throughout the supply chain by leveraging off of one another's capacities (New, 1996). According to Cravens et al. (1996) a significant supply chain management issue is not whether to establish collaborative or cooperative relationships with other organisations or actors but rather how, with which partners and what form the relationship should take.

Cooperation is of course a social process. Many psychological and environmental factors affect cooperative behaviour, just as there are many reasons why people choose not to, or are unable to, cooperate. Deliberate attempts to develop cooperation can indicate either a prior state of unreasonable uncertainty (Maxwell and Schmidt, 1975) or a desire to access 'values' that reside in other actors. Derlega and Grzelak (1982) suggest a mix of four main elements define cooperation between parties: (1) goal directed behaviour; (2) rewards for each participant; (3) distributed responses and (4) coordination. According to Blau (1975) reluctance to develop cooperative strategies indicates a prior state in which all the consequences of specific actions are recognised and the probability of their occurring accepted. While this is rarely the case, non-cooperation can also occur when the 'costs of cooperating' (i.e. specific asset, resource or transaction costs as well as social/psychological costs or compromises) with certain actors are determined or perceived to be greater than when not cooperating. Regardless of the motivation for cooperation, whether or not cooperation actually manifests between actors and the form it takes is influenced by the means, mechanisms and processes by which cooperation can be expressed (Tuomela, 2000).

Many studies in social interaction, including cooperation, systematically incorporate the social representation dimension (Abric, 1982). In the context of supply chain linkages this involves each party's perspective, role of networks and information in shaping representations, supply chain decisions, strategies and practices of each party. An essential premise is that behaviour (including cooperation) is partially determined by the way one represents the situation (Abric, 1982). 'The situation' is a unitary concept for a set of circumstances one finds oneself in. When an individual is faced with any given situation he or she will develop a representation not only of the situation as a whole but also of its components, *inter alia* the people, relationships, the tasks involved and one's self in the situation. When applied in supply chain inquiry, this set of representations provides a relational framework in which to examine how actors perceive, create and resolve supply chain tensions and establish relations of coordination.

Research Participants and Methods

Three farmer-processor groups agreed to participate in this study. One group consisted of 20 dairy farmers supplying a large and national processor with over 7000 suppliers (approximately 50 per cent of New Zealand dairy farmers). These farmers located in the Waikato and Bay of Plenty Regions of the North Island were consistently in the top 5 per cent of suppliers in terms of milk quality (i.e. low bulk somatic cell counts, no prohibited substances). In the case of the sheep meat sector two groups participated. One consisted of a small, young and successful meat processing company in the South Island with 700 sheep suppliers and 15 of their suppliers who were experienced in contract supply, particularly contracts related to premium markets for chilled lamb (S1). Over half the farmers in this group used irrigation and all were farming on the east coast lowland plains of New Zealand's South Island. The other meat group was made up of established meat processors in the lower North Island with over 2000 suppliers and a group of 24 suppliers from a general supply base (S2). These farmers were situated in the southwest lowlands and hill country in New Zealand's North Island, a much more diverse and challenging environmental setting than group S1.

The research methods consisted of (in this order) 'first' group workshops, structured questionnaires (farmers only), semi-structured interviews (farmers and processors) and a series of two further workshop meetings over eighteen months at which each of the case study groups in which both farmers and processing company staff attended. The research methods were sequenced in such a way that the results of one method would feed into the design of those that followed.

Developing Cooperation in New Zealand's Dairy and Sheep Meat Sector: Representations and the Importance of Networks and Tacit Knowledge

In both sectors farmers expressed a desire to align themselves with one processing company believing this the best strategy in the tightening supply context. Dairy farmers had little choice in this matter with respect to their processing company. Yet, they endorsed the principle and most had adopted a strategy of developing long-term relationships with a few farm input suppliers. Farmers who had personal network connections to international markets had a better understanding of the global supply 'situation' and market machinations and were more open to cooperative strategies with their respective processing companies than those without. These farmers also had a better understanding of the constraints and strategies of processing companies. However, while awareness of the role of the 'other party' in the supply chain is a precursor to forming a commitment to develop a closer relationship, it does not guarantee it, as the dairy industry exemplifies.

Similarly processing companies wanted to work more closely with farmers to capture value, although their preference was to deal with fewer, larger suppliers because of the economies of scale. These findings reflect similar findings in the supply chain management literature. In both sheep and dairy industries, there are now fewer, larger farms compared with a decade ago. Despite the alignment in farmer and processor 'representations of the market situation' there are marked differences between the dairy and sheep meat industries in their willingness and ability to develop a more cooperative supplier – processor relationship.

The Dairy Industry: The Irony of the Cooperative

The majority of dairy farmers in New Zealand currently supply milk of high quality, most of which can be further processed into a wide range of products, to a single cooperative dairy company called Fonterra. At the time of this research 90 per cent of New Zealand dairy farmers supplied one of two large dairy cooperatives, which subsequently merged to form Fonterra. While dairy farmers are aware of the potential to differentiate raw milk for use in different high value products (e.g. functional foods, nutraceuticals, bio-medical uses), they are unable to individually benefit directly from this because milk differentiation occurs at the processing level. Traceability does not currently extend to the farm. In the dairy industry's cooperative structure and current technology milk is pooled and returns are bundled. Although the costs are higher and there are no direct financial incentives for supplying milk of higher than 'standard' quality, there are indirect benefits. Producing milk with low SCC (an indicator of milk quality), for example, improves production volumes and herd health and reduces the risk of breaching milk quality standards should a production problem occur (i.e. mastitis). Furthermore, farmers gain a great deal of job satisfaction in supplying high quality milk as it is indicative of system robustness and allows them to gain 'peer respect' as a good supplier and cooperative member.

Dairy farmers indicated they would be willing to develop closer ties with a company that enabled them to manipulate milk properties and capture the extra value of doing so (e.g. low-cholesterol milk), although they weren't entirely sure what this involved. However, industry structure does not allow farmers to supply another company simultaneously and even if they could, there are currently no supply alternatives for most farmers. Even if they wanted to, there were no obvious mechanisms through which dairy farmers could express loyalty or commitment toward their processor.

Consequently, dairy farmers participating in this research (i.e. the top performers in terms of milk quality) had little interest in developing a closer relationship with the processing company. For these farmers, investing in new management or technology was directed at increasing volumes and herd worth which did not require interaction with the processing company. In fact, most farmers indicated contact with the company was usually associated with some form of negative experience and there was little need for farmers and processor to interact at all. This is, perhaps, because dairy company field officers tended to interact primarily with poor performing farmers, and apart from daily milk statistic feedback sheets most information farmers required was readily available elsewhere through a well established range of formal and informal networks. Furthermore, because farmer-processor interactions are fairly standardised throughout the industry and therefore need little attention, infrequent contact between parties is unnecessary unless a problem arises. Such cooperation between farmers and the processing company in the dairy study groups tends to take the form of co-action and minimum 'necessary' information exchange and are essentially a satisfying strategy.

Compared to the meat industry, the dairy industry does not appear to have such a well-developed relationship with its supply base, which it will need to remedy if milk supply becomes differentiated by specific qualities (e.g. cholesterol levels). Given that the New Zealand's dairy industry is based on cooperative principles it is ironic then that the development of more cooperative relations is currently constrained. However, the cooperative structure of the dairy industry is not entirely to blame for this situation. The following four systemic issues need to be addressed if the dairy industry is to take advantage of its latent the cooperative capacity: (1) the company's policy of working with farmers only when supply problems arise; (2) having a penalty-based system as opposed to an incentive-based system; (3) developing tacit knowledge about each other and working together; and (4) supplier numbers, as the company's preference was to have fewer, larger suppliers to minimise transaction and transport costs.

The Sheep Meat Industry: Developing a Capacity to Cooperate

In contrast to the dairy industry, the meat industry has a much more diverse set of suppliers (e.g. breeders, storers, finishers,) and consists of many processing companies (some of which are cooperative) and other buyers of livestock (i.e. other farmers). As such farmers currently have a number of supply options many farmers supply to multiple buyers. However, while farmers do not want to be locked into a single buyer situation, most have indicated that they would prefer to develop a closer relationship with a single processor. Similarly processing companies would like to formalise supply relations with their suppliers. In order to secure, manage and add value to supplied livestock, some meat processing companies have developed a range of different supply options (e.g. general supply, a range of seasonal and premium market contracts) which have led to the development of a more cooperative supply relationship between farmers and processing company.

For Group S1 (i.e. farmers on precise specification contracts), cooperative behaviour manifests in the form of a clear commitment from each party (i.e. bulk of supply, non-opportunistic behaviour), preferential treatment to one another (i.e. bonuses, flexibility, extra services), collaborative activity (e.g. joint planning, trial contracts) and enhanced communication and information exchanges. Group S2 exhibits some of these behaviours but not to the degree evident in Group S1.

In general, this indicates that the more specific the contract criteria (weight, fat content, bone to meat ratio, conformation, low chemical, numbers, dates, etc.), the closer the company and farmers were working together. While all farmers in this study networked to varying degrees through demonstration farms, supplier meetings, social events and the printed media, Group S1 farmers had formed an informal 'club'. This 'club' included a number of processing company staff who met to discuss and learn about contract risks and management practices. In this way the companies' and farmers' representations of the other party and their 'situation' was enhanced. Farmers said this 'club' provided them with valuable comparative information that allowed them to understand their own practices and improve their understanding of the processor and the supply situation generally. Processors gained valuable insight into the problems farmers faced in meeting contract specifications and were able to explain the constraints they were faced with.

In terms of motivation for acting cooperatively, it was very important for farmers that processing companies understand the local environmental, social and economic factors acting on farmers and attempt to accommodate these in supply agreements through risk sharing provisions. For both S1 and S2 there were several examples of the company demonstrating a commitment to its suppliers, especially in times of stress (e.g. drought, disease, currency valuation changes). Apart form the suppliers' club, Company S1 was facilitating cooperative behaviour through attempts to align representations of its supplier base, especially those on tight contracts. Company S1 was actively providing suppliers with information about market specificities. They often held open days where farmers could view videos on markets and supply chain links and even tour the processing plant. Along with other expressions of cooperation (risk sharing, preferential treatment, etc.) these gestures of cooperation allowed suppliers to form a positive representation of their supply chain partner.

Most information from the processing company augmented information farmers received through personal connections to export markets and with other farmers and friends. These network links enabled farmers to better understand market demands and supply chain pressures such as food health and safety and the need for, for example, maintenance of stock genetic history records and farm certification for traceability requirements. It also allowed them to make sheep breed and stocking rate decisions in line with market requirements and their feed system.

Learning about each other's constraints and comprehending supply chain pressures such as tighter regulatory requirements and modified price-grade or penalty rates were best achieved through face-to-face contact between two parties. For both Groups, this was mainly achieved by working closely with the company's livestock representative through whom increased information was transferred in both directions. However, for Group S1, the processing company supply and procurement *managers* had an open door policy for their suppliers, which also facilitated direct contact. Farmers were extremely loyal to the company's livestock representative whom they differentiated from the company and many had had a longer association with the livestock representative than the company.

Farmers and processing companies in Group S1 were investing time and effort in generating, recording and exchanging information that would be useful to each other's operations. In addition a 'trial contract' system was established whereby farmers considering supplying to precise specification contracts could trial a contract for season without penalty. Through interactions with the livestock representatives, processing company staff and other farmers, Group S1 farmers were developing a set of contract evaluation and negotiation skills that were not evident in Group S2. Nonetheless Group S2 were interested in developing a better understanding of the management implications and risks associated with precise specification contracts. However, while Group S2 suppliers also wanted to have a close relationship with a single processor, many were still deliberating over which one to choose from, as their predominant processor was 'nothing special'.

Conclusions

This study has shown that New Zealand farmers and processing companies are finding themselves in new economic spaces, largely defined by international market and regulatory requirements for food safety, year round availability, specific cultural qualities and volumetric limits. Interestingly, farmers and processing companies currently have similar representations of these new economic spaces. This was not the case in the mid-1990s when Paine and Sheath (1997) commented, 'there still remains an unresolved mismatch between the mentality of undifferentiated production by producers and the precise product specifications increasingly sought by processors'.

Furthermore these new economic spaces are forcing farmers and processors into more cooperative relations in order to extract greater value from production and processing processes. Again farmers and processing companies have similar representations of their relationship. In both sectors farmers expressed a desire to align themselves with one processing company believing this the best strategy in the tightening supply context. Similarly, processing companies wanted to work more closely with farmers to capture value, although their preference to deal with fewer, larger suppliers because of the economies of scale.

The alignment of representations in the above two areas (i.e. the situation and the other party) suggests a number of processes have occurred in each industry as a legacy of the agricultural reform process. The agricultural reforms removed financial and information support to farmers and exposed processors and farmers more directly to international market forces, yet resulted in significant productivity and efficiency gains. To survive and grow in this context farmers and processors were forced to develop new networking and business management capacities and improve their knowledge of the 'science' of livestock and milk production and market requirements. It is this 'forced' stepping up of capacity through greater diversity of interactions and integration of new knowledge that has allowed for the aligning of representations and has laid the platform for the development of more integrated and cooperative relations between processors and farmers. At the basis of this is the significance of a range of networks that not only allow actors to learn new technical, production and management skills but also allows them to understand market machinations and assess their own performance and the performance and compatibility of others (i.e. potential partners).

However, despite the willingness to cooperate, industry comparison discussed in this chapter shows significant differences in the ability to cooperate for mutual gain. In the dairy industry, structural constraints (i.e. a single buyer), the inability to differentiate milk at the farm-gate and through the supply chain, and infrequent positive interactions between farmers and processors creates an environment where representations of one another are only ever partial and cooperation has no way of expressing itself fully. Dairy farmers remain simple commodity producers. Cooperation is a natural human behaviour built on tacit knowledge. But how it occurs in specific settings still needs to be negotiated and learnt through trial and error, as the example of Group S1 illustrates. For the dairy industry this has created a situation where farmers and processors will need to learn how to cooperate if new differentiated supply opportunities arise.

The difference between the two sheep groups also emphasizes how cooperation is a learnt behaviour and that it requires involved parties to 'work through' the intricacies of what it means to cooperate as they occur. This case also signifies the importance of frequent and diverse interactions, and collaborating on issues that are mutually relevant (i.e. contract terms and conditions). The case of S1 also illustrates a 'snowballing' effect where initial cooperative activities tend to lead to new opportunities that allow positive reinforcement and the further development of cooperation.

Finally, conventional analysis of the pastoral and agri-food sectors in New Zealand has traditionally paid little heed to accounts of social relations between actors other than to broadly describe their occurrence and political and regulatory *raison d'etre* by way of structural relations. This may have been appropriate during New Zealand's period of agricultural reform and de-regulation. But now that the social and psychological dimensions (e.g. cooperation, communication, knowledge, learning and networking) of structural relations and the agency of actors are recognised as being critical to risk management and adaptive capacity, a more qualitative and culturally sensitive approach is called for. In this chapter I have sought to examine how supply chain actors individually interpret and collectively respond to new and emerging economic spaces through the social process of cooperation. Understanding cooperative behaviour calls for a micro-scale approach. And because it involves multiple supply chain actors embedded in different contexts, the approach must incorporate provision for relationality.

Acknowledgements

This research was funded by the Foundation for Science Research and Technology 1998–2000, administered by AgResearch and the University of Auckland. I also acknowledge the support provided by the National Institute of Water and Atmospheric Research Limited. My thanks to the many farmers and processing company staff who contributed to this study between 1998–2001, and to Professor Richard Le Heron of Auckland University, Associate Professor Mark Paine of Melbourne University and Dr Alan McDermott of AgResearch.

References

Abric, J. C. (1982), 'Cognitive Processes Underlying Cooperation', In V. J. Derlega and J. Grzelak (eds), 1982, *Cooperation and Helping Behavior: Theories and Research*, New York: Academic Press.

Blau, P. M. (1975), *Approaches to the Study of Social Structure*, New York: Free Press.

Blunden, G. (1996), 'Corporatisation and Producer Marketing Boards', In R. Le Heron and E. Pawson (eds), *Changing Places. New Zealand in the Nineties*, Auckland: Longman Paul, pp. 126-129.

Christopher, M. and Juttner, U. (2000), 'Developing Strategic Partnerships in the Supply Chain: A Practitioners Perspective', *European Journal of Purchasing and Supply Mangement*, 6, pp. 117 – 127.

Clemens, E. K. and Row, M. C. (1992), 'Information Technology and Industrial Cooperation: The Changing Economics of Coordination and Ownership', *Journal of Management Information Systems*, 9(2), pp. 9-29.

Cloke, P. and Le Heron, R. (1994), 'Agricultural Deregulation: The Case of New Zealand', In P. Lowe, T. Marsden and S. Whatmore (eds), *Regulating Agriculture*, London: David Fulton, pp. 104-126.

Conti, S. (2000), 'Small and Medium Sized Enterprises in Space: The Plural Economy', In E. Vatne and M. Taylor (eds), *The Networked Firm in a Global World: Small Firms in New Environment*, Aldershot: Ashgate. pp. 19-43.

Cooke, P. (1994), 'The Co-operative Advantage of Regions', Paper presented at the Conference on Region, Institutions and Technology: Reorganizing Economic Geography in Canada and the Anglo-American World, University of Toronto, September 1994.

Cravens, D. W., Piercy, N. F. and Shipp, S. H. (1996), 'New Organizational Forms for Competing in Highly Dynamic Environments: The Network Paradigm', *British Journal of Management*, 7: pp. 203-218.

Derlega,V. J. and Grzelak, J. (eds) (1982), *Cooperation and Helping Behavior: Theories and Research*. New York: Academic Press.

Dexcel (2003), 2001/2002 *Economic Survey of New Zealand Dairy Farmers*. Dexcel Limited, Hamilton, New Zealand.

Harland, C. M. (1996), Supply Chain Management: Relationships, Chains and Networks. *British Journal of Management*,7, Special Issue, S63-S80.

Hobbs, J. E. and Young, L. M. (2000), 'Closer Vertical Co-ordination in Agri-Food Supply Chains: A Conceptual Framework and some Preliminary Evidence', *Supply Chain Management: An International Journal*, 5(3): pp. 131-143.

Hughes, A. (2000) 'Retailers, Knowledges and Changing Commodity Networks: The Case of the Cut Flower Trade', *Geoforum*, 31(2): pp. 175-190.

Lazonick, W. (1993), 'Industry Cluster versus Global Webs: Organisational Capabilities in the American Economy', Industrial and Corporate Change, 2: pp. 1-24.

Le Heron, R., Penny, G., Paine, M., Sheath, G. Pedersen, J., Botha, N. (2001), 'Global Supply Chains and Networking: A Critical Perspective on Learning Challenges in the New Zealand Dairy and Sheepmeat Commodity Chains, Journal of Economic Geography', 1: pp. 439-456.

Le Heron, R. and Roche, M. (1999), 'Rapid Reregulation, Agricultural Restructuring, and the Reimaging of Agriculture in New Zealand', Rural Sociology, 64(2): pp. 203-218.

Livestock Improvement Corporation (2003), *Dairy Statistics 2001–2002*, Livestock Improvement Corporation Limited, Hamilton, New Zealand.

Loader, R. and Hobbs, J. E. (1999), 'Strategic Responses to Food Safety Legislation, *Food Policy*, 24: pp. 685-706.

Macleod, G. (2000), 'The Learning Region in an Age of Austerity: Capitalising on Knowledge, Entrepreneurialism, and Reflexive Capitalism', *Geoforum*, 31: pp. 219-236.

Marsden, T. and Arce, A. (1995), 'Constructing Quality: Emerging Food Networks in the Rural Transition', *Environment and Planning A*, 27(8): pp. 1261-1279.

Maughan, C. W. (1998), 'Red Meat', In M. Pickford and A. Bollard (eds), *The Structure and Dynamics of New Zealand Industries*, Palmerston North: Dunmore Press: pp. 25-52.

Maxwell, G. and Schmitt, D. (1975), *Cooperation an Experimental Analysis*, New York: Academic Press.

McMichael, P. (1996), 'Globalisation: Myths and Realities', *Rural Sociology*, 61(1): pp. 25-55.

Meat Industry Association (2000), *Annual Report 2000*, Meat Industry Association.

Morgan, K., Murdoch, J. (2000), 'Organic vs. Conventional Agriculture: Knowledge, Power and Innovation in the Food Chain', *Geoforum*, 31: pp. 159-173.

Moscovici, S. (1961), *La Psychanalyse, son Image et son Public* (2nd edition), Paris: Presses Univeritaires de France.

Murdoch, J., Marsden, T. and Banks, J. (2000), 'Quality, Nature and Embeddedness: Some Theoretical Considerations in the Context of the Food Sector', *Economic Geography*, 76: pp. 107-25.

New, S. J. (1996), 'A Framework for Analysing Supply Chain Improvement', *International Journal of Operations and Production Management*, 16(4): pp. 19-34.

Nixon, C. (1998), 'Dairy Processing', In M. Pickford and A. Bollard (eds), *The Structure and Dynamics of New Zealand Industries*, Palmerston North: Dunmore Press: pp. 87-120.

Paine, M. and Sheath, G. (1997) Personal communitcation with the author.

Pickford, M. and Bollard, A. (1998), 'Introduction', In M. Pickford and A. Bollard (eds), *The Structure and Dynamics of New Zealand Industries*, Palmerston North: Dunmore Press.

Pritchard, W. N. (1999), 'The Emerging Contours of the Third Food Regime: Evidence from the Australian Dairy and Wheat Sectors', *Economic Geography*, 74(64): p. 74.

Spekman, R.E., Kaumauff, J.W. and Myhr, N. (1998), 'An Empirical Investigation into Supply Chain Management: A Perspective on Partnerships', *Supply Chain Management*, 3(2): pp. 53-67.

Storper, M. (1997), *The Regional World: Territorial Development in a Global Economy*, New York: Guilford Press.

Trienekens, J. (1999), *Management of Processes in Chains: A Research Framework*, Unpublished PhD thesis, Wageningen Agricultural University, Netherlands.

Tuomela, R. (2000), *Cooperation*, Netherlands: Kluwer Academic Publishers, Dordrecht.

Whatmore, S. and Thorne, L. (1997), 'Nourishing Networks: Alternative Geographies of Food', In D. Goodman and M. Watts (eds) *Globalising Food: Agrarian Questions and Global Restructuring*, London: Routledge.

Wilkinson, R. M. (1998), Multilateralism and the World Trade Organisation: The Practice of Regulating International Trade, Unpublished PhD.Thesis, University of Auckland.

Chapter 10

Placing Economic Development Narratives into Emerging Economic Spaces: Project Jeep, 1996–1997

Jay D. Gatrell and Neil Reid

Perhaps one reason why regional scholars have found it easier to promulgate fuzzy concepts is that the literature has become increasingly permissive about the quality of, and the necessity to, include evidence in published research (Markusen (1999, p. 872).

Introduction

Markusen's observation is correct. But, perspective is everything. Places and regions are fuzzy concepts – especially when compared and contrasted to the precise and absolutist nature of space. Yet, the judgment that concepts are fuzzy or evidence scant is imprecise and privileges what Barnes (2001) calls the first wave of theory of economic geography. As Barnes (2001, p. 555) rightly articulates, 'second wave' epistemological threats from Marxism, Critical Realism, flexible industrialization, or other alternatives to the quantitative revolution could easily be dismissed as ideology, a value add to existing theory, or a limited re-articulation of existing literature rooted in empirical data. But the **new** *new economic geography* is a radical departure from the 'rules of the game'. As such, the cultural turn represents a considerable shift away from tradition – not merely a re-visioning of it. In this paper, we explore contemporary developments in a parallel, but related literature in economic development policy and identify cultural themes in geography. To underscore the relevance of the new economic geography and conceptual utility of culture, this paper reviews the case study of Toledo Jeep. In this analysis we focus on the period between August 1996 and July 1997 when the city of Toledo, Ohio faced the possibility of the manufacture of its signature product being relocated to a location outside of the city limits. The paper concludes by asserting the importance of local spaces, local culture and the efficacy of developing an innovative and expressive retention initiative.

Space and Place: A Contemporary Context

Notions of space and place are common in the economic geography literature and have become staple concepts in the community of critical human geography. Specifically, critical human geographers have embraced Lefebvre's Triad (1991) to understand and explain the emerging politics in urban spaces and tension that exists between space (i.e., global spaces of representation) and place (i.e., local representational spaces). In most cases, geographers emphasize the structural imperatives (most likely economic – but increasingly cultural) associated with political conflict within and between space and how global structures produce conflict in local spaces and places.

The most widely held interpretation of Lefebvre's Triad (1991) narrowly focuses on the space/place dialectic and has been conflated with the local/global dialectic. Hence, 'spatial practices' have been interpreted through a functionalist lens as subordinate to the dominant (i.e., capitalist) structure. That is, the spatial practices associated with space and global structures were theoretically privileged and in practical terms place-based and local practices dis-empowered. Such is the case in much of economic geography; local facts, details and cases are little more unimportant facts to be brushed away while economic geographers unlock more meaningful socio-spatial processes using acceptable methodologies.

However, Lefebvre's (1991) own work does not marginalize spatial practice. Rather, Lefebvre recognizes the equality of the tripartite and strives not to reduce space and place to the abstract and concrete. By failing to privilege either the space or place, many of the essentialist assumptions of radical geography are absent. That is, it is not assumed that either the conceived or lived space is more (or less) important or more (or less) empowered than the other. In contrast to the pre-ordained outcomes of strict structural interpretations of the space/place dialectic, Lefebvre's model is open to many possibilities and mirrors the complexity of regional processes. In fact, Lefebvre's own language enables a wide range of creative possibilities and potential applications.

While the rationale for, and intellectual underpinnings of a new economic geography that can be informed by an understanding of space and place is rather straightforward, the philosophical problem arises when geographers try to explain and understand spatial practice conceptually and how spatial practices may vary on the ground and in-place. In short, new economic geography is primarily concerned with the socio-spatial context (to be read institutional context), related policy outcomes, and the specific narrative used to explain observed conditions and derive a better understanding of local, regional and global processes. As a result, new economic geography's preoccupation with local spaces and places and the mechanisms and institutional contexts that shape localities and regions mandates economic geographers to confront or account for culture. While the cultural turn is much maligned, culture does matter and serves to mitigate a variety of economic and non-economic conflicts (Cox, 1988; Feldmann, 1994; Gatrell and Reid, 2002; McCann, 2002; Portz, 1990).

Despite being dismissed as too specific, fuzzy, or merely interesting, geographers and others have been slowly and steadily developing the concept of culture and the role of culture in the development process throughout the 1990s. As McCann (2002) demonstrates, culture (or some functional proxy) has been explicitly linked to observed economic conditions and the politics of local business, practices of urban regime types and the spatial practices employed by local coalitions (Figure 10.1). Across the social sciences, many examples of culture and specific couplings of time, space and tradition have been acknowledged as key determinants of local development including: (1) Malecki's (1991) business climate; (2) Saxenian's (1994) entrepreneurial ethos; (3) Zukin et al.'s (1998) urban imaginary; (4) Molotch et al.'s (2001) tradition; (5) Reese and Rosenfeld's (2001) civic culture; (6) Gatrell and Reid's (2002) cultures of production; (7) McCann's (2002) discursive and intra-urban definition of 'cultural politics of local economic development'; and (8) Jacobs' and Fincher's (1998) cultural political economy. When these concepts are repositioned within the Lefebvrian framework – the cultural imperatives of local economic development are understood to restrict policy options and define the realm of policy possibilities. As a result, everyday life in local places ceases to be merely a container for economic activity and emerges as a neo-institutional agent for change and continuity. Hence, the local business politics are derived from 'the local' and serve to structure the internal and external linkages within and between 'place'.

To understand the cultural imperatives of economic development, it is useful to consider economic development as both an instrumental and expressive process. As such, place-making, region-making and even industry-making are embedded with local meaning and embedded within local discourses. Consequently, the observed geographies of industries are seldom the predicted ones. As the brief case study of Toledo Jeep demonstrates, counter-factual cases can be more easily understood within the context of contextual (to be read cultural) factors. For these reasons, the 1995–1997 Jeep crisis and its exact resolution are unable to be understood solely within the context of empirically observed realities.

The Toledo Jeep Story

In July 1997 Chrysler announced that it was going to invest US$1.2 billion to expand and update its Jeep production facilities. The bulk of these monies would be invested in the construction of a new assembly plant. A small amount would be dedicated to refurbishing existing production facilities. Chrysler's announcement ended almost twelve months of speculation over the future of Jeep production in Toledo.

This speculation began in August 1996 when Chrysler Corporation (now Daimler-Chrysler) announced that it would be decommissioning much of the out-dated Toledo Jeep plant and replacing it with a new facility. From the outset Chrysler made it clear that the new plant would not necessarily be located in Toledo. All viable sites within a fifty-mile radius of the city would be considered. The dynamics of the possible relocation of Jeep production were complicated by the fact that the city of Toledo is bounded on the north by the state of Michigan. This meant that the potential competition for Jeep was not only between Toledo and other geographically proximate communities, but also between the geographically adjacent states of Ohio and Michigan.

The need for a new facility resulted from inefficiencies in the production system stemmed from two main sources. First, the production system was geographically bifurcated. Toledo had two Jeep plants. One was located on Jeep Parkway and the other, five miles away, on Stickney Avenue. The Jeep Parkway plant was a multi-level, 4.5 million square feet facility dating from the turn of the twentieth century. The Stickney Avenue plant was a 512,000 square foot plant, built in 1942.[1] Two Chrysler product lines were assembled at the plant – the Jeep Cherokee and the Jeep Wrangler. The Cherokee was assembled entirely at Jeep Parkway. Assembly of the Wrangler, however, was divided between the two facilities. Body frames for the Wrangler were assembled at Jeep Parkway, and then transported by truck to Stickney Avenue where chassis, engine, wheels, brakes and other parts are added. Approximately 777 Cherokees and 398 Wranglers were produced per day.

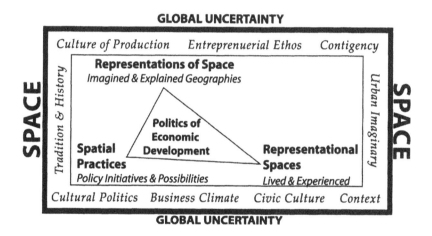

Figure 10.1   Limits to Place, Lefebvre's Triad, and Cultural Context

Second, inefficiencies resulted from the fact that the multi-level layout of the ageing Jeep Parkway facility was inappropriate for modern day assembly line production. Furthermore, the plant's paint shop (the only one in the two-plant system) had insufficient capacity and represented a major bottleneck in the Toledo production system. This bottleneck reduced the potential production capacity by several hundred vehicles per day. A new, state-of-the-art, facility would eliminate these inefficiencies.

From the city of Toledo's perspective, maintaining the production of Jeeps in Toledo was both an economic and a symbolic imperative. Jeep is one of the largest employers in the Toledo region and a major contributor to the city's tax base. In mid-1996 the two plants employed over 5,500 people. This represented over 20 per cent of the city's manufacturing jobs. Furthermore, the Jeep plants were the central cogs in Toledo's automotive network. The city has literally dozens of manufacturing plants that produce component parts for both Jeep and other automakers located in other parts of the country. Automobiles and automobile component parts production account for 44.5 per cent of the city's manufacturing employment. More importantly, because automotive salaries are considerably above the manufacturing average, the sector's share of the city's manufacturing payroll is 53.7 per cent. The economic spin-offs from Jeep's presence in Toledo are also considerable. The 4,900[v] jobs at the new Jeep plant generate $220 million in payroll (excluding overtime and profit sharing). This results in $572 million of direct and indirect spending in the local economy.

Keeping Jeep in Toledo was also critical from the point of view of maintaining the momentum of an unusually buoyant local economy. Economically, the 1980s had been a tough decade for Toledo. Thousands of manufacturing jobs disappeared from the city and the county (Table 10.1), while Northwest Ohio's unemployment rates soared as high as 14.2 per cent. The mid-1990s saw the Toledo region successfully emerge from a period of economic recession and restructuring. Unemployment rates fell and reached a 30-year low (under 5 per cent) by the end of decade. The total number of manufacturing jobs increased and real manufacturing salaries reached an all-time high. Toledo's economic resurgence was not just a locally-recognized phenomenon. In the mid-1990s it's economic vitality was being touted by the national and international press (e.g. Patti Waldmeier in the *Financial Times*).

Symbolically, maintaining Jeep production in Toledo meant keeping a product line whose history was inextricably associated with the city. The Jeep has it genesis in the hostilities of Word War II. The U.S. army was in need of a four-wheel-drive general-purpose vehicle. It invited the country's automakers to submit designs. The contract was awarded to the Willys-Overland, owners of the Jeep Parkway plant. The first military Jeep was assembled in 1941. Approximately 360,000 were produced over the next four years. The end of the war did not signal the end of the Jeep, however. Recognizing the potential of a large civilian market (particularly among returning servicemen) Willys-Overland produced the first civilian Jeep (the CJ-2A) in 1945. Over the remainder of the twentieth century the Jeep product line was continually updated to keep up with changing consumer tastes. Toledo became recognized nationally as the city that built Jeeps. Several editorials in the local daily newspaper, *The Blade*, emphasized the symbolic significance of Jeep to the city. Keeping Jeep was 'about pride and identity' (Toledo Blade, 1996). The Jeep was 'inextricably linked in the mind of the nation with the Glass City' (Toledo Blade, 1996). Losing Jeep would be both an 'economic and psychological disaster' (Toledo Blade, 1997a).

Chrysler's announcement that it was considering new plant sites outside of Toledo was not the first time that the city had faced the possibility of losing one of its major employers. Three times in the past (1986, 1987, and 1990) Toledo Jeep facilities closures were threatened, and each time Toledo Jeep survived (Gatrell and Reid, 2002). On two of those occasions (1987 and 1990) concessions on the part of the Toledo labor force saved Jeep. In the most recent crisis in 1996 however, there was a commitment and desire on the Chrysler's part to maintain the existing Jeep labor force. Toledo's Jeep labor force, in many respects, underwent a dramatic metamorphosis during the early 1990s. Quality circles were introduced, productivity has improved and worker's compensation costs and absenteeism reduced significantly (Garcia, 1996). This was the logic underlying the preference for a new plant within a fifty-mile radius of Toledo. A fifty-mile radius would keep workers within a one-hour commute.

When it became clear that Chrysler would consider shifting Jeep production outside of Toledo, the city responded by establishing a rapid response team. This 39-member team comprised a wide variety of expertise including county commissioners, economic development officials, lawyers, real estate specialists, union representatives and the Governor's office. The charge of this group, known as the Project Jeep team, was to ensure that Jeep production continued in Toledo. Project Jeep faced two major challenges. First, they had to find a parcel of land that could accommodate a new automobile assembly plant. Second, they had to put together a US$322 million incentives package that would be sufficient to entice Chrysler to continue its relationship with the city.

Chrysler specified the need for a 500-acre parcel of land. Eventually the city was able to deliver such a viable site to Chrysler. It fell short of the requisite 500 acres but was sufficient to meet the automaker's needs. The new plant was to be built on the existing Stickney Avenue site, immediately adjacent to the plant already located there. The original Stickney site was 230 acres. Toledo proposed increasing the size of the site to 430 acres. Adding 200 acres to the existing site was not cheap however, and ultimately cost Toledo taxpayers US$137.5 million. The major site acquisition costs involved the relocation of eighteen businesses, eighty-three residential homes and two railroads that occupied a portion of the expanded site. Toledo used its power of eminent domain to remove the offending residences and businesses from the site (Chavez, 1997). Although Toledo originally budgeted US$19.55 million for relocation costs they ultimately cost US$45.3 million. The majority of this cost overrun was the result of the Toledo failing to adequately estimate the costs of relocating the eighteen businesses. In November 1997 Toledo had estimated business relocation costs at US$13.3 million, but the actual cost was over US$35 million. As a result of underestimating business and other site improvement costs, including environmental clean-up costs and costs of constructing and widening access roads, Toledo had to borrow monies from the State of Ohio and the U.S. Department of Housing and Urban Development (HUD). As a result, Toledo ended up paying over US$60 million in finance charges to manage the incurred debt.

In July 1997 Chrysler announced that it had chosen Toledo as the location for its new Jeep plant. The new facility was effectively going to be an extension of the Stickney Avenue plant. The new plant would include a new body shop, paint shop, sludge/paint mix building, and a trim/chassis/final assembly building. The opening of the new facility in April 1991 coincided with the introduction and launch of Jeep's newest product line – the Jeep Liberty. The Liberty replaced the Cherokee. When Chrysler announced that Jeep would be remaining in Toledo the local newspaper reiterated the symbolic importance of Jeep to the city. The decision to remain in Toledo was a 'destiny realized', and with it an 'enormous psychological cloud' was lifted from the city (Toledo Blade, 1997b).

Chrysler's commitment to make a $1.2 billion investment in Toledo brings with it an emotional lift to this community that is difficult to overstate. Some companies, some trademarks are so identified with the community of their birth that to move them anyplace else seems sacrilege. So it is with Jeep (Toledo Blade, 1997a).

Table 10.1   Major Manufacturing Job Losses in Toledo Metropolitan Area, 1980–1990

Company	Reason for Job Losses	Year(s)	Number of Jobs
Libbey-Owens Ford	Plant Closure	1982	2500
Champion Spark Plug	Lay-offs	1980–1989	955
Midland-Ross	Plant Closure	1980	350
DeVilbiss Company	Plant Closure	1989	350
Toledo Scale	Lay-offs and Plant Closure	1982,1984	325
Nekoosa Packaging	Plant Closures	1989–1990	286
Bingham Stamping	Plant Closure	1985	275
Gulf Oil	Plant Closure	1981	235
Dana Corporation	Lay-offs	1986	225
Schindler Elevator	Plant Closure	1989	225

Source: Regional Growth Partnership.

Not surprisingly, the incentives package and its associated miscalculations were just targets of considerable criticism. One Toledo councillor likened the incentives package to a 'Christmas wish list for Chrysler' (McKinnon, 1999a). The Mayor and other economic development officials however, remained adamant that Toledo had gotten a good value for its incentives dollars. In arguing their case Jeep proponents focused attention on the various economic spin-off benefits generated as a result of Chrysler's decision to keep Jeep in Toledo – the large number of construction employees required to build the new plant, the new jobs created by suppliers relocating their operations from outside to inside the city in order to meet the stringencies of just-in-time (JIT) delivery, and the decision by DaimlerChrysler to build a new parts warehouse and distribution center within the city limits (Brickey, 1997). Given the earlier focus on the symbolic importance of retaining Jeep it may seem ironic that the Mayor emphasized the economic benefits of retaining Jeep in his post-decision defense of the incentives package. However, when one examines the nature of much of the post-decision criticism, the Mayor's stance is entirely understandable. In the aftermath of the euphoria of maintaining Jeep there was significant focus on the opportunity costs of doing so. Debate in the Toledo City Council, for example, considered how the monies dedicated to keeping Jeep would impact the city's general operation and capital improvement funds (Baessler, 1999).

Just as Toledo's economic rebirth had become the focus of the national and international press during the mid-1990s, so too did the Jeep incentives package. The Castle Coalition, a grassroots activist group, listed the Jeep incentives deal as being responsible for one of the top ten abuses of eminent domain in the United States during the late1990s (Castle Coalition, 2002). Local attorney Terry Lodge then sued the City of Toledo. Mr. Lodge filed the lawsuit on behalf of the eighteen families who had been forced to relocate in order to make way for the new Jeep plant. Mr. Lodge was supported by Peter Enrich, a law professor at Boston's Northeastern University and nationally known community activist Ralph Nader. The lawsuit argued that the incentives package was unconstitutional as it violated the commerce clause of the US constitution. Although the lawsuit was ultimately unsuccessful it put Toledo, Ohio in the national spotlight once again. The feelings of many in the Toledo economic development community are perhaps best summed up by Donald Jakeway, President of the Regional Growth Partnership (a Toledo-based economic development agency). Responding to incentives package critics Jakeway commented that he 'would hate to think what would have happened, and what we'd be doing today, and what kind of hole we'd be crawling out of if they [Chrysler] hadn't made the commitment' (McKinnon, 1999b).

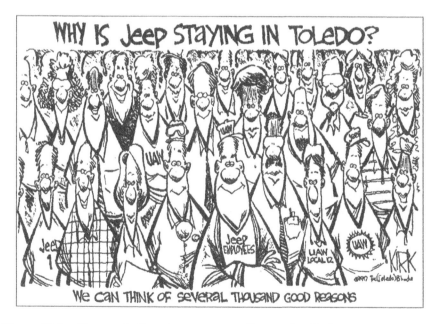

Figure 10.1   Economic Development as an Expressive Endeavour

Ultimately the new Jeep plant sits on Stickney Avenue as a visible symbol of both Toledo's industrial past and its future. The product line that is uniquely Toledo remains in the city. The newest member of the Jeep family, the Liberty, is recognized by a number of consumer magazines as one of the best Sport Utility Vehicles (SUVs) on the market. The new plant is a paragon of efficiency and has been touted by some auto analysts as a potential contender for the most efficient automotive assembly plant in the state of Ohio – no simple feat given that Honda has two assembly plants in the state. The deal that ensured that Jeep would remain in Toledo was identified as one of the top ten facility location deals in the world for 1997, while the decision to remain in the city, on a brownfield site, was characterized as a 'major U.S. auto manufacturing counter-trend' (Lyne, 1998).

The counter-intuitive case of Toledo and Toledo Jeep suggests that the decision-making process and the discourse that framed it during the 1996–1997 crisis were unique. While much of the empirical evidence associated with the Toledo case is consistent with other rustbelt communities (i.e., declining manufacturing employment and the disappearance of major plants and firms), the competition for local capital investment and the location were not defined merely as urban labor markets and/or the deceptively simple 'problem' of local dependence. Instead, the labor market issue and local dependence (in the strictest sense of jobs) were not 'in play'. Rather, the preservation of place, meaning, and an industrial icon *in place* were the primary drivers that shaped a new policy regime that was primarily an expressive process.

While certainly the materiality of the crisis and its potential implications for local workers and locality were very much real, the community appeal and structure of the debate was to positively reinforce the long relationship and historical bonds that connected Jeep, the workers, Toledo city and all residents to one-another. As such, the dominant narratives on the crisis were distinct from previous ones. Whereas the competition had been other places, the competition was functionally symbolic, as the workforce would be preserved. The potential did exist for the facility to move a few miles north into Michigan. Nevertheless, public opinion and debate was structured around Toledo – as a city and a metropolitan region – and the notion of community and shared infrastructure. In the end, the public discourse become embodied in and concretized with the formation of a special Mayoral taskforce known as 'Project Jeep'. Unlike traditional business coalitions or networks of association associated with the local dependence literature, the Toledo case was comprised of city officials, county leaders, the regional development corporation, chamber of commerce, the United Auto Workers, Toledo Jeep (the facility – not necessarily the corporation per se), the Port Authority and several other community leaders. Finally, the inter-state competition mandated that regional efforts be coordinated and supported by the state and representatives from the Governor's Office were included.

Place making and meaning making are the end result and inevitably become the currency of contemporary economic development policy. That is, economic development is a discourse on change and continuity – in much the same way economic geography is a discourse. But economic development's place-bound geography enables the cultural components to come to the fore. Indeed, Project

Jeep was an expressive (as well as instrumental) policy network. For example, the language of 'Project Jeep' was linked to the corporation's military history. Likewise, the organization of the rapid response team included key labor actors. This reality reflects the community's long labor history and the politician's understanding of these key actors. While these observations may seem self-evident, they are still valid and aid our understanding of the 1996–1997 crisis. Hence, we believe the politics of everyday life and place can re-arrange the economic and non-economic priorities of local decision makers by appealing to shared meanings, understandings and ideals. Similarly, the notion of locality as institution – or as we have suggested elsewhere, local cultures of production – are a useful device for understanding and exploring the non-economic drivers of regional change and continuity. While culture, place, and similar fuzzy concepts are certainly based on scant evidence, economic geographers, policy makers and others should not be so cavalier as to dismiss or ignore the imprecise nature of the lived world. Indeed, the lived world of Toledo's thousands of workers, their families, tavern owners and toolmakers.

Conclusion

The Jeep crisis represents a new sophisticated place-based strategy that combined a counter-intuitive brownfield site with a traditional incentives package to preserve old jobs and grow new jobs in a successful attempt to retain important and symbolic anchor firm – Jeep – against all odds and industry norms. While capital recruitment and retention politics may vary over time and across space, the appeal of Project Jeep was its initiative derived from a shared history and a sense of identity that had long been forged between the specific firm, workers, residents and the entire community. More importantly though, the post-Keep Jeep era has been marked by a re-birth of a city, rust-belt industry and a new wave of economic development that is not merely instrumental and spatial – but also an expression of place, identity, and pride.

> The setting is Toledo, Ohio – the most middle-American of cities. It is a town where the smokestacks have names, where the architecture is relentlessly industrial. Outsiders see Toledo as a cliche of Rustbelt dreariness. Insiders understand that grey can be beautiful (Waldmeir, 1996).

References

Baessler, J. (1999), 'Council OK's Plan for Capital Upgrades', *Toledo Blade*, 12 May, pp. 13-24.

Barnes, T. (2001), 'Retheorizing Economic Geography: From the Quantitative Revolution to the "Cultural Turn"', *Annals of the Association of American Geographers*, 91: pp. 546-565.

Brickey, H. (1997), New Auto Plant called Boom for Building Trades, *Toledo Blade*, July 30, 3-A.

Castle Coalition (2002), Government theft: The top ten abuses of eminent domain, 1998–2002 (www.castlecoalition.org).

Chavez, J. (1997), 'Stickney Plant's Neighbors Accept Need for Relocation', *Toledo Blade*, July 29, 3-B.

Cox, K. and Mair, A. (1988), 'Locality and Community in the Politics of Local Economic Development', *Annals of the Association of American Geographers*, 88: pp. 307-325.

Feldman, M. (1994), 'The University and Economic Development: The Case of Johns Hopkins University and Baltimore', *Economic Development Quarterly*, 8: pp. 67-76.

Garcia, C. (1996), 'Trade Secrets: Global Markets spur Toledo's Turnaround', *Policy Review*, 77, May/June (www.policyreview.org).

Gatrell, J. and Reid, N. (2002), 'The Cultural Politics of Economic Development: The Case of Toledo Jeep', *Tijdschrift voor Economische en Sociale Geografie*, 93: pp. 397-411.

Jacobs, J. and Fincher, R. (1998), 'Introduction', In R. Fincher and J. Jacobs (eds), *Cities of Difference*, New York and London: Guilford Press: pp. 1-25.

Lefebvre, H. (1991), *The Production of Space*, Oxford: Blackwell.

Lyne, J. (1998), 'The Strategic Art of the Deal: SS's 1997 Top 10', *Site Selection*, April/May (www.siteselection.com).

Malecki, E. (1991), *Technology and Economic Development: The Dynamics of Local, Regional, and National Change*, London: Longman Scientific and Technical.

Markusen, A. (1999), 'Debates and Surveys: Fuzzy Concepts, Scanty Evidence, Policy Distance: The Case for Rigour and Policy Relevance in Critical Regional Studies', *Regional Studies*, 33: pp. 869-884.

McCann, E. (2002), 'The Cultural Politics of Local Economic Development: Meaning-making, Place-making, and the Urban Policy Process', *Geoforum*, 33: pp. 385-398.

McKinnon, J. (1999a), 'Is Toledo Paying Too Much to Keep Jeep?', *Toledo Blade*, September 12(1): p. 10.

McKinnon, J. (1999b), 'Jeep Benefits to Area Wide-ranging', *Toledo Blade*, February 21, A-17.

Molotch, H., Freudenburg, W. and Paulsen, K. (2000), 'History Repeats Itself, But How? City Character, Urban Tradition, and the Accomplishment of Place', *American Sociological Review*, 65: pp. 791-823.

Portz, J. (1990), *The Politics of Plant Closings*, Lawrence, KS: University Press of Kansas.

Reese, L. and Rosenfeld, R. (2001), 'Yes, But...: Questioning the Conventional Wisdom about Economic Development', *Economic Development Quarterly*, 15: pp. 299-312.

Saxenian, A. (1994), *Regional Advantage: Culture and Competition in Silicon Valley and Route 128*, Cambridge, MA: Harvard University Press.

Toledo Blade (1996), 'Chrysler Says that Jeep could Move', *Toledo Blade*, October 15, p. 1, p. 4.

Toledo Blade (1997a), 'Step Up and Save Jeep', *Toledo Blade*, January 1, p. 1.

Toledo Blade (1997b), 'A Destiny Realized', *Toledo Blade*, July 30, 1997, p. 1.

Waldmeier, P. (1996), 'Grey is Beautiful: The Experience of Toledo, Ohio Reflects the Rebirth of America', *Financial Times*, 31 December, p. 10.

Zukin, S., Baskerville, R., Greenberg, M., Guthreau, C., Halley, J., Halling, M., Lawler, K., Nerio, R., Stack, R., Vitale, A., and Wissinger, B. (1998), 'From Coney Island to Las Vegas in the Urban Imaginary: Discursive Practices of Growth and Decline', *Urban Affairs Review*, 33: pp. 627-655.

Chapter 11

Israel as a Post-industrial Space of Work and Leisure: A Value Stretch of Lifestyle Attributes

Baruch A. Kipnis

Background and Scope

This chapter explores the work and leisure lifestyles of Israelis associated with the rise of a post-industrial globally oriented economy that began in the late 1990s. This period is considered 'Israel's high-tech revolution' and Israel was seen as a high-tech giant and the second Silicon Valley (Karp, 1998). At that time Israel was ranked fifth in the world in its number of start-up firms and first in the number of its start-up firms per 1000 population (Perman, 2000), recruiting some $US 4-5 billion in FDI (foreign direct investment). Yet, in Israel as well as elsewhere, the early twenty first century is considered to be the end of the high-tech era.

What has made Israel so special in its post-industrial globally linked high-tech development? Since the late 1980s Israel has gradually associated itself with the '*mega markets*' of the global economy: the European Union, North America, and the West Pacific Rim. The core of this development has been Greater Tel Aviv, a world city in evolution (Kipnis, 2001), equipped with a complex of specialized producers' services, information and expertise needed for integrating and supporting the global production environment. In addition, Tel Aviv offers diversified social, cultural, and economic possibilities for attaining quality-of-life assets (Short, 1996; Veltz, 1997). All are viewed as 'psychic rewards' (Buswell, 1983) needed for a white-collar environment of high-income, knowledge-intensive young people, the leading agents of a global economy. Many workers belong to the nation's elite, behaving as a 'Transnational Capitalist Class' (Sklair, 2000). A few also belong to the 500 to 600 Israeli [global] Super Rich described by Beaverstock, et al. (2002). In 2003 three quarters of the wealthy Israelis resided in Greater Tel Aviv as well as nearly half of Israel's population.

A number of other factors helped Israel become a post-industrial, globally affiliated high-tech center: (1) The abolition of the Arab boycott on firms that invested in Israel has turned Israel into an investment paradise for FDI; (2) Israel's role as an 'economic bridge' between the EU (European Union) and NAFTA (North American Free Trade Agreement) allowing American firms to enjoy custom allowances when selling their products to EC and vice versa, as long as their products contain substantial Israeli value added as specified by each FTA (Free Trade Area); (3) The absorption of over one million immigrants during the 1990s, many of them well educated individuals in science, engineering, humanities and performing arts, boosting Israel's post-industrial economy and its R&D high-tech capabilities; (4) IDF's (Israel Defense Forces) role in creating a high-tech ambience and training young Israelis to become high-tech leaders (Perman, 2000; Hiltzik, 2000); and (5) The inherent 'labour reproduction' capabilities of Israelis to improvise, invent and innovate. This capacity, outcomes of the social-cultural heritage and necessities, might bear a few negative 'zigzag' behavioural patterns, primarily when managerial and marketing capabilities are involved. This has proven to be a pivotal for the development of the nation's high-tech start-ups economy (Hiltzik, 2000; Treen, 2001). Thus, at the start of the twenty first century 85 per cent of Israel's high-tech firms were located in Greater Tel Aviv and more than 81 per cent of the then leading industries, communication, information technology were located there.

Israel's accelerating entry into the world economy has seen profound structural shifts in employment and in industrial mix, an increase in FDI, and expanding exports in quantities, mix and destinations. Since late 1980s industrial production, mainly in high-tech, has more than doubled. Manufacturing R&D spending reached 3 per cent, placing Israel among the leading high-tech, start-up intensive countries (Arazi, 1998; Karp, 1998; Kipnis, 2001). Israeli innovations are placed in products of multinationals in the fields of computers, optics, communication, information systems, medicine, software and even consumer goods (Achsat, 1998). High-tech giants including Intel, Microsoft, Digital and IBM have located R&D labs in Israel (Maor, 1998). In the late 1990s, over 80 per cent of Israel's products were exported from or imported to global mega-markets. Since 1993 FDI to Israel has more than tripled, revealing cross investment patterns (Dolev and Sarel, 2000; Cox, 2001). While most FDI originated in the USA, growing amounts arrived from the EU and Asia, primarily Japan.

A restructuring towards higher status occupations and advanced service industries followed. Between 1988 and 1998 total employment in Israel increased by 43 per cent but the percentage of scientific and other academic workers both in finance and business services doubled. Among the main causes of this shift was the absorption of highly educated Russian, many with scientific and engineering knowledge bases. These transformations exacerbated unemployment, most of it structural, estimated at 11 per cent in mid 2004 (Basok, 2004). A worrisome symptom and post-industrial phenomena is that foreigners from developing and semi developing countries account for 10 per cent of Israel's current labour market.

Such socio-economic and cultural changes are not new in world terms (Castells, 1996). Harris (1996) shows how peoples lives are increasingly constituted by a sea of self-reflexive signs manifest in buildings, clothes, cars, consumer goods, films, videos and television. Israel is no exception. Indeed, before the peak of Israel's post-industrial globally oriented phase, the *Globes Economics Daily* (April 29, 1997) reported on the Israelis' hyper-consumption-oriented lifestyles, resembling many aspects of Sklair's (2000) *'transnational capitalist class'*.

This chapter considers the lifestyle concept in a post-industrial society context in which *work* and *leisure* lifestyle attributes play a pivotal role in shaping place development strategies. Our interest is in how Israeli post-industrial service-intensive society lifestyles and values affected the way people work and recreate and influenced people's consumption patterns. Three studies employing the same questionnaire and the same methodology using the *value stretch model* were carried out between 1999 and 2002. The sampled interviewees were asked to assign their subjective assessment to 72 lifestyle attributes derived from the Globes article and from other lifestyle studies. The sampled populations were undergraduate students from five Israeli universities, a control group of older students engaged in enrichment programs who resided in three Haifa neighbourhoods on the northern slope of Mount Carmel, and a group of hi-tech employees. The following issues are discussed: (1) What are the many faces of the concept of lifestyle, and where are the 'work' and 'leisure' profiles of lifestyle attributes ranked among six other profiles of lifestyle attributes?; (2) Do people value their subjectively perceived lifestyle attributes of '*work*' and '*leisure*' differently?; and (3) What are the main lifestyle attributes of '*work*' and '*leisure*' and do they vary among different social groups? Do they vary among different social groups?

What are the elements of the post-industrial milieu? First, there is a heavy dependence of control over information and knowledge and on the ability to support the smooth operation of its complex global networks of production. This has led to a growing need for specialized labour in the 'quaternary' and the 'quinary' sectors. The values that these two sectors assign to their profession, to their place of work, and to their mode of employment have evolved into a main determinant of their work setting and lifestyle. The 'quinary' and the 'quaternary' sectors have created increasing demand for 'tertiary' labour in order to perform the still necessary less complex lower status services. These features are usually portrayed as rational, consumption-oriented and value-loaded. In this context post-industrial culture preaches liberalism, equality, feminism, and a sustainable environment, and it values commodified personal cultural and leisure activities.

Conceptualizing Lifestyle

Lifestyle studies aim to identify behavioural patterns and indicators of culture, believed to be *class- and place-differentiated*. Their outputs have focused on a variety of aspects of human lives, such as health, diet, safety, aging, marketing, advertising and work and leisure. From a spatial economic development stance, the outputs of lifestyle studies might turn into a valuable planning input and a viable implement in advancing our understanding of our culture and environment. In accepting the role of lifestyle attributes as a planning input, we must acknowledge Schwartz's (1996) proposition that young people are the leading agencies of change, therefore the most appropriate social group to identify needs and scenarios for short- and long-range plans.

The Many Meanings of 'Lifestyle'

The concept of lifestyle has many meanings. The Oxford Online Dictionary (2002) describes lifestyle as human characteristics, while a Google search shows 11 million Internet sites identified as *lifestyle,* covering areas such as health, diet, sports, work, safety, and many others. Early definitions that could tell us more about what lifestyle means include those of Max Weber (cited by Tumin, 1970) and of Mitchell (1983). Both linked the individual's lifestyle and that of his/her social affiliation group. Weber referred to lifestyle as a mode of conduct, dress, speech, thought, and attitudes, modes that could help define various 'honour' groups and serve as a model of behaviour for those who aspire to be members of these groups. Tumin further extended Weber's definition to incorporate into his own a range of distinctive institutional behaviour patterns such as family styles, styles revealing value orientation to the world, and styles reflecting ways of inter-personal and inter-group conduct. Mitchell, employing VALS (Values and Life Styles) methodology, established a link between lifestyle types and marketing.

Contemporary Lifestyle Studies

Many contemporary lifestyle studies identify and explain the patterns of behaviour, actions and conduct of people. They reflect on, but do not necessarily justify, the manners of human beings in order to reveal their values and aspirations, and they explicate why they behave the way they do (Chaney, 1996). Moving from the individual to the group, the lifestyle of a social group mirrors its affiliates' experiences, the realities of their lives, their heritage and their values. The many faces of a group's lifestyle and the spatial environment it occupies could be associated with its nickname and its associated images. Examples are 'yuppies' (young urban professionals), 'buppies' (black yuppies), 'yuffies' (young urban failures), 'swells' (career women), 'dinkies' and 'sinkies' (double/single income no kids) (Short, 1996).

A recent conceptual shift from class to status in politics and in marketing has led the generic sociological term 'lifestyle' to emerge with a new meaning (Cahill, 1994). It means 'individuality, self-expression, self-fulfilment, self-realization, and a stylistic self-consciousness'. Under the term 'lifestyle', people are no longer regarded as 'ordinary' and seeking class solidarity, but as having 'self-interest' and being capable of doing something about their needs on their own. In politics, social class has ceased to be the major determinant of people's vote. In marketing new definitions of people have emerged according to their age groups, their personal aspirations, and their inherent 'lifestyle shopping' habits (Cahill, 1994). In the shopping mode customers identify their needs according to the models displayed in the catalogues. Market research firms now target people in terms of their 'lifestyle' and classify consumers accordingly, including those concerned about brand prestige; those who try to be up to date; the status seeker; the rational man; those who have a sense of humour; those who are independent and/or honest; and those who are primarily concerned with sensory benefits (Cahill, 1994).

Mitchell's (1983) study established the best-known typology, known as the Nine American Lifestyles. Lifestyle attributes according to Mitchell clarify who we are as individuals, consumers and as a nation; they explain where we go and why; they expound why some people are strong leaders, why others are successful businesspersons or brilliant artists, and why others do not have these capacities. They tell us why we like some people but dislike others, why we trust a few and distrust others, and why we favour a given product but reject others. Employing a VALS – *psychological development methodology*, Mitchell established a hierarchy of four main groups of lifestyles divided into nine subgroups.

The media's role in forming lifestyle patterns of primarily young people has also attracted social scientists' attention. Rosengen (1994) assumed that the media are used in a complex matrix involving different socialization 'actors', these being the young person, his/her family, his/her peer group, and his/her school and ascribed to the actor, whose action is determined by his/her values, interests and tastes, the power of selecting among media-induced alternatives; hence the media's power in shaping the lifestyle of the young. Versantvoort (2000) associated lifestyle with labour supply by establishing lifestyle as a primary factor in explaining a person's behaviour dynamic factor that acts as an *independent variable* in his/her family, work, and leisure, and as a consumer. This idea could explain the individual's or the group's work behaviour, and help determine a community's labor supply. In addition, it could explain how members of that community would maintain their family life and make use of their free time. She maintains that such a view significantly differs from the one used in marketing, which frames lifestyle as a *dependent variable* whose patterns reflect the characteristics of the society involved, and as the main predictor of the person's way of using time and money.

Veldet and Fiddler's (2002) *lifestyle performance model* applies lifestyle attributes as a planning implement. The model assumes that lifestyle, as a personal way of living, comprises a range of daily life activities congruent with the needs of the individual and with norms of the socio-cultural framework to which he/she belongs. Each individual develops activity patterns that can be described as his/her lifestyle, simulating an inter-play between the person's intrinsic needs, desires, and expectations of his/her living conditions and of the environment he/she wishes to live in, and his/her ability to attain them. Some of the elements of the *lifestyle performance model* resemble those of the *value stretch model* proposed in this chapter.

Israeli Lifestyle Studies

A number of Israeli studies (available only in Hebrew) have identified a change in values from work and solidarity to affluence, hedonism and individualism. This work has shown that 'class', a leading denominator for social stratification, had already been replaced by other determinants such as ethnicity and orthodoxy and identified three lifestyle clusters (*a superior*, *a popular*, and *a religious*). The studies include the lifestyle of the Israeli artist, the lifestyle of the Israeli secular society and a series of marketing studies (Ziv, 1998).

The Value Stretch Model

Interviewed persons were asked to indicate their subjective evaluation of the 72 lifestyle attributes placed on the three elements of the *'value stretch' model* (Figure 11.1). Della-Fave's (1974) model accommodates values given to each of the attributes on a scale from 5 (very important) to 1 (not important at all). Given these values, the measured average gaps between the model's values indicate the person's propensity to compromise over a given lifestyle attribute. From the scores for the elements and from the gaps one can calculate for any social/demographic subgroup the average value (score) of each one of the elements and gaps of that group. See Kipnis and Aspis (1994), Kipnis and Mansfeld (1986) and Mansfeld (1992a; 1992b) for earlier applications of the model.

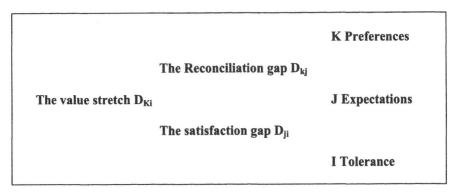

Figure 11.1   The Value Stretch Model

Source: Schnell and Kipnis 1989 following Della-Fave, 1974.

The Elements of the Model are:

- *Preferences – K.* The highest level of a given attribute a person seeks to attain over a long-term horizon of 20-25 years.
- *Expectations – J.* The level of a given attribute that a person expects to attain in a short-term horizon of 5 years, assuming he/she is ready to mobilize his/her resources and energies to this end.
- *Tolerance – I.* The lowest level of an attribute a person is willing to accept, assuming that his/her expectations cannot materialize. One may refer to this level as the present level of the lifestyle attribute under consideration (Kipnis and Mansfeld, 1986); or the person's last experience (Mansfeld, 1987); or as the minimum requirement or the most essential level for survival in the case of a public policy (Schnell and Kipnis, 1989).

The Gaps of the Model are:

- *The Reconciliation gap* D_{kJ} indicating the difference between the values assigned to an attribute at the level of preference and the values allocated to it at the level of expectation.
- *The Satisfaction gap* $D_{Ji,}$ measuring the difference in the values assigned to an attribute at the level of expectations and value given by an individual to his/her tolerance level.
- *The value stretch* D_{ki} is the sum of the reconciliation gap (RG) and of the satisfaction gap (SG).

Data and Statistical Measures

The data used here were compiled from three case studies using the same questionnaire and 'value stretch model' methodology. The first study (1999) was of students at five university campuses and in two control groups of middle-aged and elderly people who participated in External Studies enrichment programs at the University of Haifa and the Open University. The study yielded 304 useable questionnaires; its main hypothesis was that age and gender tend to influence the relative value of the lifestyle attributes.

The main hypothesis of the second study (2000) was that interviewees would assign different values to their lifestyle attributes according to their neighbourhood's socio-economic characteristics. This Haifa study yielded 404 questionnaires. This study explored whether Haifa's Jewish residents in three neighbourhoods located down the northern slope of Mount Carmel tended to value the lifestyle attributes differently. The uppermost neighbourhood lies on the top of Mount Carmel and comprises a mixed-age population is relatively affluent. The lowest neighbourhood is a low to lower middle class community comprising mostly adults or seniors. The middle slope neighbourhood has traditionally been the most hard core of Jewish Haifa and is a mixed neighbourhood of secular, ultra-orthodox and newly arrived immigrant Jews, alongside Arabs, who gradually are occupying the western edge of the neighbourhood. The research, aimed primarily at the Jewish population, surveyed 'Little Moscow', where many of the new immigrants of the 1990s had first settled.

The third study (2002) was aimed at hi-tech workers. Its hypothesis was that those employed in R&D would allot different values to their lifestyle attributes from those allotted by their colleagues who were not R&D workers. It was designed during the 'boom' of Israel's high-tech industry but fieldwork occurred during its downturn (Kipnis, 2002). Due to the time elapsed between 1999 (the first sample) and 2002, and probably due to the high-tech crisis, only 47 of the original 72 lifestyle attributes were found to be relevant. The attributes found unrelated were those that had become commonplace in most work environments such as the use of cellular phones for work. Another side effect of the high-tech crisis was that some of its hidden impacts influenced the values allocated with some of the attributes.

Analysis

Lifestyle Profiles

To examine the relative magnitude of various 'families' of lifestyle attributes in the eyes of the interviewees the 72 attributes were grouped into 7 'families' or lifestyle 'profiles'. Note that some attributes were affiliated with more than one profile. Table 11.1 shows the rank order of the seven profiles in each of the three samples. The rank of preferences (K) of the three samples is almost identical. Exceptions are the *consumption* profile of the Haifa sample, and the *personal attitudes* and *leisure* profiles of the high-tech sample. Of interest is the relatively high value scored by the *family* profile, notwithstanding the fact the divorce rate has been growing, and the relatively small value scored by the *consumption* profile, despite the fact that high consumption patterns characterize the behaviour of post-industrial men.

Table 11.1   The Average Preferences (K level) and of the D_{kj} and D_{ji} Gaps of Lifestyle (Profiles of the Three Samples)

Students' sample			Haifa sample			High-tech sample		
K	D_{kj}	D_{ji}	K	D_{kj}	D_{ji}	K	D_{kj}	D_{ji}
Family-related lifestyle attributes								
4.032	0.219	0.199	4.058	0.147	0.214	4.062	0.062	0.194
Personal attitudes-related lifestyle attributes								
3.655	0.139	0.128	3.668	0.064	0.090	4.111	0.076	0.243
Work-related lifestyle attributes								
3.532	0.238	0.226	3.486	0.132	0.249	3.613	0.193	0.320
Residence-relates lifestyle attributes								
3.392	0.275	0.236	3.388	0.191	0.230	3.009	0.255	0.290
Leisure-related lifestyle attributes								
3.199	0.184	0.247	3.376	0.126	0.150	3.232	0.374	0.224
Personal status-related lifestyle attributes								
3.011	0.263	0.226	2.991	0.137	0.220	2.903	0.169	0.287
Consumption-related lifestyle attributes								
2.677	0.503	0.530	3.060	0.500	0.564	2.733	0.651	0.835

K= Preferences; D_{kj} = Reconciliation gap; D_{ji} = Satisfaction gap. All D_{kj} and $D_{ji\ values}$ > 0.3 are underlined.
Source: Calculated by the author.

In considering the relative legitimacy of the lifestyle profiles, one should also examine their propensity of concession disclosed by their *reconciliation* and *satisfaction* gaps. The D_{kj} (average reconciliation gap) and D_{ji} (average satisfaction gap) reveal these in Table 11.1. A lifestyle profile with large D values, namely large D_{kj} or large $D_{j\,I}$, or both, indicates that the interviewees were ready to compromise on attaining it in the long- and/or the short-term. Between the two gaps the $D_{j\,I}$ is the most sensitive, revealing a high propensity of concession in many lifestyle profiles over the short-term horizon. If a concession threshold of D= 0.3 signifies a large propensity to compromise, then the consumption profile leads the list, with all its Ds much above 0.3. Among the students group ($D_{kj} > D_{ji}$) many were unemployed or holding temporary jobs. In Haifa, where quite a few of the interviewed were young people or new immigrants ($D_{kj} < D_{ji}$) that had not yet stabilized their work environment and were ready to compromise over unskilled employment (many of the immigrants, despite the high-level education, have not yet managed to fulfill their job potential). The hi-tech employees in the midst of the crisis in their industry showed the largest propensity to concession over their work expectations, with $D_{ji} > 0.3$. However, their long-range preferences (expressed by a relatively small D_{kj}) might be a sign of their trust that the current industry crisis would pass and their professional skills would be in demand.

The leisure profile of both the students and the people of Haifa tended to be consistent, where $D_{ki} < D_{ji}$. This means that the interviewees' leisure expectations were relatively close to their preferences. By contrast, they testified that if in the short term they would not be able to materialize their expectations, they would tolerate a lower level of leisure activities. An exception is the case of the hi-tech workers. With the impact of industry crisis in mind, they were ready to concede on the level of their consumption expectations $D_{ji} = 0.835$, on some of their expected work related attributes $D_{ji} = 0.320$, and even on a few of their residence expectations $D_{ji} = 0.290 > D_{kj} = 0.255$. Aware of the efforts required to regain the above essential lifestyle attributes (work, housing and consumption) at a time of future economic recovery, they were ready to lower their leisure preferences expressed in their $D_{kj} > D_{ji}$.

Work and Leisure Lifestyle Profiles

Two lifestyle profiles, *work* and *leisure*, were examined to evaluate their possible integration into economic development strategies for regions near the climax of a post-industrial milieu. Both profiles had importance for people living in a post-industrial society and were influential factors in advancing their region's economic development. Table 11.2 shows the attributes affiliated with work and leisure lifestyle profiles along with their preference (K), expectation (J), and tolerance (I) values, all ranked according to the values of K. Table 11.2 also shows the standard deviation of the K, J, and I values of each of the attributes, and the R coefficient of Spearman's rank correlation.

Table 11.2   Lifestyle Attributes of Work and Leisure profiles

Profiles' Attributes	The average values of the elements			The standard deviation of the values of		
	K	J	I	K	J	I
Work-related attributes[1]						
Professional advancement	4.244	4.244	3.952	0.858	0.897	1.129
Convenient working conditions	4.153	3.957	3.660	0.930	0.984	1.181
To work in my own profession	4.121	3.953	3.601	1.019	1.087	1.266
Work with tenure	4.036	3.832	3.591	1.066	1.103	1.206
Freedom of initiative at work	4.026	3.833	3.516	1.038	1.054	1.202
Short commuting distance	3.964	3.800	3.544	1.019	1.039	1.147
Have a meager position	3.525	3.314	2.999	1.231	1.177	1.225
Earn much money	3.167	2.974	2.685	1.425	1.342	1.299
Self employed	3.039	2.781	2.647	1.423	1.398	1.364
Salaried employment	2.931	2.925	2.840	1.214	1.321	1.276
Frequent trips abroad	2.916	2.813	2.571	1.345	1.243	1.144
Work from home	2.596	2.463	2.309	1.255	1.176	1.152
Spearman's rank correlation R coefficients						
	R values between the average scores of the model elements			R values between elements' average standard deviation		
The pair of variables	K and J	K and I	J and I	K and J	K and I	J and I
R values	0.972	0.972	0.965	0.965	0.524	0.692
Leisure-related attributes						
Have regular vacations	4.221	4.033	3.845	0.953	0.995	1.094
Hosting friends at home	4.172	4.075	3.948	0.825	0.856	0.952
Engage in sports activities	3.828	3.740	3.571	1.159	1.159	1.213
Have (a) creative hobby(ies)	3.748	3.606	3.433	1.197	1.188	1.236
Lectures and courses	3.617	3.480	2.218	1.123	1.084	1.158
Internet for leisure	3.530	3.413	3.203	1.345	1.323	1.335
Go out to movies	3.431	3.337	3.155	1.139	1.128	1.153
Watch TV	3.416	3.310	3.146	1.064	1.059	1.121
Weekend abroad	3.275	2.998	2.764	1.304	1.259	1.282
Go out to pubs and clubs	3.065	2.968	2.787	1.282	1.251	1.237
Season ticket for theatre	3.020	2.820	2.571	1.296	1.212	1.188
Dine at expensive restaurants	2.994	2.762	2.518	1.286	1.215	1.207
Go out to sports events	2.811	2.713	2.602	1.382	1.339	1.309
Have a season ticket for concerts	2.582	2.448	2.304	1.227	1.147	1.117
Own a yacht	2.229	2.079	1.971	1.294	1.202	1.156
Spearman's rank correlation R coefficients						
	R values between the average scores of the model elements			R values between elements' average standard deviation		
The pair of variables	K and j	K and I	J and I	K and J	K and I	J and I
R values	0.996	0.821	0.825	0.957	0.786	0.900

K= Preferences; J= Expectations; I= Tolerance. Attributes Ranked by Average Preference (K) Values.
Source: Field surveys 1999, 2000, and 2002.

The work- and leisure-related attributes tend to reveal different consistencies in their value stretch model's elements and in the rank order of the elements' standard deviation. Of the two, the rank order of the work-related attributes is more consistent than that of the leisure-related. The former scored R values greater than 0.95; the latter scored a large R between K and J (R= 0.996) but R= 0.825 and 0.821 for J and I and for K and I respectively. In contrast, the R values of the standard deviation show different patterns. They are more consistent in the case of leisure, but less so in the case of work-related lifestyle attributes.

The R values suggest that respondents assigned different values to the value stretch model's elements as they moved down the model's stretched time horizons. They were more consistent in allocating the values in the case of work-related attributes, but at the cost of large variance between the values. The opposite pattern prevailed in the leisure-related attributes case. The interviewees ranked the attributes' elements differently, but the variance between the values was smaller. A possible interpretation of the results for place strategy planning could be that people place similar values on work attributes regardless of their time of occurrence, but they tend to differ, probably according to their professional status, gender, or age, in the values they place on each attribute. This seems not to be the case with leisure. When asked to appraise how important a leisure attribute was for them, interviewees did not hesitate to place his/her personal value on each element of the leisure life style attributes according to the attribute's relevance to him/her at a given point of time. However, the variance between the scores of the attributes was small, regardless of the interviewee's personal taste determined by age, gender, or profession.

Essential Work-Related Lifestyle Attributes

Of the 12 work-related lifestyle attributes only eight were ranked among the first five (Tables 11.3A and 11.4A). The same attributes, albeit in different order, appear in almost all the socio-economic and demographic subgroups. Of the eight attributes, only three had a weighted rank of more than 39, including: 'To have professional advancement opportunities at work' (weighted rank 58); 'To work in my own profession' (weighted rank 40); 'To work in a place having convenient working conditions' (weighted rank 39). Those that followed and all scored low weighted ranks were: 'To have freedom of initiative at work'; 'To have a work position with tenure'; 'To have short travel distance from home to work'; 'To have a managerial position'; 'To earn much money'.

These results suggest that contemporary economic development policy for advanced economies ought to concentrate on developing employment openings geared to the professional potential of the population involved, with preference given to those attributes important to young people who are at the entry stage to the local labour market. The strategy must also provide conditions suitable for professional advancement, convenient work facilities and apt environment.

Table 11.3   Five Highest-ranked Work and Leisure Lifestyle Attributes by Sample, Gender, Age and Type of Employment

11.3A: Work related attributes

Attributes	Attributes	Attributes
All the sampled population Professional advancement To work in my own profession Freedom of initiative at work Convenient working conditions Short commuting distance	*Males* Professional advancement Convenient working conditions To work in my own profession Short commuting distance Work with tenure	*Seniors (age > 51)* Convenient working conditions To work in my own profession Professional advancement Short commuting distance Work with tenure
Students Professional advancement To work in my own profession Convenient working conditions Freedom of initiative at work To earn much money	*Females* Professional advancement Convenient working conditions Freedom of initiative at work To work in my own profession Short commuting distance	*High level jobs* Professional advancement Convenient working conditions To work in my own profession Short commuting distance Work with tenure
Haifa Professional advancement Convenient working conditions Work with tenure To work in my own profession Short commuting distance	*Young (age < 35)* Professional advancement To work in my own profession Convenient working conditions Work with tenure Freedom of initiative at work	*Low level jobs* Professional advancement Freedom of initiative at work Convenient working conditions To work in my own profession Work with tenure
Hi-tech Professional advancement Freedom of initiative at work Have a management position Short commuting distance To work in my own profession	*Adults (age 36-50)* Professional advancement Convenient working conditions Freedom of initiative at work Work with tenure To work in my own profession	*Not employed* Professional advancement To work in my own profession Convenient working conditions Work with tenure Freedom of initiative at work

11.3B: Leisure related attributes

Attributes	Attributes	Attributes
All the sampled population Have regular vacations Hosting friends at home Engage in sports activities Have (a) creative hobby(ies) Participate in lectures/courses	*Males* Have regular vacations Hosting friends at home Engage in sports activities Have (a) creative hobby(ies) Participate in lectures/courses	*Seniors (age > 51)* Hosting friends at home Watch TV Have regular vacations Have (a) creative hobby(ies) Engage in sports activities
	Females Have regular vacations Hosting friends at home Have (a) creative hobby(ies) Engage in sports activities Participate in lectures/courses	*High level jobs* Have regular vacations Hosting friends at home Engage in sports activities Have (a) creative hobby(ies) Participate in lectures/courses
Haifa Have regular vacations Hosting friends at home Engage in sports activities Have a creative hobby (ies) Watch TV	*The young (age < 35)* Have regular vacations Hosting friends at home Engage in sports activities Have a creative hobby (ies) Participate in lectures/courses	*Low level jobs* Have regular vacations Hosting friends at home Engage in sports activities Have a creative hobby (ies) Participate in lectures/courses
Hi-tech Have a creative hobby (ies) Have regular vacations Engage in sports activities Hosting friends at home Go out to movies frequently	*Adults (age 36-50)* Have regular vacations Hosting friends at home Engage in sports activities Have (a) creative hobby(ies) Participate in lectures/courses	*Not employed* Have regular vacations Hosting friends at home Engage in sports activities Participate in lectures/courses Have (a) creative hobby(ies)

Source: Field surveys 1999–2002.

Important Leisure-Related Lifestyle Attributes

Fifteen leisure-related lifestyle attributes were isolated out of the 72 surveyed attributes (Table 11.2), but only seven were mentioned among the first five (Tables 11.3B and 11.4B). Of those, only three scored relatively high: 'Have regular vacations' (weighted rank 57), 'Host(ing) friends at home' (weighted rank 47) and 'Engage in sports activities' (weighted rank 33). It is important to note too, that six of the seven attributes were oriented to popular or home-associated leisure activities. The only one attribute that bore some cultural or intellectual flavor was 'To participate in lectures and courses' (weighted rank 11). This reflects the growing need for on-the-job training, a basic requisite for many post-industrial occupations. It is also a sign of the growing hunger for intellectual enrichment in the educated public or in those aspiring to narrow education gap of their early years, evidenced by the popularity enrichment programs have gained from the rising number of educated retirees.

Table 11.4   Distribution of Weighted Ranks of Work- and Leisure-related Lifestyle Attributes

11.4A: Work related attributes

The five highest ranked Attributes	The rank					Weighted Rank*
	1	2	3	4	5	
Professional advancement	11		1			58
To work in my own profession		5	2	3	2	40
Convenient working conditions	1	5	4	1		39
Freedom of initiative at work		2	3		2	19
Work with tenure			1	3	4	13
Short commuting distance				3	3	9
Have a management position			1			3
Earn much money					1	1

11.4B: Leisure related attributes

The five highest ranked Attributes	The rank					Weighted Rank*
	1	2	3	4	5	
Have regular vacations	10	1	1			57
Hosting friends at home	1	10		1		47
Engage in sports activities			10	1	1	33
Have (a) creative hobby(ies)	1		1	9		21
Participate in lectures and courses				2	7	11
Watching TV		1			1	5
Go out to movies frequently					2	2

* The weights are 1=5; 2=4; 3=3; 4=2; 5=1.
Source: Calculated by the author.

In terms of an economic development strategy, the image of the post-industrial person as a heavy consumer of leisure, one who is capable and ready to spend both time and money to satisfy his/her leisure expectations, might evolve into an effective economic development instrument. However, as a strategy implement, one must distinguish the activities of a few urbane consumers of culture (who go to theatre and concerts or take a weekend abroad or to dine in luxurious restaurants), from those of the majority of post-industrial people, who create a wider demand for popular leisure activities.

Concluding Remarks

The chapter has inquired as to whether '*work*' and '*leisure*' lifestyle attributes, stretched along short and extended planning time horizons, could serve as input for a 'place' economic development strategy. At this point it is essential to suggest that the actual scored values and the measured gaps were significantly different. These differences discovered in all the known (to the author) value stretch studies reveal that in the lifestyles literature, attributes are 'place and class differentiated'. Another point of concern is how one should move from the individual interviewed person to a 'class' or to a 'status' group. This question can be answered by Schnell and Kipnis (1989) methodological response to utilize a stratified analysis in order to identify the most meaningful social groups for whom an averaged or a weighted value could be attached for each one of the assigned scores of the value stretch model. These could serve as place and class differentiated inputs for planning a social policy planning.

The relatively low scores gained by the consumption related attributes and the relatively high scores of the family oriented ones require further scrutiny. As to the second, the family related, where the interviewees' assigned high values to '*live as a couple*', '*raise children*', '*spend time with the family*', and to '*gender equality*' needs explanation. In Israel, as in most advanced economies, divorce rates have significantly increased, reaching close to the 10,000, nearly one third of all marriages in 2001(the most recent year for which data are available). Without detailed deliberations, one may conclude that the highly scored attributes and the divorce rates are closely linked. An equal and close partnership in family life has gained the same level of legitimacy as divorce has. Therefore, if the marriage does not work well according to the above lifestyle preferences, divorce inevitably becomes an legitimate act.

Sobel (1981) examined whether work and leisure lifestyle indices tended to be ranked higher than those of consumption. The argument was that notwithstanding the relatively higher weight of work- and leisure-related aspects of life as opposed to consumption, their salience over consumption requires further elaboration. The rationale behind Sobel's statement is that unlike consumption, work does not reflect a great deal of choice. Moreover, even though most people view work as a significant rewarding activity, the rewards are not from the work itself but from its social meanings, primarily from the person's ability to consume.

Sobel also questioned the belief that the reduced number of working hours means more time for leisure. He argued that commuting and activities at home consume much of the saved hours, and that the remaining time is not used for leisure fully. He concluded that the argument for leisure cannot rest upon a quantitative assessment of free time, given that the utilization of free time often involves prior or simultaneous consumption. Despite higher wages and shorter working hours, most free time activities appear in the form of consumption. In conclusion, the utilization of free time also bears out the contention that it is closely associated with consumption. Thus Sobel's findings, 20 years on, still have saliency. In fact, and thanks to Sobel, our research agenda is to probe those who gave a high score to the attributes of the consumption profile, and whether they match the elites defined by Sklair (2000) and by Beaverstock et al. (2002).

References

Achsat, H. (1998), 'Invest in Geeks', *Israel's Business Arena – Globes*, January 22.

Almog, O. (2004), 'The Jewish-Secular-Veteran Population in Current Israel – a new Typology of Lifestyles', *The Geographical Research Forum*, forthcoming.

Arazi, D. (1998), 'Three Spokes in the Wheel', *Israel's Business Arena – Globes*, January 22.

Basok, M. (2004), The Number of Unemployed Has Reached a Climax of 290,000, Haaretz, 04.23.2004.

Beaverstock, J. V., Hubbard, P. J., and Short J. R. (2002), 'Getting Away With It. The Changing Geographies of the Global Super-Rich', *Research Bulletin*, 93, *www.lboro.ac.uk/gawc/rb/rb/93.html.*

Buswell, R. J. (1983), 'Research and Development and Regional Development: A Review', In A. Gillespie (ed.), *Technological Change and Regional Development*, London: Pion, pp. 9-22.

Cahill, M. (1994), *The New Social Policy*, Oxford: Blackwell.

Castells, M. (1996), *The Rise of the Network Society*, Oxford: Balckwell.

Chaney, D. (1996), *Lifestyles*, London: Routledge.

Cox, J. (2001), 'Israeli Tech Start-Ups Cross Over to Delaware: More than 1,000 Firms Stage Alarming Exodus to Secure Funds, Avoid Taxes', *USA Today*, January 23.

Della Fave, R. (1974), 'Success Values: Are They Universal or Class-Differentiated?', *American Journal of Sociology*, pp. 153-169.

Dolev, G., and Sarel, E. (2000), 'Start-up Exodus', *Upside*, 12(9): pp. 147-156.

Harris, D. (1996), *A Society of Signs*, London: Routledge.

Hiltzik, M. A. (2000), 'Israel's High-Tech Boot Camp: The Army', *Los Angeles Times*, August 24. In Israel seed, www.israelseed.com.

Jacobs, E., Scheepers, P. and Felling, A. (1992), 'Life-styles as Social Cultural Patterns? A Description of Material and Cultural Life-styles in the Netherlands in 1990', Paper Presented at the Meeting of the ISA Research Committee on Social Stratification, Italy, May 14-16.

Karp, M. (1998), 'Not a Powerhouse Yet', Israel's Business Arena – *Globes*, January 22.

Kipnis, B. A. (2001), 'Tel Aviv, Israel – A World City in Evolution: Urban Development at a Deadened of Global Economy', *Research Bulletin*, #57, at GaWC site: http://www.lboro.ac.uk/gawc.

Kipnis, B. A. (2002), 'The Global Crisis and Israel's High-Tech Industry', *Research Bulletin*, #72, in GaWC site: http://www.lboro.ac.uk/gawc.

Kipnis, B. A. and Aspis, Y. (1996), 'Defining Needs for Neighborhoods Services in Arab Urbanizing Settlements of Israel: A Value Stretch Model in Social Policy Planning', *Social Security*, 3: pp. 31-51.

Kipnis, B.A. and Mansfeld, Y. (1986), 'Work-Place Utilities and Commuting Patterns: Are they Class or Place Differentiated?', *Professional Geography*, 38(2): pp. 160-169.

Mansfeld, Y. (1987), 'Destination-Choice and Spatial Behaviour of Tourists: Evaluating the Potential of Psychological-Geographical Collaboration in Geography of Tourism Research', *Geography Discussion Papers*, pp. 20-44.

Mansfeld, Y. (1992a), 'Tourism: Towards a Behavioural Approach', *Progress in Planning*, 1(38): pp. 91-92.

Mansfeld, Y. (1992b), 'Group Differentiated Perceptions of Social Impacts Related to Tourism Development', *Professional Geographe*, pp. 140-151.

Maor, R. (1998), 'Israel as Technology Incubator', *Israel's Business Arena – Globes*, January 22.

Mitchell, A. (1983), *The Nine American Lifestyles: Who We Are and Where We Are Going*, New York: Macmillan.

Perman, S. (2000), 'Start-up Nation'. *Economy Now*, 1(6): pp. 134-150.

Rosengen, K. E. (1994), 'Culture, Media and Society: Agency and Structure, Continuity and Change', In K. E. Rosengen (ed.), *Media, Effects and Beyond: Culture, Socialization and Lifestyles*, London: Routledge, pp. 3-28.

Schnell, I. and Kipnis, B.A. (1989), 'Well-Being in a Pluralistic Society: Toward a Policy-oriented Methodology', *Geoforum*, 3(20): pp. 303-313.

Schwartz, P. (1996), *The Art of Long View*, New York: Doubleday.

Schwartz, W. and Schwartz, D. (1998), *Living Lightly. Travel in Post-Consumer Society*, Oxfordshire: Jon Carpenter.

Short, J.R. (1996), *The Urban Order*, Cambridge: Blackwell.

Sklair, L. (2000), 'The Transnational Capitalist Class and the Discourse of Globalization', In *http://www.hp.com/*. Also in *The Cambridge Review of International Affairs*.

Sobel, M.E. (1981), Lifestyle and Social Structure: Couples, Definition, Analysis, New York: Academic Press.

Tumin, M. (1970) *Reading on Social Stratification*. Prentice Hall: Engelwood-Cliffs, NJ.

Treen, D. (2001), 'The HR Challenge for the Hi-Tech Start-Up', *Ivey Business Journal*, 65(3): pp. 10-12.

Veldet, B. and Fiddler, G. (2002) *Lifestyle Performance: A Model for Engaging the Power of Occupation Thorofare*. Slack: NJ.

Veltz, P. (1997), 'The Dynamics of Production Systems, Territories and Cities', In F. Moulaert and A. J. Scott (eds), *Cities, Enterprises and Society on the Eve of the 21st Century*. London: Pinter, pp. 78-96.

Versantvoort, M. (2000) *Analyzing Labor Supply in a Life Style Perspective*. Rotterdam.

Yaniv, N. (2000), Application of the Value Stretch Methodology in Plan Evaluation: Case study of Israel 2020 National Plan, Ph.D. Thesis, Department of Geography, University of Haifa.

Ziv, Y. (1998) 'What is your style?', *The Insurance Agent* 80, pp. 26-27 (in Hebrew).

Chapter 12

Electronic Waste, Global Value Chains and Environmental Policy Response in China

Tong, Xin

Introduction

Management of the ever-increasing quantities of end-of-life or used electronic equipment (e-waste) has become a global issue in recent years. This issue is of particular significance for China for two reasons. First, among developing countries, China is a major destination of the e-waste exported from the developed countries. Serious conflict now exists between the goals of environmental protection and local economic development in the coastal areas where e-waste recycling activities are concentrated. Second, China is also one of the largest manufacturers of electronic products in the world, and the global mandate on the management of end-of-life electronic equipments will affect the competitiveness of the electronics industry in China.

This chapter begins by showing that environmental regulations and the locational dynamics of recycling activities are normally omitted in global value chain analyses. This omission has particular institutional roots, but these are changing. The chapter then examines the e-waste problem as it has emerged in China, explaining the current situation of the e-waste recycling activities in mainland China, the influences on the electronic industry and the reactions of the Chinese government to developments.

Global Value Chains, Environmental Regulations, and Locational Dynamics of Recycling

Recycling has existed as long as human society and plays a range of roles in our economic system. Yet it has rarely been examined in the industrial geography literature. This gap is unjustified because the present growth of international recycling is as important in some economies as the development of agricultural and consumer product markets (Beukering, 2001). From the viewpoint of local development advocates, recycling as an industrial sector is increasing, creating employment and attracting investment; while from the view of the environmentalists, recycling is an important strategy for alleviating the pressures of society on the environment. Why, then has recycling been neglected so far in industrial geography? There are two reasons, and they are interrelated with each other.

First, recycling, which was integrated with the processes of production and daily life of traditional human society, has been separated and left out in the development of mass production and consumption in the industrialized world. General attitudes toward waste generated in everyday life and the way we dispose of such wastes have also changed dramatically in last several decades (Strasser, 1999). The separation between the production stages and the waste disposal stages of the products excluded recycling activities from the consciousness of industrial geographers, who mainly focus on the production stages.

Second, this separation has led to, and been strengthened by, modern urban waste management systems. During the end of nineteenth century and the beginning of twenty-first century, along with the fast urbanization and industrialization in the western countries, waste management in cities faces the possibility of market failure. In order to improve the health and environmental conditions in cities, local governments in more and more cities are taking responsibility of household waste management (Gandy, 1994). Considering waste management in public policy terms could benefit recycling activities that are not profitable in the pure market economy. However, this institutional transformation also alleviated the responsibility of private producers and consumers to dispose the waste they generated.

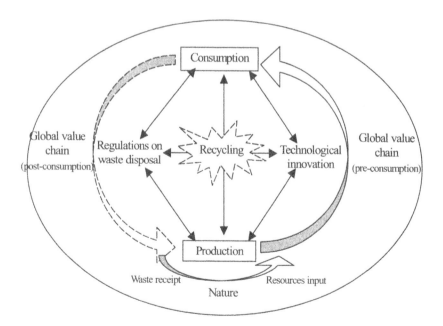

Figure 12.1   Missing Dimensions of Global Value Chains

The mode of production characterized by mass production, mass consumption and mass abandonment was associated with a particular mode of regulation on waste disposal activities, in which recycling was not only neglected in industrial geographies, but marginalized in the mainstream economic analysis on industrial development. The unbalanced relations between the pre- and post-consumption stages in the global value chains can be strengthened by the regulations on waste disposal, thus hindering technological innovations in recycling (Figure 12.1).

Although recycling is important for environmental protection, it is not a clean industry itself and is often a serious pollutant. International recycling, especially that associated with the transport of hazardous waste from developed countries to less developed countries has attracted some attention (Held et al., 1999; Davis, 1993; Greenpeace, 1993; OECD, 1994). Environmentalists and economists disagree with each other on this issue. Environmentalists believe that the spatial disparity of environmental regulations plays an important role in the locational dynamics of recycling activities. According to the 'pollution heaven' hypotheses, the higher disposal costs caused by the increasingly strict environmental regulations in developed countries could drive pollution industries in these countries, including many recycling activities, to move to the less developed world where disposal requirements are more lenient.

A World Bank report (1993) illustrates the economic perspective. It indicated that there is scarce evidence to show that the spatial distribution of waste industries has changed dramatically in last decades, moving from the North to the South, or from the countries with strict environmental regulations to those less restricted. The growth of waste industries in most developing countries results from domestic industrialization. Other economic factors, such as labour costs, rather than the disparity of environmental regulations more aptly explain the locational dynamics of this industry.

This conflict has its root in the worldwide expansion of the current mode of capitalist commodity production in which the South has followed the unsustainable way of development in the North. Many international organizations have tried to prevent the hazardous waste trade from the North to the South. This has been helped by the Basel Convention which provides a list of commonly acknowledged hazardous wastes, and requires all member countries to ban the trade of these wastes from the developed to developing countries. But such efforts have met with great difficulties when they have conflicted with the local pursuit of economic growth.

Importantly, environmental policy principles relating to waste have changed noticeably since the 1970s. First, the focus has extended from the control in production stage characterized by 'end-of-pipe' resolutions to the assessment of the full lifecycle impacts of products or services with systematic approaches. Second, the measures go beyond governments' commands and controls to include more economic incentives and voluntary agreements among the stakeholders. Third, international cooperation has tackled cross-border pollution.

Among the new environmental policy principles, which entered public policy less 10 years ago is the idea of Extended Producer's Responsibility (EPR). This approach is aimed at problems in the management of end-life-products.

Lindhqvist (2000) provides a formal definition of Extended Producer Responsibility, stressing that EPR is an environmental protection strategy designed to reach an environmental objective of a decreased total environmental impact from a product, by making the manufacturer of the product responsible for the entire life-cycle of the product and especially for the take-back, recycling and final disposal of the product. Thus EPR is implemented through administrative, economic and informative instruments. As Lindhqvist points out, the composition of these instruments determines the precise form of the EPR.

According to the OECD (2001), the main feature of EPR policy is the shift of responsibility (physically and/or economically; fully or partially) upstream toward the producer and away from municipalities. This is based on the idea that the producer has control over their products (here producer refers to manufacturers, distributors, wholesalers, as well as anybody who has control of the products in the commodity chain).

EPR has been applied in package recycling, end-of-life vehicle management, end-of-life electronics tack-back schemes, and so on. This regulatory approach is significant for the electronic industry where enterprises face fast development of technology, frequent upgrades and in-built obsolescence. The application of EPR in the management of e-waste is beginning to influence the pattern of innovation, production, consumption and recycling in the electronic industry.

At present, 16 countries have passed versions of take-back legislation on e-waste. According to Raymond Communication, an international consultant company specialized in recycling market, similar legislation will be established in another 28 countries in the coming five years, covering most markets of electronic products in the world. How is China responding to e-waste in environmental policies?

E-waste Recycling in China: Ecological Dumping or International Recycling?

Recycling of e-waste, is an economically useful but environmentally hazardous activity, due to the toxic substances contained in the scraps (Lin et al., 2002). Two broad categories are listed by the Basel Convention on the Control of Transboundary Movements of Hazardous Waste and Their Disposal (the 'Basel Convention'): (1) heavy metals such as glass with high-lead content in CRTs (cathode-ray tubes), mercury used in PCBs (polychlorinated biphenyls), etc.; (2) Brominated Flame Retardants (BFR) prevalent in the plastics used in electronics to prevent the products from catching fire, which can release toxic substances during incineration. The profits of e-waste recycling mainly come from the sale of precious and non-ferrous metals extracted from scraps in the secondary market. Without proper pollution control equipment and techniques, the extraction of such metals from PCBs and plastic-coated cables often leads to serious pollution. The residuals from the extraction processes also contain hazardous substances that require proper disposal.

The disassembly of end-of-life equipment is labor intensive and low value-added, squeezing the profit margin in countries with higher incomes. The investment on pollution control equipment and techniques is so large that it cannot be supported just by the revenue from the sale of the secondary materials that are recovered from the scrap. Moreover, from the environmental perspective, the international transport and end-of-life disposition of e-waste confers spatially disparate costs and benefits to consumers in developed countries as well as recyclers in developing countries.

The environmental pollution stemming from import e-waste recycling activities in China drew media attention with the publication of 'Exporting Harm: The High-Tech Trashing of Asia', an on-line report jointly prepared by the Basel Action Network (BAN) and Silicon Valley Toxic Coalition (SVTC) on Feb. 25, 2002. This report exposed the well-hidden trade of high tech trashes from developed to developing countries. According to this report, over 90 per cent of the scrap computers that the recyclers collect from US users are exported to Asia's developing regions. From this, about 80 per cent goes to coastal areas in Mainland China. This means China has become the largest acceptor of the e-waste dumping from developed countries (Puckett and Byster, 2002).

The report by BAN and SVTC has generated much Internet debate. Similar topics became the hot issue on domestic public media in China. Many coastal areas where e-waste scrapping activities were prevalent, such as Huangye in Hebei province, Nanhai in Guangdong province and Taizhou in Zhejiang province, had massive negative exposure in the public media (Dai, 2002; CCTV, 2002).

Widespread criticism on the Internet contrasts with the attitude of government authorities in charge of the import e-waste management in China. The State Environmental Protection Agency (SEPA) promulgated a declaration in September, which denied that pollution in Guiyu resulted from the import e-waste scrapping, declaring that it mainly came from domestic consumption. However, according to our interviewees, the government is requiring stricter inspections of imported recyclable goods, especially in the seventh category, which includes most of the e-waste.

The government's contradicting attitudes and actions reflect the dilemma in local economic development in China. Generally speaking, the import of large amount of e-waste reflects two development imperatives in China: the demand for low-cost raw materials to alleviate domestic shortage and the need to promote labour-intensive industries to generate employment opportunities for the unskilled labour force in rural areas.

From an economic view, the development of international recycling has its incentives. However, from an environmental protection standpoint, the hazardous waste dumping is called 'recycling', transferring ecological burdens from one place to another. Even in recycling, the unbalanced distribution of the costs and benefits in products' full life cycle can make such trade unjustified.

Should the import of e-waste be considered a form of ecological dumping or a way of international recycling? The different answers to this question mean different policy implications for various levels of government. In order to answer this question, we consider why e-waste imports are concentrated in some areas in coastal China.

Emerging Patterns

A huge demand for cheap materials in China has arisen since the advent of economic reforms and border opening began in the late 1970s. The importation of secondary materials has continued to increase, so much so that China has become one of the largest importers of these goods in the world.

Most e-waste recyclers in China are township or village owned enterprises that employ unskilled workers. They are concentrated mainly in rural places near seaports, where there is convenient access to the supply and market, yet far away enough to escape the inspections and controls of government authorities.

These rural recyclers have played a vital role in local industrialization because in the early stages of the market transition in China, most raw materials such as iron and steel, nonferrous metals and plastics were controlled by central planning and only available for state-owned enterprises. It was extremely difficult for most enterprises owned by townships, villages, or privately owned enterprises in rural areas to acquire industrial materials from formal distribution channels, and they had to rely on secondary materials.

The local market demand for secondary materials has become the main economic motive for e-waste recycling in the eastern coastal regions. An interviewee (2003) from Taiwan stated, 'Import e-waste recycling was controlled strictly in Taiwan twenty years ago, just like the situation in the mainland China at present. We came to the Mainland in late 1980s, among the first tier of investment from Taiwan Island to the Mainland, mainly due to the increasing labor cost and strict environmental regulations in Taiwan. Our first plant was settled in Guangdong, where we imported most of the materials from overseas, and did the disassembling in China. All secondary materials were exported back to Taiwan after processing.' He added, 'However, we had established this plant near Shanghai in early 1990s. All of the secondary materials are consumed locally. Our customers found us themselves. We have established a local business network and hope to continue our business here, although the labor cost advantage is diminishing and the requirement on pollution controls are also increasingly strict in this region.'

Unfortunately, environmental concerns are still the main constraints on the development of e-waste recycling in this region. According to a survey conducted by the SEPA, e-waste recycling has become *the* main source of pollution in many localities in coastal China since early 1990s (*China Economic Times*, 1995). This led the government to take urgent actions to restrict, if not ban, the e-waste import and scraping in China.

Late in 1995, the State Council issued an 'urgent notice' asking the State Environmental Protection Administration (SEPA), State Administration for Entry-Exit Inspection and Quarantine (SAIQ), Ministry of Foreign Trade and Economic Cooperation (MOFTEC) and other agencies to develop regulations to deal with imported waste. The Interim Provisions on Wastes Import and Environmental Protection (the Interim Provisions) was promulgated in March 1996. This restricted the import of hazardous waste that had been used as raw material and prohibited imports of other forms of hazardous waste. Some 460 enterprises from thousands of applicant recyclers were selected as certified importers and processors under the Interim Provisions.

On January 26, 2000, SEPA, together with MOFTEC, SAIQ and the General Administration of Customs, issued a Notice mandating a complete ban on the import of scrap computers, panel displays, kinescopes and other electronic equipment, effective April 1, 2000. Many provinces, however, have found the ban ineffective. The reasons are simple. Government agencies have insufficient resources to implement the regulations, and the command and control approach is unlikely to fundamentally alter the basic forces that give rise to the environmental problems in the first place.

The actual number of small enterprises engaged in the import e-waste scraping activities is much larger than the approved number. Since the import of e-waste often takes the name of metal scraps or electronic products, it is difficult to get the exact quantity of the total imports. The Beijing Zhongse Institute of Secondary Metals (2002) estimates that in 2001 there were 700,000 tons of imported e-waste in the Yangzi River Delta.

The underground economy could be large. For example, a family enterprise in Luqiao, using discarded computer monitors to make television sets, supplies 200 units per month to an appliance store. A market for refurbished electronic products involving over 1000 disassembling and processing enterprises has existed in Nanhai city in Guangdong province for a decade. In an inspection in Qingyuan City in Guangdong province, more than 14,000 companies were detected to have been selling used had disks to Guangzhou.

Given that the electronic products industry has become the largest exporter of industrial goods in China, producers have begun to worry about overseas market barriers resulting from the mandate on product take-back schemes. Although the government has reacted to the rise of electronics production and e-waste recycling, the labor-intensive assembly and disassembly activities in both stages in the lifecycle of electronic products have located in Mainland China. The global transport of e-waste has intimate linkages with the globalization of electronics production; the problem associated with the links cannot be solved separately. Since it is the unbalanced distribution of costs and benefits within the products' full lifecycle value chains that leads to the shabby conditions of the recycling activities, a transformation of legal frameworks and institutional infrastructure could help China to build an environmentally and economically sound e-waste recycling system.

In 2002 a Commission jointly organized by the Ministry of Information Industry, SEPA, and the State Economic and Trade Committee was asked to devise regulations on e-waste management according to the EPR concept. The aim is to incorporate market incentives into the management of the life cycle of such a global class of products. The draft Regulatory Approaches on the Pollution Control in Electronic and Information Products was released for public comment in June 2003. In this draft, the producers are required to choose recyclable materials and environment friendly designs in production, and to label the contents of material on the products. A 2006 deadline was set to replace toxic substances in the electronic products, matching the timetable of the EU WEEE (European Union waste electrical and electronic equipment) directives. The Regulatory Approaches on End-of-life Household Electronic Equipment is also being prepared. This aims to get producers and distributors to accept responsibility and take back the end-of-life products they sold on the market.

According to the new regulations, the producers will play a key role in the national e-waste recycling system. However, the debates continue. Many large companies complain that the profits margin in manufacturing has been squeezed in the domestic price war on market share. Additional burdens are unacceptable. In contrast to the reluctant domestic producers, many MNCs such as Motorola, Nokia, HP and Epson began to voluntarily promote their own take back scheme. A spokesperson from Nokia said, 'Such actions could benefit the image of the company in the mind of Chinese people ... and it is also the duty of Nokia as a corporation citizen in the world.'

The behaviour of the large MNCs could have effects on the development of local recycling enterprises. For example, MNCs in Beijing such as Motorola, Nokia, HP, and IBM have to dispose the e-waste they generate in their daily working in a proper way according to the requirement of ISO14000. They looked for organizations qualified to do this job. The only facility for industrial hazardous waste disposal in Beijing is limited to disassembling. The PCB scraps are sent to Korea or Singapore for further processing. Other recyclable materials, such as glass, plastics, metals in electronic wires, and so on go to recyclers in Hebei province and Zhejiang province. 'If the new regulations on e-waste management come into enforcement, the business prospect will be much more brilliant, and we will consider investing on technological upgrading.' said a respondent in this facility, 'However, at present, only a few MNCs (multi-national corporations) in Beijing need such services, the domestic users have not taken this issue seriously.'

The domestic producers, who are to expand their market share out of China, have noticed the regulatory transformation in waste policy overseas since late 1990s. For example, Haire, a well-known household electronic appliances producer in China, has set up its global strategy. The company has cooperated with the China Consumer Electronics Institute to track the development of e-waste policies in their target foreign market, and actively participates in the construction of relevant national legal systems in China.

However, there is still a gap between the electronics producers and recyclers, for the traditional rural recyclers do not have equipment and techniques to reach the environmental standards required of electronics producers. On the one hand, electronics producers complain about the extra burden the new regulations will put on them while on the other hand, the traditional recyclers find their business niches diminishing due to the ban on the import of e-waste.

Conclusion

China is exploring a path of green development to reduce the ecological footprint of national industrialization and make growth sustainable. In reality, however, the conflicts between local economic development and environmental protection are so intense that the government often finds itself in a dilemma. The unbalanced distribution of costs and benefits in the full lifecycle of products from the environmental perspective is strengthened by economic globalization. The environmental conflicts are increasingly transnational, and traditional environmental regulations constrained only within national borders cannot be fully effective in this context.

In the case of e-waste management, more and more countries have adopted the new resolutions based on the EPR principle, including China. Such 'top-down' transfers of regulatory approaches led by the central government of developing countries like China are mainly modelled after 'best-practice' approaches employed in developed countries. In fact, the three key concerns in the construction of e-waste recycling institutional infrastructure are: environmental protection in the consumption of electronics products; environmental sound technology innovation of the electronics producers, as well as promotion of the recycling industry; and the involvement of non-government forces and the inter-sectoral collaborations among enterprises, which are as important as the direct actions of the government agencies. In many other countries, public actions often precede those of government and enterprises. However, a low-level effort from non-government forces in China limits the effectiveness of environmental policies. Large inputs from civil society including industry based volunteer activities are required to realize the green development objective.

Acknowledgements

This research was supported by the National Natural Science Foundation of China (No.40071028). I thank Prof. Wang Jici of Peking University, my dissertation advisor, for her guidance and generous support for field work.

References

Beukering, P. J. H. (2001), Recycling, International Trade and the Environment: An Empirical Analysis, Dordrecht: Kluwer Academic Publishers.

China Economic Times (1995), Gao wuran hangye yong xiang Zhongguo (High pollution industries pouring in China). February 28th, 1995.

CCTV (2002), Jiaodian Fangtan: Chadu laiji diannao (Focus Interview: prevention against the import discarded computers). May 18th, 2002.

Dai, X. L. (2002), 'Muji: Diannao yanglaji jin Zhongguo yihou' (Report of the Import discarded in China). *Computer Newspaper*, February 26th, 2002.

Davis, C. (1993), *The Politics of Hazardous Waste*, Englewood Cliffs: Prentice Hall.

Gandy, M. (1994), *Recycling and the Politics of Urban Waste*, New York: St. Martin's Press.

Greenpeace (1993), *The International Trade in Toxic Waste: An International Inventory*, Washington: Greenpeace International.

Held, D., Mcgrew, A. and Goldblatt, D. (1999), *Global Transformations: Politics, Economics and Culture*, London: Polity Press Limited.

Lin, C. K., Yan, L. and Davis, A. N. (2002), 'Globalization, Extended Producer Responsibility and the Problem of Discarded Computers in China: An Exploratory Proposal for Environmental Protection', *Georgetown International Environmental Law Review*, 14(3), pp. 525-576.

Lindhqvist, T. (2000), *Extended Producer Responsibility in Cleaner Production*, Lund: Lund University Press.

OECD (1994), 'Transfrontier Movements of Hazardous Waste', *Statistics 1991*, Paris: OECD.

OECD (2001). *Extended Producer Responsibility, a Guidance Manual for Governments*. Paris: OECD.

Puckett, J. and Byster, L. (2002), *Exporting Harm: The High-Tech Trashing of Asia*, BAN and SVTC.

Strasser, S. (1999), *Waste and Want: A Social History of Trash*, New York: Metropolitan Books.

World Bank (1993), *International Trade and the Environment*, Washington: World Bank.

Chapter 13

Environmental Symbiosis and Renewal of Old Industrial Districts in Japan: Cases of Kawasaki and Kitakyushu

Atsuhiko Takeuchi and Hiroyasu Motoki

Introduction

A fundamental responsibility of human beings in the twenty-first century is to incorporate environmental symbiosis into sustainable development. Attempts to plan sustainable regional industrial systems will be assisted by investigation drawing on both ecological and economical points of view. That is to say, the construction of a new paradigm is required, taking up technological development together with the socialization of industry as a premise. The ideas or behaviour concerning people's production and life are subject to change depending on the conditions of the respective countries or regions.

In Japan, an island country situated in the Asian monsoon region, human existence has been maintained in a unified style that conforms with nature. The notion of 'oneness of human and nature' has ruled people's life for a long time. However, a great change has occurred with remarkable industrialization since the 1960s, and the natural circulation system is now collapsing in many areas, resulting in serious environmental pollution. In response to this general situation, the formation of a new environmental symbiosis by examining the behaviour of industries and people has become an important subject in Japan.

This chapter investigates the renewal of old industrial districts by examining policies emphasizing environmental symbiosis. This development strategy has meant new spatial relations as industrial space is transformed into a different economic space. Here, the new economic space is defined as a space characterized by innovative new economic factors such as knowledge intensive industries converted from that dominated by old industries.

We conducted a survey in two districts, Kawasaki in the Tokyo metropolitan industrial region, and Kitakyushu in western Japan, focusing on the governance of leading iron and steel makers, and the strategies and behaviour of the local governments).

The Formation of Geographical Paradigms for Sustainable Development

In forming a new paradigm of the industrial system, it is necessary to investigate the current globalization trend. The notion of globalization infers an overwhelming scientific conformance in a period in whereby none of the entrepreneurs will be antagonistic to the implied international common rules. However, the ideas or behaviour concerning the people's production and life are subject to change depending on the conditions of the respective countries and regions. So-called tacit knowledge (Nonaka and Takeuchi, 1995) and sensitivity, in particular, are strongly linked to the notion of individual natural and socio-cultural conditions. It is,therefore wise to consider different regional conditions in the formation of new global paradigms. Needless to say, there are many factors that should be strictly standardized from a global point of view, such as intelligent proprietary rights, environmental restrictions, etc. From such a standpoint, debate begins with the premise of considering sustainable development and renewal of old industrial district in Japan.

Premises Relating to Sustainable Development in Japan

For the consideration and realization of a country's sustainable development, it is important to examine the origins of its society and culture together with its natural condition, to draw on the fundamental elements of the Japanese system of society, production and life. Although political, economic and cultural influences from overseas have frequently been applied to Japan, many traditions relating to the fundamental pattern of Japanese culture and basic ideas regarding environmental symbiosis remain. Since the Meiji Restoration in 1868, Japan's industrialization has been fully expedited by state-guided strategies. The number of employees in the industry increased together with the introduction of Western lifestyle. However, this does not imply that people's views or the foundation of Japanese production systems became westernized.

Since the 1960s, a drastic change has taken place in the fundamental style of production practices and people's lives. Thanks to industrialization, people's income increased remarkably and they rapidly adopted a more American way of life. The landscape, traditional agriculture and relationships between farming villages and cities have impacted severely upon ecological systems. This transformation has been assisted by the attitudes of many Japanese people who have become contemptuous of traditional environmental symbiosis ideals. However, the aforementioned change has happened only during the past forty years of Japan's long history. At the beginning of this century Japan is becoming aware of the necessity to forge a path of sustainable economic and industrial development. This is an opportunity for Japan to promote sustainable economic development by reconsidering former erroneous industrialization, while looking towards recovery of ecological systems.

An indispensable contribution to sustainable development can be made by re-aligning the industrial complexes that tend to cause environmental problems.

The number of the enterprises with an ISO14001certification is rapidly increasing in Japan (Braun, 2002) and implies that companies are becoming more environmentally consciousness. How to build up new economic spaces by the regeneration of old industrial districts is thus an urgent issue.

Industrialization of Japan and Heavy and Chemical Industrial Complexes

In the mid-nineteenth century, Japan was willing to rapidly introduce Western technology to accomplish industrialization. Since the beginning of twentieth century, emphasis has gradually been put on heavy and chemical industries, paralleling the strengthening expansion of the industry. Most of the heavy and chemical plants were located in coastal districts because they were convenient locations for the import of raw materials. In the 1960s there was a huge amount of extra investment in the heavy and chemical sector. A rapid increase in the heavy and chemical complex caused severe destruction of the environment (Takeuchi, 1999). This resulted in the acceleration of serious trials on pollution in the most of heavy and chemical industrial districts.

In the mid-1980s, enterprises that lost international competitive power due to the appreciation of the yen were compelled to change their management strategy. Especially in the iron and steel industry, rationalization is promoted, taking up large-scale reorganization of production and radical conversion of enterprise strategy as a pillar (Takeuchi, 1992). The re-alignment was accompanied by a change in the characteristics of industrial districts.

Since the 1990s, global environmental problems have become the most important themes. For this reason, individual enterprises have been asked to carry out sustainable industrial expansion for further global competition in light of global environmental problems. Especially for TNCs, industrial expansion continue to strengthen R&D functions, technology transfer among enterprises, the unification or alliance with domestic or overseas enterprises, and contribution to the countries to which advancement is made with environmental preservation in mind. This is, as it were, the construction of a new paradigm of an international industrial system. It is closely related to the movement of domestic plants and government to the renewal of old industrial districts directed toward new economic spaces. With this situation in mind, we have investigated two districts as examples.

Kawasaki District in the Tokyo Metropolitan Region; Renewal of Heavy and Chemical Industrial Complex

Kawasaki district is situated on the western side of Tokyo bay, and is close to Haneda (Tokyo) Airport. In Kawasaki district, heavy and chemical industry plants have been built on reclaimed land since the beginning of the 20th century, particularly after World War One. The leading enterprise in this district, JFE (formerly NKK), is the second largest iron and steel maker in Japan. JFE and other plants of petro-chemical and chemical plants were constructed one by one to form

Japan's largest heavy and chemical complex. Kawasaki district, characterized by the heavy and chemical complex, had long been regarded as the core of Tokyo's metropolitan industrial region (Ohgouchi,1964). However, this initial idea created by economists was based on desk work, and was later corrected dramatically by empirical field survey research conducted by economic geographers. The district has become a raw material producing corner in the Tokyo region. With this in mind, the true nature of the district should be taken into the consideration and reflected in policies.

The formation of the heavy and chemical industrial districts in Kawasaki district has also created serious pollution problems, as well as the largest and most serious pollution trial in Japan was held for several years. The main issue of the trial's dispute was regarding characteristics of the industrial district. In Japan, both economists and governments have mistakenly named the heavy and chemical industrial complex 'kombinat', a term used in the former USSR. Although the plants are close to each other and share the same infrastructure, each individual enterprise is different in terms of its specific location. It is impossible to distinguish individual business administration entities (Takeuchi, 1990). The industrial district can never be simple enough to be called a cluster. This is due in part because the economic environment has begun to change since the second half of the 1980s, especially as international competition intensified and the enterprises were compelled to execute rationalization. In this situation the behaviour of the enterprises constituting the complexes effected a drastic change in their own location behaviour. As a result, local government policies were altered as well. Kawasaki district is always under the strong influence of Tokyo. As both capital and business core of Japan Tokyo has a huge market a potential melting pot of various elements. Kawasaki district is attempting to transform it self into a new economic space with new elements.

Changes in the functions of the industrial complexes have become remarkable since the 1990s. The first reason for this is the progress of rational placement of the production, and the transfiguration of such placement into a knowledge-intensive production and environment-correspondence production has been attained. JFE once had a state-of-the-art plant in Fukuyama (Hiroshima) in western Japan and unification and alignment of the plants' products was promoted. As a result, the number of the employees rapidly reduced from 40,000 to 5000 and extensive land in this district became simultaneously idle. Former NKK merged with Kawasaki Steel in 2002 to become JFE. Currently, JFE has a project under way to strengthen a total production system. In Kawasaki district, JFE adopted a fundamental policy to not only strengthen the R&D agencies related with established iron and steel technology, but also specialize the specific and highly-evaluated products maximizing the conditions located in the Tokyo region. The same is true of other enterprises specializing in chemistry and petro-chemical plants.

Needless to say, the industrial realignment in Kawasaki district is also related with the whole of Tokyo Bay Re-development Project (Takeuchi, 1999). The individual enterprises are willing to strengthen R&D functions that have been shaped up as pioneers for the improvement of high-technological and scientific skills in this district, and are ambitious enough to promote a new policy to specialize them as their national or international technology centres. On the sites where JFE's (formerly NKK's) plants were located, development of a strategy based on technological expansion by JFE's own accord is now in progress. The strategy consists of projects concerning the expansion of so-called environmental business such as the recycling of household electric appliances, plastic products and a new energy development. JFE is also contributing a great deal to the abatement of environmental problems overseas through its technology. As a matter of course, cooperation with local governments is indispensable for the promotion of the aforementioned projects.

The second reason is Tokyo's impact. As Tokyo functions become heightened year by year, attention is paid to the Kawasaki Port as a stronghold for the distribution of merchandise and re-development of the Tokyo Bay area. Kawasaki district is in close proximity to Haneda airport and is therefore expected to enjoy its popularity as the location required for new business. Furthermore, as the extension of Southern Tokyo, a technological complex of the machinery industry (Takeuchi and Mori, 2001) is in expansion and the R&D medical equipment and apparatus agencies are located here.

The industry in Kawasaki district had traditionally been a huge income source for Kawasaki City and was under the JFE's strong influence. In contrast, since the 1970s, the heavy and chemical industry has been placed in an awkward position due to the pollution they caused. The enterprises or plants were in an antagonistic relationship with local governments or inhabitants. However, since the end of the twentieth century, Kawasaki's municipal government has endeavoured to commence renewal of the industrial district under an explicit policy closely together with JFE. Kawasaki's current policy promotes renewal by shifting its stance from dependence on the huge heavy and chemical industrial complex to a powerful knowledge intensive new economic space including the reform of old industries. To be more concrete, it has demanded a project that will keep the environment clean and knowledge creative to permit the city containing in itself and a variety of new industry as a concept taking up new employment creation as a 'Super Eco-Town' (ecological town). The project is one of one of two in the country approved by the national government in 1997. Kawasaki district is now changing its functions to a new economic space entirely different from the conventional heavy and chemical industry complex.

Kitakyushu District in Western Japan; from the Iron and Steel Complex to Eco-Town

Kitakyushu district in western Japan is the largest iron and steel complex in the provincial area. Both the process of development together with the characteristics of this industrial district and the course of the renewal in recent years is utterly different from Kawasaki district. The district's industrial activities started with the establishment of a state-run iron and steel in 1901 with a view to building up armaments and the growing needs. The production of the Yawata plant was expanded in an extremely wide stride to secure a monopolistic position throughout the country. Immediately before World War Two, this enterprise absorbed many other steel makers' enterprises in Japan to become monopolistic giant Nippon Steel. Up until the 1950s Nippon Steel was the only integrated-operation plants in Japan with blast furnaces, with the exception of NKK in Kawasaki. The expansion of the iron and steel industry in Kitakyushu (Yawata) district was remarkable and state-of-the-art gigantic plants were built up one by one from the Yawata area facing the inner gulf to the Tobata area facing the outer sea. Thus Kitakyushu's position as a pivotal point for Japan's iron and steel industry appeared to be immobile (Takeuchi, 1966). However, since the 1970s the importance of the iron and steel production in this district has decreased.

A number of reasons account for the area's decline. They include the fact that Kitakyushu is far from the metropolitan areas which form the main markets for the machinery industry. Raw material imports have had to be sought from remote countries such as Brazil and Australia. Large-scale vessels were therefore introduced for transport, but because the inner gulf is not deep enough, the large scale vessels cannot come alongside the Yawata area berth. To avoid such difficulties, Nippon Steel built state-of-the-art plants in the peripheries of Tokyo and Nagoya regions. The production in Kitakyushu district was simultaneously reduced. Nippon Steel had to promote further rationalization of production owing to the steep appreciation of the yen since 1985, and completely closed the blast furnaces in Yawata area and retained only one in Tobata area where big vessels were able to come alongside the berth. As a result, the number of the employees reduced from more than 50,000 to less than 10,000.

After the 1990s, competition with foreign iron and steel makers became severer each year. Nippon Steel's projects for the rationalization of production and withdrawal from Kyushu were further accelerated. Assisted by such location withdrawal strategies, Nippon Steel came to possess a huge unused reclaimed land. Although Nippon Steel started a major renewal project to promote various businesses other than steel in 1985, almost all of the new businesses such as electronics or information were located exclusively in Tokyo. in contrast with Kitakyushu where only a big leisure facility was constructed in the former site of a blast furnace (Takeuchi, 1992). Although Nippon Steel's business priority was to effectively utilize the sites, the area was too large for the strategy to progress smoothly. Meanwhile as Kitakyushu City and its enterprises had grown under the strong influence of Nippon Steel, closure of the major plants severely shocked the local economy.

Kitakyushu was also known as one of the Japanese cities where pollution was most serious. In the 1960s, the sky over Kitakyushu district was called 'the vault of heaven with seven-colours of smoke' and fish never habited the inner gulf that was 'sea of death'. Nevertheless, the district was free from judicial concern over pollution due to Nippon Steel's dominance in the local economy. However, since the 1980s, complying with the environmental problems has become a serious and difficult assignment for enterprises. The case is quite the same with the local governments, and they were commonly obliged to cope with the severe environmental problems. Meanwhile, cries for addressing the global environmental problems began to be uttered in the 1990s, and the environmental symbiosis became a pivotal subject of the economic activities.

Nevertheless, the resurrection of Kitakyushu district which is located far from major market areas appears far more difficult than in Kawasaki. In this situation Nippon Steel, which once behaved as if it has been a solemn monarch, was forced harmonise with all the factors in this district. Under the mayor's strong leadership, the city of Kitakyushu plans to expand the existing plants and raise the environment related businesses together with Nippon Steel, adopting environmental symbiosis as an organizing principle. Following this concept the conversion of old industrial district into a new economic space was promoted as a pivotal strategy by the tight cooperation of local government, Nippon Steel, and mutual trust relationships.

The fundamentals of the project lie in the integration of waste measures, environmental conservation measures, and industry promotion policy into overall regional industrial policy. The project is sustained by fundamental research for technological development, experimental studies, and the commercialization of the project. Many facilities are being built up in accordance with recycling projects in the comprehensive environmental industrial complex for commercialization (e.g., schemes for plastic PET bottles, office equipment, automobiles, home appliances, fluorescent tubes, medical waste, wood and plastic wastes and mixed construction waste). The highest level of recycling technology has been adopted and is being used in all of these facilities.

In these facilities, supply sources of the materials are sought in western Japan including Kitakyushu. Thus the largest complex of the 'Venous industry' in Japan is formed here (Togawa, 2001). Concentration of the R&D recycling related divisions is also in progress. Kitakyushu, the typical enterprise city of Nippon Steel which once enjoyed 'gray' prosperity (a reference to the sky-covering smoke emitted from chimneys) is now being resurrected as a model district proud of environmental symbiosis, enjoyable and ecologically healthy. At present there are twenty-six environment related businesses with R&D in the city. These include not only industrial facilities but also there is an environmental museum and various environmental education programs are being offered. Nippon Steel is also contributing a great deal to the global environmental symbiosis through its technology and Kitakyushu is supporting such cooperation with many cities all over the world.

Incidentally, as for the operation of the recycling plants, material procurement is a difficult problem to solve. As Kitakyushu is far from major markets, it is putting many resources into the procurement of raw materials and adopting the system of repeating tough competition and cooperation with Kawasaki, currently the main recycle centre in the eastern Japan. The location of the recycling industry and such renewal project as Eco-Town is one of the new and key economic geography issue linked to re-formation of economic space.

Conclusions

Globalization should be promoted bearing in mind the natural, socio-cultural conditions of individual regions. In Japan where people have historically remained symbiotic with nature, sustainable development is a way to approach the conversion from industrialism into ecological management. For the sustainable development of Japan's industrial systems, the large scale old industrial districts such as Kawasaki and Kitakyushu are an exceedingly significant factor. In the two districts, two leading enterprises have cooperated with the local governments and residents to establish a subsidiary for the purpose of socialization. They also intend to make resurrection as the Eco-Town by forming *a mutually trustable relation among governments, people and enterprise.*

Under the leadership of the local governments, both districts are making resurrection with R&D organ and environment related industry as pillars by taking advantage of the human resources, technology and various infrastructures possessed by the leading enterprises.

The leading enterprises in the two districts are making vast strides to reduce the output of environmentally harmful chemicals, and furthermore they are realizing environmental symbiosis at a global level taking responsibility for the conditions of respective countries or regions. Such behaviour exhibited by the two enterprises is aimed at harmonizing industrialism with environmentalism and could be considered a TNC prototype of this century. The recent actions of the two districts forming a new economic space is a path leading to Japan's traditional environmental symbiosis and is a great step towards constructing a new paradigm for global sustainable development. The new direction of economic geography in this century is to investigate the paradigm for sustainable regional development through detailed empirical research with environmental symbiosis as a premise.

References

Braun, B. (2002), 'Building Global Institutions; The Role of Management Standards in the World Economy', Paper presented for the IGU Commission on 'The Dynamics of Economic Spaces', South Africa, pp. 1-20, paper available from authors.

Nonaka, I. and Takeuchi, H. (1995), *The Knowledge-Creating Company*, Oxford: Oxford University Press.

Ohgouchi, K. (1964), *Production System of the Keihin Industrial Region*, Tokyo: Tokyo University Press.

Takeuchi, A. (1966), 'Decline of Industrial Production in Kitakyushu District', *Geographical Review of Japan*, 33(10): pp. 665-679 (In Japanese).

Takeuchi, A. (1990), 'Character of Kawasaki Coastal Industrial Region', *SINCHIRI (New Geography)*, 38(2): pp. 23-36 (In Japanese).

Takeuchi, A. (1992), 'Strategic Management of Japanese Steel Manufacturing in the Changing International Environment', In D. E. Hussey (ed.), *International Review of Strategic Management*, Willy: Chichester.

Takeuchi, A. (1999), 'Revitalization of Tokyo–Bay Area and Formation of New Industrial Complex', *Report of Researches, Nippon Institute of Technology*, 29(3): pp. 1-9.

Takeuchi, A. and Mori, H. (2001), 'The Sustainable Renovation of the Industrial Complex in Inner Tokyo; The Case of the Japanese Machinery Industry', In R. Hayter and R. Le Heron (eds), *Knowledge, Industry and Environment*, Aldershot: Ashgate, pp. 337-354.

Togawa, K. (2001), *Car and its Recycle*, Nikkan Jidousya Sinnbunnsya. Tokyo.

Chapter 14

Environmental Regulation and Economic Spaces: The Mexican Leather and Footwear Industrial Districts

Raul Pacheco and Hadi Dowlatabadi

Introduction

Understanding how industrial sectors and individual firms respond to external shocks and pressures is necessary in order to design strategies for adaptation to new economic and environmental conditions. A number of forces have an effect on the way industries and whole economies shift their production patterns to create new economic spaces. Amongst those forces, changes in the political, economic and social landscapes are considered the most relevant drivers of structural change. In this chapter we examine the restructuring of less developed countries by documenting the impact of at least one other factor, namely, direct environmental regulatory pressure.

We begin by examining the case of the leather and footwear commodity chain in Mexico. These industries are geographically concentrated in the central cities of León and Guadalajara. Over 60 per cent of the total national leather production and over 40 per cent of the total national footwear production in Mexico is generated in León, while in the figures for Guadalajara hover between 30 and 25 per cent. These two regions make up the most important Mexican leather and footwear clusters or industrial districts and exhibit characteristics considered typical of an industrial district (Harrison, 1992; Markusen, 1996), namely: high concentration of firms within a specific geographical location, great degree of interconnectedness amongst firms, small and medium sized firms within the cluster, and regionally cooperative forward and backward linkages between firms.

Industrial districts offer an opportunity to examine the delicate balance between environmental protection and the promotion of economic development. Because firms within the cluster are inextricably linked, governments must ensure that any policies to be implemented (be it industrial, environmental or both) take this high degree of inter-connectedness into account. Shutting down highly pollutant factories that provide employment to surrounding communities may create negative impacts far beyond direct job losses. Policies that impact any link in the supply chain can lead to impacts on other industrial firms both up- and down-stream (buyers/suppliers). This is particularly so when the degree of interdependence is high and the strength of inter-firm ties is intense.

Hide tanning, for example, utilises considerable amounts of water and chemicals. Tanneries significantly impact on their surrounding environment. Leather and footwear industries worldwide are characterized by their high degree of geographical concentration (Sorenson and Audia, 2000; Rabellotti and Ciarli, 2002). Firms in this commodity chain have developed strong inter-firm ties, particularly supplier-buyer linkages both forward (with retailers) and backward (with suppliers).

This chapter highlights the impact of direct environmental regulatory pressure in certain economic spaces, namely the leather and footwear industrial districts in Mexico. It also attempts to provide guidance to policymakers by showcasing the relevance of a number of restructuring drivers often neglected in mainstream literature. Acknowledging the variety of forces shaping structural change and the extent to which the restructuring dynamics are a process of continuous 'smooth-sailing' or punctuated equilibrium 'shock-and-recover' will help us to design smart growth strategies that are agreeable with environmental, societal and political considerations.

Background: The Mexican Leather and Footwear Industrial Clusters

León is located northwest of Guanajuato State within the so-called Bajio, a region that had historically favoured agricultural development (Calleja-Pinedo, 1994). The whole production chain that encompasses footwear and leather (from raw hides to retailing) has been considered the most important industrial activity in León for at least the last 70 years (Iglesias, 1998). Although the origins of this tradition of leather-making and footwear production are not well documented, historical records show some shoemaking activity in León since the 17th century. Since 1830, the leather, footwear and shawl-making industries have prospered, marked by clustering in 'barrios' or neighborhoods (Ruelas, 2002). Leather and footwear could be found in the heart of downtown León's Barrio Arriba. Many small shoe factories, shawl-making workshops and smithery shops could be found in the Coecillo (slightly north-east of downtown León), while yet more shawl factories could be found in San Miguel (in the southern part of the city) (Ruelas, 2000; Archives of Leon, 1998). The Second World War solidified the leather and footwear industry's position, because a high percentage of US domestic consumption came from Mexican imports (Martínez and Ortíz, 2000).

In the mid 1990s, the tanning industry in León felt increasing pressure regarding environmental concerns when the North American Free Trade Agreement (NAFTA) came into force on January 1, 1994. This pressure was exacerbated in December 1994 with the death of 40,000 birds in the Silva reservoir, just downstream from León. Also, as the number of dams on the Turbio River increased, the region, particularly León, faced water shortages threatening the long-term survival of traditional tanning practices. This implies that there are two environmental-related issues with the tanning industry: resource availability and environmental quality/pollution control. Priority has, however, been given to environmental quality, as it was the major concern of environmentalists and government officials at the time when these events began.

The tanning industry was one of many that felt such pressure with the incorporation of Mexico into the General Agreement on Trade and Tariffs (GATT). The negotiation, which started in 1986, marked the beginning of an intense process of market liberalization. GATT required Mexico to lower trade barriers and open its internal markets to international competition. This had a significantly negative impact on Mexico's domestic footwear producers. While the significant increase in imports resulted in a more than ten fold monetary increase from US$ 13.7 million in 1987 to US$ 145.2 million by 1993, there was a decline in the domestic industry (Rabellotti, 1999). An increasingly high threat of substitution by its main customer in the value chain, the footwear industry, has led Leon's tanning industry to a crisis point. Given this situation, these simultaneous market and environmental pressures need to be addressed if these allied industries are to remain viable in this geographical region.

Guadalajara, also located in the central region of Mexico, was founded in 1532. Originally known as the 'New Galicia', the city has grown to become the second largest in Mexico and has 'annexed' three other cities: Zapopan, Zapotlanejo and Tonalá. The Guadalajara metropolitan region was traditionally considered an agricultural state, although by the end of the 18th century it had a significant number of shawl-making, shoe-making and leather crafting workshops (Ayala Castellanos and Flores Peredo, 1992). Currently, Guadalajara's industrial landscape is predominantly dominated by small and medium-size enterprises (SMEs) (Cota-Yañez, 1997).

The industrialization process in Guadalajara followed three stages (Arias, 1980; Cota Yañez, 1997): (1) Before the 1930s, and up until the late 1950s, Guadalajara's industrial platform was oriented to basic goods; (2) In the 1970s, a phase of industrial specialization occurred, with a focus on intermediate goods; and (3) From the 1970s to the 1980s, the industrial focus was on final consumption goods (tertiary).

By 1930 Guadalajara had quickly become the second Mexican hub for leather and footwear manufacturing, with approximately 60 tanneries (mostly specialized in non-bovine leather manufacturing) and about 700 shoe factories (mostly specialized in women's footwear) (estimates based on interviews with stakeholders in the Guadalajara cluster, conducted during June and July, 2003). Guadalajara's leather and footwear industries are still considered relevant contributors to the region's economic development. But while both Guadalajara's and León's industrial districts have faced increased market pressure, only León's cluster has met with tight direct environmental regulatory pressure.

Drivers, Responses, Trajectories: An Integrated Framework to Understand Industrial Restructuring

Because many scholars have used the term 'restructuring', it is important to define the term and the context within which it is being used. Knutsen (1998; 2000) understood restructuring as a response by firms to crises and structural changes, as well as a means to maintain and enhance competitiveness with more continuous change. Knutsen indicates that restructuring occurs at the firm level more than at the industry level. We argue that restructuring can occur at three levels: individual plants, firms and industry-wide. It is difficult to situate a particular firm within a specific restructuring scale. However, the net effect of structural change leaves the firm, the industrial sector and the geographic region in a different state than before.

Structural changes imply a 'substantial reorganization of economic, industrial and social processes and relations' (McGrath-Champ, 1999, p. 237). Changes in market, economic and geographical structures are among the various dimensions of industrial restructuring. Resource re-allocation, downsizing, vertical integration and/or dis-integration, changes in labour relations and movements of skilled labour are all elements of a restructuring process.

Understanding restructuring and its associated and varied dimensions requires a thorough analysis of causal relationships between the factors that lead to structural change and their interplay. Increased competition due to vanishing borders and globalization can, for example, force firms to choose new operational strategies. These may range from specialization in a particular production process and reaping economies of scale, to developing flexible production facilities and seeking advantages of fast movers. Technological changes within an industrial process can drive some firms out of business as their processes become obsolete and their capital base too depleted to invest in new technology or other means of production to remain competitive in the marketplace.

Analyses of structural change may support one of two competing models of dynamics: (1) that structural change comes about as a smooth and continuous process with incremental changes; or (2) that structural change is the result of responses of the system to external shocks, creating sharp, distinctive points of reconfiguration.

To empirically test either theory, we need to examine restructuring as a dynamic process, where changes may occur incrementally or in sharp, punctuated-equilibria. In a dynamic analysis, we must trace the history of each industrial district in order to understand the multiple factors that have defined the path of development to industrial activities in any particular location. We then need to estimate the degree to which each factor has been relevant for restructuring outcomes and what effects they may have on potential future scenarios. To do so we compare the restructuring trajectories of the leather and footwear clusters in León and Guadalajara, and in doing so, demonstrate the need to broaden the types of drivers that could affect restructuring.

To examine the relevance of environmental regulation as a restructuring driver, we use the Drivers-Responses-Trajectories (DRT) framework. As shown in Figure 14.1, external forces, or *drivers*, influence the way the system behaves altering its state. When subjected to pressure, the system responds through a variety of strategies called *responses*. As firms implement adaptive strategies, the cluster changes. Economic agents (firms in this case) respond in different ways to the same pressure signals. It may be wise for a small-scale tannery in downtown León to close operations based on their assessment of their own inability to cope with stringent environmental regulation and the likelihood of strict sanction that would lead to plant closure by authorities. Alternatively, shutting down would be an unlikely (and somewhat irrational) strategy for a large tannery located in the outskirts of León, as it may have already implemented a certain number of measures lessen its negative environmental impacts and have more stable revenue streams than that of a micro-tannery.

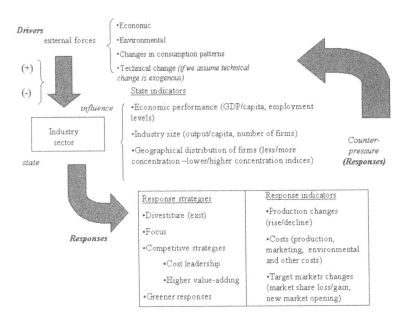

Figure 14.1   The Drivers-Responses-Trajectories Framework to Analyse Industrial Restructuring

Source: (Pacheco, 2004).

The restructuring *trajectory* of the whole industrial sector is therefore a combination of the strategies of micro, small, medium-sized and large firms. Whether the entire sector (as a whole) will decline is dependent on the combined effect of such strategies and the responses over time to external challenges of all firms as an aggregate. It has been argued, for example, that the firms within an industrial district share such a strong interconnectedness that some 'stronger' plants are able to pull 'weaker' plants to help them survive.

It is important to recognise that smaller size firms will take different restructuring trajectories than bigger size firms. Small-scale industries' strategies to cope with sudden changes in the macroeconomic environment may, or may not, be as well suited as large-scale industries'. Furthermore, within the same industrial sector, it is possible that larger firms will reduce their production levels whereas smaller firms may only shift their production patterns and/or technologies. As a result, the restructuring strategy is dependent not only on firm size but also on its internal core capabilities (Pacheco, 2004).

Restructuring trajectories, as defined here, are pathways of change that firms, industrial sectors and regions adopt over time. De-industrialization is one example of a restructuring trajectory, while consolidation and resizing of an industrial sector is yet another. We limit our examination to structural change within the two geographical regions of León and Guadalajara in central Mexico within the leather and footwear commodity chain. Re-locating industrial activities is considered one of the most common restructuring trajectories. Moving plants from one city to another, or from one country to another, are other approaches that some firms take in response to changes in the macroeconomic environment.

Environmental Regulation as a Restructuring Driver

While other restructuring drivers have been previously analysed at length elsewhere (Hayter, 2000), perhaps one of the first works that emphasised the importance of environmental constraints was Collins' (1998). In a study of the global pulp and paper industry, Collins (1998, p. 403) writes that 'the implications of environmentalism for changes in the spatial pattern of industry have to be considered in a much broader framework than in terms of the costs of environmental regulation only'.

The importance of environmental issues on the form that industrial restructuring takes within an economy was first outlined by Gibbs (1996). He argues that there has been a traditional disconnection between economic restructuring and environmental performance. He calls for an application of the notion of sustainable development, and argues that environmental problems are, at times, the result of inadequate economic restructuring. He believes that adopting regulation theory as a working framework allows us to integrate economic, social and environmental concerns, thus leading to 'better' industrial restructuring.

While it does not directly linking restructuring to environmental pressure, the 'pollution haven hypothesis' correlates changes in geographical location of firms with pollution at a broad level (Cole Elliot et al., 2000). According to the pollution haven hypothesis, pollution-intensive firms tend to migrate from countries or regions with stricter environmental regulations to countries or regions with more relaxed environmental regulations. If this hypothesis is true, tighter regulations will drive polluting firms away. While there is some evidence that supports the pollution haven hypothesis, it only does so with certain trading pairs of countries. Cole and his co-authors are quick, however, to reveal evidence contradicting this hypothesis as a broad generalization.

The notion of restructuring as a form of 'industrial metabolism', espoused by the German research group of Binder et al. (2001), indicates that a 'dematerialization' strategy drives structural changes (which they understand as the rise and decline of dirty industries). They call for an industrial policy that recognizes the challenges that dematerialization and structural changes bring to regions under conditions of restructuring. This industrial policy should be harmonised with environmental policy if the broader goal is to comply with environmental, social and political considerations altogether.

Hayter's (2000) study of the restructuring of the forestry industry emphasises the need to further our understanding of resource constraints, particularly as this paradigm is not usually considered in mainstream economic geography literature. Furthermore, Hayter and Le Heron (2002) have more recently posed the notion of a migration from a purely techno-economic paradigm to a 'green' techno-economic paradigm, exploring the validity of a 'green' paradigm for industrial geography.

We build on the aforementioned works and argue that, in addition to considerations of paradigmatic changes, behavioural changes as a result of increased environmental regulatory pressure should be considered as drivers of restructuring (Pacheco, 2004). Our basic tenet is that the restructuring trajectories of geographically concentrated industries can be affected by increased environmental regulation. We empirically test our proposition by assessing the responses of tanneries to increasing environmental regulation and the new spatial configuration of the industrial region where these tanneries are located.

Comparing Direct Regulatory Pressure in the León and Guadalajara Clusters

From 1992 to 2003, environmental regulation has played a key role in driving structural changes in the León leather and footwear cluster, while it has had very little effect on the Guadalajara cluster, as shown in Figure 14.2. To study how the clusters responded to environmental regulatory pressures, we compared the number of inspections.

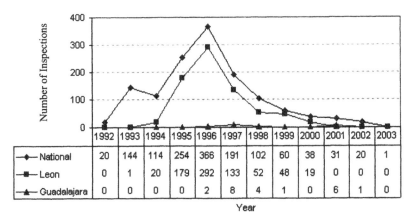

	1992	1993	1994	1995	1996	1997	1998	1999	2000	2001	2002	2003
◆ National	20	144	114	254	366	191	102	60	38	31	20	1
■ Leon	0	1	20	179	292	133	52	48	19	0	0	0
▲ Guadalajara	0	0	0	0	2	8	4	1	0	6	1	0

Year

Figure 14.2   Comparative View of Total Annual Number of Inspections to Tanneries from 1992–2003

Figure based on data disaggregated by industrial district.
Source: (Pacheco, 2004).

Environmental authorities increased the pressure on tanneries by performing a higher number of inspections to verify their compliance with environmental pressure (Pacheco and Dowlatabadi, 2003). It is important to note that in the year when the most inspections were carried out in Guadalajara (1997), the difference in environmental pressure is quite substantial (133 inspections of tanneries in León in 1997 versus 8 in Guadalajara). While the regulation that prescribed tanneries' solid wastes as hazardous encompassed the industry at a national level, inspections were much more frequent in the leather cluster in León than in the Guadalajara cluster.

Several options to partially mitigate the tanning industry's environmental impacts have been suggested by environmental agencies. These include, either individually or in combination, the following: (1) implementation of wastewater treatment systems in each plant; (2) collection and disposal of solid wastes in hazardous waste landfills; (3) adoption of cleaner technologies for leather manufacturing; (4) relocation of tanneries outside the geographical boundaries of León in an industrial park named Parque Industrial Ecológico de León (PIEL); (5) limiting tanneries within the city boundaries to only buy wet-blue (leather already tanned) and only perform wet-end processing (re-tanning, dyeing and fat-liquoring) up to finished product (leather). It is estimated that about 88 per cent of the total volume of tannery wastewater discharged to municipal sewers comes from the beam house and tanning stages and about 12 per cent comes from the wet-finishing.

Small-scale tanners processing raw hide to finished leather strongly rejected the relocation options citing lack of capital to move from their current location to industrial parks. Discussions between tannery owners and environmental agencies regarding relocation initially began in 1992/1993. All tanneries in the León downtown core were asked to relocate entirely to PIEL by the end of 1997. Relocation would imply moving the 'wet' part of the process (i.e. beam house-tanning-wet finishing) to industrial parks with adequate, collective wastewater treatment facilities.

System Responses and Restructuring Trajectories in León and Guadalajara

Given that signing GATT and NAFTA was an action undertaken by the Federal government of Mexico, their effects were perceived in the Guadalajara cluster as having the same intensity as those affecting the León cluster. However, since the product mix and the target markets of both clusters were significantly different, the strategies each cluster followed to face the challenges posed by increased market pressures were also different. In the case of footwear manufacturing in Guadalajara, shoemakers decided, according to the Jalisco Chamber of Commerce President, to continue to concentrate on women's shoes and high-price, low-volume products. In the case of leather production in Guadalajara, since the number of tanneries is significantly lower than that of León, and given that their product mix is much more diversified, tanneries in Guadalajara chose to concentrate on mid- to high-price leather. Furthermore, as indicated by one tanner with over 40 years in the business, tanners in Guadalajara were already looking at León's footwear industry as a potential market for their leather (Alfrez, 2003).

As for the footwear industry in León, the trade association (Chamber of Footwear in Guanajuato, CICEG) commissioned a project to analyse the competitiveness of the leather and footwear cluster in León. The report focuses almost entirely on the León footwear industry and, as a result, has very little appeal to tanners. Furthermore, it entirely neglects the importance of resource constraints and resource availability in León.

In León the tanneries have had a range of responses to increased levels of environmental pressure. The list is lengthy: (1) relocating to industrial parks; (2) signing voluntary agreements for environmental auditing and designing/implementing action plans to produce 'greener' leather; (3) signing an agreement to dispose of their hazardous wastes in an authorised 'Sludge Park'; (4) changing to cleaner production processes; (5) implementing waste treatment processes; (6) 'Officially withdrawing operations' (i.e., functioning illegally without paying taxes or appearing on any official registries); and (7) shutting down.

It is also noteworthy that the trade associations (like the Chamber of Tanners) successfully lobbied the government to extend the relocation period for approximately 15 tanneries to 2000. Data on the relocation of tanneries indicates that approximately 200 plants, out of 800 in total, had agreed to relocate by 1999 (though this is not 25 per cent of the production). Although the Chamber of Tanners in León (CICUR) signed a voluntary agreement (*Convenio del Rio Turbio*) with government officials from municipal, state and national-level environmental agencies, this agreement has yet to be fully implemented.

Nevertheless, available data indicate that there has been at least some degree of response by the system. Our interviews and data analyses confirm our hypothesis that environmental regulation drove tanneries in León to undergo structural changes that have reshaped the whole regional economy. While it is still early to assess the extent to which this reshaping took place and what the final form deriving from it will be, regulatory pressure did indeed play a significant role in the restructuring trajectory of tanneries in León.

Conclusions

In this paper we demonstrate that increased environmental regulatory pressure played a role in the way the tanneries within the León cluster underwent restructuring processes. While regulatory pressure is not the only restructuring driver affecting these clusters, it is one that has not been given enough attention to in the past. Through our research we gained insights in two areas, urban and cluster restructuring.

With respect to urban restructuring, the city of León followed a restructuring trajectory that predominantly saw the cluster remain as a 'core centre for leather and footwear' (Pacheco, 2004), while Guadalajara reached a strong degree of diversification. That is to say, while the degree of specialization in Leon increased, it decreased in Guadalajara (Rodriguez Bautista and Cota Yañez, 2001). The footwear and leather industries in Guadalajara chose to pursue a 'niche' strategy, which would potentially yield much better results than through price competition.

The government of León and the state government of Guanajuato chose to implement a number of strategies and invest on a core plan to boost the regional economy by taking measures which would increase the competitiveness of footwear and leather firms within the cluster. This strategy but it is also a result of lobbying efforts by local entrepreneurs, particularly those from the footwear industry.

The restructuring trajectory of León is quite different to Guadalajara's, and has predominantly became a 'Mexican Silicon Valley' (Pozos Ponce, 1996) where the relevance of the leather and footwear industries was perhaps considered secondary. The restructuring trajectories of both clusters were the result of a different dynamic, even though both clusters were subject to the same economic shocks.

In this regard, it is important to note that both clusters underwent a punctuated-equilibrium type of restructuring trajectory. As shown in our analyses, the clusters responded to external shocks by undergoing structural changes that shaped their potential futures. Recognising this aspect of industrial restructuring is a key to understanding the dynamics of structural change within industrial regions.

References

Ayala Castellanos, M. D. L. L. and Flores Peredo, L. (1992), 'Guadalajara en la época colonial', *Guadalajara en el umbral del Siglo XXL*, J. Arroyo Alejandre and L. A. Velázquez (eds), Guadalajara, México: Universidad de Guadalajara/H. Ayuntamiento de Guadalajara, p. 407.

Binder, M., et al. (eds) (2001), *Green Industrial Restructuring*, Berlin: Springer.

Calleja-Pinedo, M. (1994), *Microindustria: Principio y soporte de la gran empresa. La producción de calzado en León*, Guanajuato, Guadalajara, Mexico: Universidad de Guadalajara.

Cole, M. A., et al. (2000), The Environment, Trade and Industrial Restructuring: Revisiting the Evidence, Birmingham: University of Birmingham.

Collins, L. (1998), 'Environmentalism and Restructuring of the Global Pulp and Paper Industry', *Tijdschrift voor Ecoomische en Sociale Geografie*, 89(4): pp. 401-415.

Cota Yañez, M. D. R. (1997), 'Las pequeñas y medianas empresas manufactureras jalisciences ante la apertura comercial', J. Arroyo Alejandre and A. de León Arias, *La internacionalización de la economía jaliscience*, Guadalajara, Mexico: Universidad de Guadalajara/UCLA Program on Mexico/Juan Pablos Editor: pp. 83-116.

Gibbs, D. (1996), 'Integrating Sustainable Development and Economic Restructuring: A Role for Regulation Theory?', *Geoforum* 27(1): pp. 1-10.

Harrison, B. (1992), 'Industrial Districts: Old Wine in New Bottles?', *Regional Studies*, 26(5): pp. 496-483.

Hayter, R. (2000), Flexible Crossroads: *The Restructuring of British Columbia's Forest Economy*, Vancouver: UBC Press.

Hayter, R. and Le Heron, R. B. (eds) (2002), *Knowledge, Industry and Environment: Institutions and Innovation in Territorial Perspective*, Aldershot: Ashgate.

Iglesias, E. (1998), *Las industrias del cuero y del calzado en México*, México, D.F., Instituto de Investigaciones Económicas UNAM.

Knutsen, H. M. (1998), 'Restructuring, Stricter Environmental Requirements and Competitiveness in the German, Italian and Portuguese Tanning Industry', *Norsk Geografisk Tidsskrift*, 52(4): pp. 167-180.

Knutsen, H. M. (2000), 'Environmental Practice in the Commodity Chain: The Dyestuff and Tanning Industries Compared', *Review of International Political Economy*, 7(2): pp. 254-288.

Markusen, A. (1996), 'Sticky Places in Slippery Space: A Typology of Industrial Districts', *Economic Geography*, 72(3): pp. 293-313.

Martínez, A. and Ortíz, A. (2000), 'Factores de competitividad, situación nacional y cadena productiva de la industria del calzado en León, Guanajuato', *Economía, Sociedad y Territorio*, II: 7: pp. 533-568.

McGrath-Champ, S. (1999), 'Strategy and Industrial Restructuring', *Progress in Human Geography*, 23(2): pp. 236-252.

Pacheco, R. (2004), 'Drivers, Responses, Trajectories: An Integrated Assessment of the Mexican Leather and Footwear Industries' Restructuring', Unpublished PhD Dissertation, Resource Management and Environmental Studies, Vancouver: British Columbia: Canada: University of British Columbia.

Pacheco, R. and Dowlatabadi, H. (2003), Industrial Restructuring, Globalization and Environmental Pressure in the Leather and Footwear Commodity Chain in León, México, 99th Annual Convention of the American Leather and Chemists Association, Greensboro, NC, USA.

Pozos Ponce, F. (1996), *Metrópolis en reestructuración: Guadalajara y Monterrey 1980–1989*, Guadalajara, México: Universidad de Guadalajara.

Rabelloti, R. (1999), 'Recovery of a Mexican Cluster: Devaluation Bonanza or Collective Efficiency?', *World Development*, 27(9): pp. 1571-1585.

Rabellotti, R. and Ciarli, T. (2002), 'The Dynamics of the Footwear Sector in Four Latin American Countries: Argentina, Brazil, Chile and Mexico', *Quaderni del Dipartimento di Economia, Istituzioni, Territorio*, Ferrara, Italy: pp. 1-27.

Rodríguez Bautista, J. J. and Cota Yañez, M. D. R. (2001), 'Efectos de la restructuración económica en la Zona Metropolitana de Guadalajara', *Comercio Exterior*, 51(7): pp. 634-651.

Sorenson, O. and Audia, P. G. (2000), 'The Social Structure of Entrepreneurial Activity: Geographic Concentration of Footwear Production in the United States, 1940–1989', *American Journal of Sociology*, 106(2): pp. 424-461.

Chapter 15

Concepts of Regional Collaboration as Points of Entry into Regional Institutional Analyses

Martina Fromhold-Eisebith

Introduction

Regional systems of collaboration have been *widely* discussed as crucial promoters of economic success and innovativeness for quite some time. A growing number of concepts connect to that central idea, associated with the notions of cluster, industrial district, learning region, innovative milieu, regional innovation system, social capital and others. Recently subsumed under the term Territorial Innovation Models/TIM (Moulaert and Sekia, 2003), these concepts can be seen as constituents of a new economic geography which reveals important mechanisms in the rise of new economic spaces, in terms of agglomerations of competitive firms shaped by industrial restructuring, technological change and political forces. In fact, several concepts were mainly constructed inductively, generalising from successful real world examples (e.g. industrial district, cluster, innovative milieu), whereas others arrived through deduction from theoretical constructs followed by empirical investigation (e.g. regional innovation system).

For the evolution of new economic spaces the wide range of concepts referring to regional systems of (innovation-oriented) collaboration (Cooke et al., 2000; Sternberg, 2000), make it difficult however, to determine what exactly researchers should be looking for and against which theoretical background the results should be interpreted. In many respects the new economic geographies explaining new economic spaces bear a 'patchwork' character, and very few endeavours have been made to develop a systemic analytical framework that bridges these theories (Lagendijk, 2001: Moulaert and Sekia, 2003). As models of regional collaboration increasingly serve as guidelines for policies of regional economic promotion (especially cluster, innovative milieu and learning region), conceptual deficiencies get transferred to the practical field as well and lead to confusing mixes of applied notions and measures (in line with Markusen's (1999) accusation of 'fuzzy concepts, whimpy policies'). By systematically relating selected approaches to one another, a more sophisticated base for analyzing as well as politically promoting new economic spaces could be constructed.

This chapter explores how an explicit juxtaposition and combination of different concepts of regional collaboration may lead to a refinement and differentiation of our knowledge on crucial types of actor relationships and resulting economic advantages. It argues that the exploration of distinctions, complementarities as well as overlaps of notions brings about new insights into factors of regional success, particularly regarding the complementary role of different categories of interaction. The chapter however, can only provide one more tile to a large, widely unfinished mosaic of tasks.

The following section briefly discusses the general supposition in favour of a systemic approach combining various concepts of regional collaboration. The next section gives an example by examining the two concepts of *creative/innovative milieu* and *social capital* with regard to potentials of combination and integration. The two approaches show some overlap as both emphasize the importance of socially embedded relationships for creating a supportive environment for successful firms, but bear distinctions that turn their combination into a useful basis for better explaining and governing the functions of trustful relationships in promoting regional restructuring and innovation. A further section illustrates the relevance of the depicted conceptual connection for regional institutional analysis and policies by referring to the case of Germany's Aachen region. The transformation of Aachen from an old to new economic space is better understood when milieu and social capital relationships are regarded in conjunction. The conclusion summarizes major ideas for a roadmap ahead.

Concepts of Regional Collaboration as System Elements

Once the assumption that increased regional cooperation supports innovativeness and economic prosperity became popular in the 1980s, an increasing number of concepts were drawn into what became the 'TIM family' (Lagendijk, 2001; Moulaert and Sekia, 2003). Some concepts mark the beginnings of this conceptual association, such as industrial district (Asheim, 1996) and innovative milieu (Bramanti and Ratti, 1997), while others have followed in later years and show different foci, such as cluster (Porter, 2000), regional innovation system (Cooke et al., 2000) or learning region (Hassink, 2001). The trend has continued with the recent introduction of the idea of social capital into the discussion of regional economic collaborative advantages (Maskell, 2000; Taylor and Leonard, 2002). On the one hand, ongoing conceptual amplifications are welcome because they extend our frontiers of knowledge about factors of regional economic success constituting new economic geographies. But on the other hand, a lacking of willingness by most scholars to relate different approaches to one another induces a growing confusion over the meanings and demarcations of various notions (Grabher and Hassink, 2003).

Empirical case studies that analyze the role of actor collaboration for innovation driven regional development usually refer to a certain conceptual base (for instance, Cooke et al. (2000) to regional innovation systems). This overlooks research which concentrates on other approaches, and may therefore miss out on insights relating to other concepts. Another consequence is that different notions are mainly associated with different regional examples, which makes it particularly difficult to distinguish inter-conceptual variations from inevitable inter-regional ones. Using the central terminology of this book it can be said that almost each new economic space still tends to produce its own economic geography in terms of a broad conceptual model. More importantly we need one consistent new geographical system of models which allows the evaluation of all new economic spaces.

But the perception is growing that distinctions and relations between concepts of regional collaboration have insufficiently been explored for research and policy purposes. Two attempts by geographers are especially noteworthy: Moulaert and Sekia (2003) trace and compare theoretical, conceptual and terminological building blocks of seven TIMs, sketching a comprehensive picture of perceived links; Lagendijk (2001) categorizes inherent ideas of the 'TIM family' according to 'three stories' about regional salience. The view of a complementary relationship of concepts is also put forward by Hwang (2002, 208), who notes that several regional theories: 'differ with each other in the mechanism of agglomeration, the role of firms, and evolutionary tendencies. Each theory has its own strength and weakness.' Hwang regards various concepts as parts of an interconnected system, as no theory alone can explain the complicated phenomenon of innovation-based regional development.

Combining different concepts of regional collaboration might improve analysis and policies concerning the formation of new economic spaces because insufficiencies of the one or the other theory can be balanced. This implies a systems view, which differs from the generic and epistemological account on various components of TIM delivered by Moulaert and Sekia (2003). Instead of their sophisticated theoretical approach, a more practically oriented one that considers a limited number of crucial factors might be useful. Figure 15.1 attempts to visualize this idea of a system of complementary concepts focusing on features of regional collaboration. It depicts the differing emphases of notions –addressing hard or soft infrastructure, economic or socio-cultural institutions – which need to be taken up in conjunction, in order to assist analysis or promote all types of actor relationships that influence regional economic renewal. Theoretically, other dimensions/axes could be added to the coordinate system, for instance, regarding the scope of linkages, their degree of influence on innovation. Accordingly, the qualities associated with different concepts of collaboration should all be conceived as (in the ideal case) characterizing one and the same region, simultaneously or evolutionarily. As each notion points out, only certain cooperative qualities of new economic spaces, despite some redundancies should complement each other also from a practical perspective.

This requires explicit investigation of conceptual distinctions and complementarities so as to discern the relevant aspects that might be part of analytical and political approaches. In the following example the complexity of the task is reduced as only two concepts of collaboration are considered, those of innovative milieu and social capital. Important conceptual links may emerge from comparing notions, as was achieved by Asheim (1996) who identified an evolutionary relationship of industrial districts and learning regions, and Hassink

(2001) who points out consistencies of regional innovation systems and learning regions. The following section determines qualities of the milieu and social capital approaches that appear to be important for a systemic view on concepts of regional collaboration.

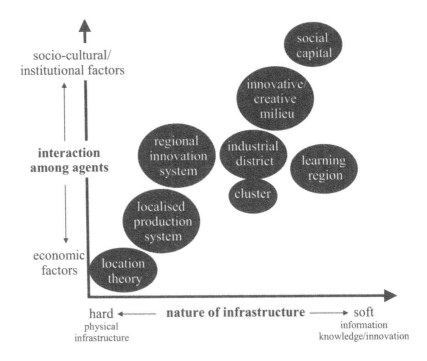

Figure 15.1   A Systemic Approach to Concepts of Regional Collaboration

Source: Depiction by the author based on Hwang 2002, p. 109, modified.

Systemically Combining Innovative Milieu and Social Capital

Both the innovative milieu and social capital concepts emphasize the function of personal relationships for successful firm development (Fromhold-Eisebith, 2004). Yet, they are associated with different, unlinked circles of debate. This includes the milieu with the Groupe de Recherche Europeen sur les Milieux Innovateurs (GREMI) group of researchers who have been investigating the phenomenon collectively for two decades (Bramanti and Ratti, 1997), social capital with a diverse set of social and political scientists (regarding conceptual origins; Bourdieu and Wacquant, 1992) and (regional) economists who have recently introduced this idea into contexts of industrial development and innovation (Maskell, 2000). Both notions display differing sets of ideas on some common ground, which offers good opportunities to find complementary aspects that can be systemically combined in order to better understand the roles of social relationships for the emergence of new economic spaces.

The milieu approach tries to explain how a good regional institutional endowment (universities, research laboratories, public support institutions and firms) in connection with efficient inter-organisational interaction and co-ordination lead to positive outcomes in terms of large numbers of innovating enterprises. The focus lies on the potential of creativity and learning which emerges from trustful information exchanges between various regional agents. Accordingly, a central GREMI definition identifies the innovative milieu as:

> the set, or the complex network of mainly informal social relationships on a limited geographical area, often determining a specific external 'image' and a specific internal 'representation' and sense of belonging, which enhance the local innovative capability through synergetic and collective learning processes (Camagni, 1991, p. 3).

The common GREMI framework, however, has not thwarted its members from producing various conceptions of the milieu. Another definition, for instance, sees its qualities essentially incorporated in the intersection of dynamic technology development (urging companies to innovate), changing patterns of organisation (e.g. in local production systems or structures of governance), and advantages of spatial proximity (e.g. social, cultural and knowledge-related coherence) (Crevoisier, 2001).

This chapter uses Camagni's milieu based definition emphasizing patterns of personal interaction (Fromhold-Eisebith, 2001). Accordingly, three sets of elements mark innovative-creative milieus: actor relationships in a regional framework, social contacts that enhance learning processes, and image and sense of belonging. The first set accentuates the fact that cooperation and information exchange between key actors of economic development are facilitated by their location in proximity to each other in the same region. This allows for easy and frequent face-to-face contact, which supports informal or formal collaborations possibly entailing innovation. To capitalize on creative potential, the contact network should include decision makers representing different types of organisations, such as manufacturing or service firms, universities, research labs, administrative bodies, agencies of industrial promotion and others (Maillat et al., 1993). This provides a particularly good seedbed for mutual inspiration and the combination of complementary resources, eventually generating new technical solutions, enterprises and programs of industrial promotion. GREMI stresses the crucial quality of innovative milieus to induce and coordinate economic change and the regrouping of productive assets (Crevoisier, 2001; Bramanti and Ratti, 1997). Although the region provides an important framework for actor contacts, successful milieus are also open to exogenous know-how inflows for enriching the circulation of information.

The second set of milieu qualities relates to specific advantages of socially embedded learning processes. Exchange of know-how and acceptance of other people's advice are favoured by good informal contacts between individuals marked by mutual trust. Under such conditions confidential and non-routine information circulates instantly, uncertainty is reduced, and learning and innovation are accelerated. The effective combination of professional and private acquaintance provides easy access to strategically important inputs as well as emotional backup for entrepreneurial decisions to innovate (motivation, encouragement, recognition). Accordingly, the trustful relationships that characterise milieus need to grow unassisted over time, leaving little hope for proactive 'milieu-enhancing' policies.

In the third set of milieu features the actors are aware of forming a coherent unity, demonstrating it to the outside in terms of a collective image that can be used for regional marketing. Sense of belonging also determines the spatial borders of the milieu, which has its limits where social coherence fades out (Maillat et al., 1993). It fulfils an important function by harmonising the individuals' differing professional interests, directing them towards common goals of locality development. Milieu relationships are often activated by upcoming industrial crises that call for joining forces.

The notion of social capital is analogous to the notion of milieu, and defined as 'the sum of the resources, actual or virtual, that accrue to an individual or a group by virtue of possessing a durable network of more or less institutionalised relationships of mutual acquaintance and recognition' (Bourdieu and Wacquant, 1992, p. 119).

Whereas this definition identifies the term with the favorable results of people's socially embedded interaction, others equate social capital with the underlying forces that trigger interaction with the resulting communities themselves (Lin, 2002). The exact meaning and content is still a matter of debate. The notion often refers to actors' deliberate engagements in associations or other institutions that support societal groups or a local population. This turns social capital into a favourable asset of an entire region (although the term originally does not have a spatial focus) where it helps to collectively solve shared social or economic problems.

The main quality of relevant relationships is seen in their capacity to transmit information in certain circles, which invites the application of the concept to innovation-driven development issues (Landry et al., 2001; Lesser, 2000). Additionally, the community-related and creating connotations of social capital must be pointed out, which also produces obligations and expectations among group members. The term closely connects to the idea of embeddedness (Taylor and Leonard, 2002). Maskell (2000) therefore explicitly distinguishes the socially integrating interaction associated with social capital from the information flows in company networks. Social capital implements social norms, often constraints of activity, which create closed networks marked by reliability and reduced competition. As a consequence, it sustains its qualities in the case of changing tasks, when actors continue to have this resource available. Thus, it carries a dual character as 'lubricant' and 'glue' (Anderson and Jack, 2002).

Social capital is considered an important asset especially for companies that operate in the vertically disintegrating, innovation-driven network economy (Landry et al., 2001; Lesser, 2000; Maskell, 2000). Hence firms often purposefully engage in its creation, expecting support for the coordination of business routines and the acquisition of know-how. The resulting communities follow common norms for acceptable behaviour, internally diffuse helpful information, constrain opportunism and enable cooperation. In sum, social capital is associated with strong inter-firm ties, certain interpersonal dynamics (around trust and reciprocity) and a common context, language and code of behaviour of integrated individuals (shared terms and experiences) (Lesser, 2000).

The key question now becomes how the innovative milieu and social capital concepts can be figured as elements of a systemic approach which uses their differing features as points of entry into an improved analysis of regional cooperative institutions. Both notions stress the importance of trustful personal relationships for learning and innovation, but also show complementarities (Fromhold-Eisebith, 2004). Given that each concept in isolation inadequately explains the functions of informal collaboration in regional development, examining them together offers a way forward. Major complementary aspects of milieu and social capital relate to four categories representing important relational elements in innovation-based regional development: general purpose of interaction, type of actors and composition of group, main task in the realm of innovation, and time-related character of interaction (Table 15.1). In a graphic depiction analogous to Figure 15.1 both concepts would hold different positions within a coordinate system defined by four dimension axes.

Table 15.1   Distinctions and Complementarities of Innovative Milieu and Social Capital

	Innovative/creative milieu	**Social capital**
general purpose of interaction	to induce and manage change and implement new plans or programmes	to sustain elements of stability and reliability in a changing environment
type of actors and composition of group	heterogeneous network of decision makers from various private and public organisations (firms, universities, administration)	homogeneous community mainly including the senior staff of firms (of the same or related industrial sectors)
main task in the realm of innovation	to get from invention to innovation, from idea to commercialisation	to master the management of the firm and to remain in the (innovative) business
time-related character of interaction	selective one-time efforts and project-related joint activities	constant maintenance of relationships in the course of regular meetings

Source: Depiction by the author.

In the first category, the milieu concept focuses on the interaction between organizations in creating innovative complexes and in changing the direction of regional development. This, however, overlooks that firms, subject to a shifting environment, need stabilizing elements in order to sustain a successful business.

This stability is represented by social capital, which by nature maintains and reproduces the structure of pre-existing relationships. It is therefore critical especially 'to the success of individuals working in a fast-paced ... and highly knowledge-intensive environment' (Lesser, 2000, p. 4), where continuing changes in collaboration opportunities and levels of competition pose a challenge especially to smaller firms. In this context social capital provides the counterweight of a familiar community of partners of the same wave-length and shared norms.

In line with the dichotomy of change and stability, innovative milieu and social capital differ also with respect to the composition of actor groups (Table 15.1). Milieus mainly rely on relationships of heterogeneous actors of differing institutional affiliation, as a prerequisite for bearing creative outcomes by newly regrouping previously unconnected resources and competences. The common ground and shared norms that mark social capital, however, grow on a foundation of homogeneity promoted by the often closed and institutional character of contact circles (Landry et al., 2001). This asset therefore appears to be best represented in communities of sectorally related firms, which might be incorporated as industry associations or sector-specific interest groups (Maskell, 2000).

Accordingly, milieu and social capital relationships fulfil differing tasks in the realm of innovation. In its logic of change the milieu mainly aims at enabling the move from invention to innovation, from idea to commercialisation or from business plan to new enterprise (Maillat et al., 1993). But companies need other kinds of support as well, to become and stay profitable. A reliable base of social capital helps them master corporate management and stay in business innovatively. Many issues that are associated with social capital relate to important everyday routines that are not at the core of the innovative capabilities of companies. Such issues often represent particular weaknesses of young technology firms: support in questions of organisation and marketing, cross-sale of products, sharing of common reservoirs of skilled labour or provision of financial assistance. Firm communities are better than milieus because they provide information about competitors and industry trends or advice from experienced incumbent companies (Maskell, 2000). But these ties are not ideal for opening up new sources of know-how and inspiration (Lesser, 2000), which requires their combination with a milieu. Consequently, the time-related character of interaction differs between innovative milieu and social capital regarding the frequency and regularity of contacts. Milieu relationships get activated in a rather selective way for certain project efforts such as implementing new programs of regional development or moving an invention to innovation. Social capital needs to be constantly cultivated which involves a regular maintenance of community contacts.

Exemplifying the Systemic Nature of Innovative Milieu and Social Capital

The Aachen example illustrates the central assumption of this chapter, that combining complementary ideas of the milieu and social capital, provides a more comprehensive framework for analysing the role of trustful collaboration in regional development.

Germany's Aachen area (population 1.2 million) may be regarded as a new economic space due to its transformation from an old industrial region into an agglomeration of new technology firms, now comprising over 800 enterprises in information technology, engineering consulting, medical and biotechnology, and other fields. The region ranks among the five most dynamic in Germany in terms of per-capita entrepreneurship (Sternberg and Bergmann, 2003, p. 38) and features an outstanding concentration of high tech firms (Licht and Nerlinger, 1997). Decisive drivers of restructuring have been triggered by different kinds of socially embedded actor interaction (besides other factors, for instance, relating to market or technology development) which show qualities either of milieu or social capital relationships (Fromhold-Eisebith, 2004).

In line with the innovative milieu model, infrastructure endowment has formed a major base of Aachen's development achievements. Several major academic and research institutions are located here, in particular the University of Technology (RWTH) Aachen. Public initiatives have added important elements, notably a dozen technology and start-up centres in the wider area. From this a growing numbers of spin-off firms, mostly established by alumni of the RWTH, have strongly shaped the regional take-off in technology industries.

Collaborative efforts have been a crucial part of these processes, some of which indicate a creative milieu. Important impulses for change have come from new collective initiatives by key actors representing different regional institutions such as industrial chambers, public promotion agencies, higher education and research, banks and other companies. They have combined their competencies and resources based on pre-existing personal, trustful contacts (originating, for instance, from graduating from the same university department or from memberships in local Lions Clubs). Common objectives of regional development, triggered by the urge to restructure the economy, harmonise differing interests. This has supported the creation of regional innovations in terms of new instruments of industrial promotion and the founding of technology firms. Actors' forces have been joined in a rather temporary way, as, over time, a consecutive row of renewed missions, projects and institutions must be produced to keep the region moving ahead.

One outcome of such milieu effects is Aachen Corporation for Innovation and Technology Transfer (AGIT), a public-private agency for promoting innovation and technology transfer in the Aachen area (www.agit.de/English). AGIT combines complementary competencies of stakeholders from over a dozen different regional organizations. The agency has created new infrastructure and other approaches to technology-driven regional development stimulating entrepreneurship and technology transfer. As a consequence, more milieu effects have been activated, such as increased regional application and commercialization of know-how from academia by innovating industries, based on socially embedded collaboration of university departments and spin-off firms. A more recent public-private initiative, the 'GründerRegion Aachen' that focuses on new firm formation, renews and carries on objectives initially designated to AGIT and coordinates activities of close to twenty organizations (www.gruenderregion.de).

But to understand relational success factors in the Aachen case, another type of trustful collaboration system needs to be regarded which is insufficiently captured by the milieu concept. When new technology firms grow older, they increasingly require sector-specific support and consulting over management, staff acquisition, sourcing of inputs, marketing, legal framework or other issues, which can hardly be provided by the change-oriented milieu. This assistance is rather provided within more homogeneous groups of companies by age and/or sector, sharing problems and objectives. Accordingly, firms require the stabilizing effects of social capital, reducing competition and enabling collaboration.

In the Aachen region this has come from several sector-specific industry associations such as plastics processing, information technology, biotechnology and automotive supplies, in addition to informal contact systems. Their main objective is to offer a forum where entrepreneurs can regularly meet personally, discuss common matters of concern, exchange information and build reliable networks of support and friendship. As most company executives are RWTH alumni, there is already a good deal of basic pre-existing shared values and language. Collectively creating innovations, though, is hardly at the heart of those contacts which, nevertheless, link potential competitors. Activities are meant to provide common assets from which every member can profit. Some sectoral associations are connected to the milieu, as they include representatives from the university or the local chamber of industry. But there is minimal political promotion for this important complement in the system of collaborative structures in the Aachen region.

Conclusions

This chapter argues that concepts of regional collaboration are complementary elements in a wider systemic framework for regional institutional analysis. It argues that a systems view on all regional relational theories or the 'TIM family', respectively, appears to be an appropriate way to synthesize a new economic geography that adequately addresses the differentiated character and variations of a wide range of new economic spaces. While one concept may fully capture only one set of relevant factors and neglect others, other concepts probably fill the gaps, and in combination they attend to all necessary simultaneous or evolutionary processes. Variability between economic spaces could be traced back to differing degrees of influence of different models within the systemic framework. To underpin these still tentative assumptions research should go in at least two major directions.

First, as the search for conceptual distinctions, complementarities and options for combination has been exercised here regarding innovative milieu and social capital, the same needs to be done with other TIM family members (Lagendijk, 2001; Moulaert and Sekia, 2003). In order to reach a sufficient depth of comparison, it is advisable to pick up only two or three notions at the same time. It might be promising to more explicitly analyze conceptual distinctions, for instance, between regional innovation system and learning region with respect to evolutionary means of coordination, between geographical cluster and industrial district with respect to the social embedding of value chain linkages, or between innovative milieu and industrial district with respect to differing involvements of certain actor groups.

Second, the complementary nature of various concepts of regional collaboration deserves to be further explored by evaluating the success story of one new economic space against an entire set of possibly applicable theories. With regard to the Aachen example, important additional features of regional restructuring may emerge when the analysis is extended to collaborative features that mark regional innovation systems, sectoral clusters and learning regions. This comprehensive approach helps to identify 'policy gaps' and improve regional development policies as well. Public authorities tend to concentrate on one 'fashionable' conceptual guideline and change-oriented instruments, but should be prompted to put more focus on essential complementing tasks.

However, growing diversities and inconsistencies of concept definitions accompanied by diminishing terminological clarity make system-oriented differentiations increasingly difficult (Markusen, 1999; Moulaert and Sekia, 2003). This has surely also affected the author's analysis, as we all perceive conceptual literature through our personal lens and detect elements in selective ways that corroborate our own hypotheses. The amount of literature on some models renders profound systematic comparison almost impossible: How can a concise account of the innovative milieu adequately capture the major facets of a notion which has been discussed by over two dozens of researchers in several books and numerous journal articles? This chapter draws a strong distinction between typical milieu and social capital qualities, a distinction that becomes blurred when other literatures are included (Fromhold-Eisebith, 2004). Nevertheless, by actively fitting several notions into one analytical system we can reverse the ongoing and confusing amplification of meanings, so reducing each concept of regional collaboration to its expedient core content.

References

Anderson, A. R. and Jack, S.L. (2002), 'The Articulation of Social Capital in Entrepreneurial Networks: A Glue or a Lubricant?', *Entrepreneurship and Regional Development*, 14 (3), pp. 193-210.

Asheim, B.T. (1996), 'Industrial Districts as "Learning Regions": A Condition for Prosperity', *European Planning Studies*, 4, pp. 379-400.

Bourdieu, P. and Wacquant, L. (1992), *An Invitation to Reflexive Sociology*, Chicago: University of Chicago Press.

Bramanti, A. and Ratti, R. (1997), 'The Multi-Faced Dimensions of Local Development', In R. Ratti, A. Bramanti and R. Gordon (eds), *The Dynamics of Innovative Regions: the GREMI Approach*, Aldershot: Ashgate, pp. 3-45.

Camagni, R. (1991), 'Introduction: From the Local "milieu" to Innovation through Cooperation Networks', In R. Camagni (ed.), *Innovation Networks: Spatial Perspectives*, London: Belhaven Press, pp. 1-9.

Cooke, P., Boekholt, P. and Tödtling, F. (2000), *The Governance of Innovation in Europe. Regional Perspectives on Global Competitiveness*, London and New York: Pinter.

Crevoisier, O. (2001), 'Der Ansatz des kreativen Milieus. Bestandsaufnahme und Forschungsperspektiven am Beispiel urbaner Milieus', *Zeitschrift für Wirtschaftsgeographie*, 45: pp. 246-256.

Fromhold-Eisebith, M. (2001), 'Kreatives Milieu', In E. Brunotte et al. (eds), *Lexikon der Geographie*, Heidelberg: Springer (CD-ROM).

Fromhold-Eisebith, M. (2004), 'Innovative Milieu and Social Capital – Complementary or Redundant Concepts of Collaboration-Based Regional Development?', accepted for publication in *European Planning Studies*, forthcoming.

Grabher, G. and Hassink, R. (2003), 'Fuzzy Concepts, Scanty Evidence, Policy Distance? Debating Ann Markusen's Assessment of Critical Regional Studies', *Regional Studies*, 37: pp. 699-700.

Hassink, R. (2001), 'The Learning Region: A Fuzzy Concept or a Sound Theoretical Basis for Modern Regional Innovation Policies?', *Zeitschrift für Wirtschaftsgeographie*, 45: pp. 219-230.

Hwang, J. S. (2002), 'Characteristics and Development of Industrial Districts: The Case of Software Clusters in Seoul, South Korea', In R. Hayter and R. Le Heron (eds), *Knowledge, Industry and Environment. Institutions and Innovation in Territorial Perspective*, Aldershot: Ashgate, pp. 107-124.

Lagendijk, A. (2001), 'Three Stories about Regional Salience: "Regional Worlds", "Political Mobilization" and "Performativity"', *Zeitschrift für Wirtschaftsgeographie*, 45: pp. 139-158.

Landry, R., Amara, N. and Lamari, M. (2001), 'Social Capital, Innovation and Public Policy', *ISUMA – Canadian Journal of Policy Research*, 2: pp. 73-79.

Lesser, E. L. (2000), 'Leverating Social Capital in Organizations', In E.L. Lesser (ed.), *Knowledge and Social Capital: Foundations and Applications*, Oxford: Butterworth Heinemann, pp. 3-16.

Licht, G. and Nerlinger, E. A. (1997), 'New Technology-Based Firms in Germany: A Survey of Recent Evidence', *Research Policy*, 26: pp. 1005-1022.

Lin, N. (2002), *Social Capital: A Theory of Social Structure and Action*, Cambridge: Cambridge University Press.

Maillat, D., Quévit, M. and Senn, L. (eds) (1993), Réseaux d'innovation et milieux innovateurs: un pari pour le développement regional, Neuchâtel: IRER.

Markusen, A. (1999), 'Fuzzy Concepts, Scanty Evidence and Policy Distance: The Case for Rigour and Policy Relevance in Critical Regional Studies', *Regional Studies*, 33: pp. 869-884.

Maskell, P. (2000), 'Social Capital, Innovation, and Competitiveness', In S. Baron, J. Field and T. Schuller (eds), *Social Capital. Critical Perspectives*, Oxford: Oxford University Press, pp. 111-123.

Moulaert, F. and Sekia, F. (2003), 'Territorial Innovation Models: A Critical Survey', *Regional Studies*, 37: pp. 289-303.

Porter, M. (2000), 'Locations, Clusters, and Company Strategy', In G.L. Clark., M.P. Felsman and M.S. Gertler (eds), *The Oxford Handbook of Economic Geography*, Oxford: Oxford University Press, pp. 253-274.

Sternberg, R. (2000), 'Innovation Networks and Regional Development – Evidence from the European Regional Innovation Survey (ERIS): Theoretical Concepts, Methodological Approach, Empirical Basis and Introduction to the Theme Issue', *European Planning Studies*, 8: pp. 389-407.

Sternberg, R. and Bergmann, H. (2003), *Global Entrepreneurship Monitor*. Unternehmensgründungen im weltweiten Vergleich. Länderbericht Deutschland 2002, Cologne.

Taylor, M. and Leonard, S. (eds) (2002), *Embedded Enterprise and Social Capital: International Perspectives*, Aldershot: Ashgate.

Chapter 16

Negotiating Culture and Economy in High-technology Industries: Governance through Intellectual Property in New Economic Spaces

Marcus A. Doel, Kevin G. Rees and Tamsin E.C. Davies

Patents: From Representation to Performativity

Economic geographers recognise that researching the geography of the so-called 'knowledge economy' and its constituent knowledge-intensive industries is hampered by a paucity of appropriate data sets. The study of knowledge *per se*, and of innovation in particular, is no exception. One source of data, however, affords researchers potential insight into the geography of the knowledge economy: patents.[1] Krugman (1991, p. 53) famously claimed that 'Knowledge flows ... are invisible; they leave no paper trail by which they may be measured and tracked'. Echoing Griliches' (1990, p. 1702) oft-quoted claim that 'patent statistics remain a unique resource for the analysis of the process of technical change', Jaffe and Tratenberg (2002, p. 12) responded to Krugman by observing 'that patent citations do constitute indeed a "paper trail" of knowledge spillovers, though one that is incomplete and mixed in with a fair amount of noise'. In this chapter we critique this 'representational' approach to patents, and offer instead a 'performative' consideration of the *work* that patents and patenting do within the 'knowledge economy'. We do so by considering the case of two high-technology industries in South Wales: medical instruments and biotechnology, and compute-software.

Slater et al. (2000, p. 339) estimate that over 40 million patents have been published. The world-wide liberalization of the criteria for patentability, in the 1990s, has stimulated patent applications, particularly in the US, whose current 'stock' of patents already exceeds 6 million. Not only are patent records specifically concerned with proprietary claims over the production and dissemination of knowledge and innovation, and underpinned by robust legal processes to ensure their validity and reliability, they also contain a wide range of spatially referenced information about inventors, inventions and assignees. Researchers are using these data to identify which individuals, firms, sectors, places, regions and nations are responsible for the creation and commercialization of specific forms of (patented) knowledge, and thence to determine their relative performances and comparative advantages (e.g.

Acs, et al., 2002; Jung and Imm, 2002; Worgan and Nunn, 2002). Given the aspiration of virtually every locality to be part of the 'knowledge economy', such studies are invaluable to policy makers, especially in relatively 'peripheral' regions such as Wales (Welsh Assembly Government, 2002).

Whilst patent records are underused in economic geography (although see Breschi, 2000; Santangelo, 2002), a relatively recent yet fairly well developed econometric and scientometric literature exists: the former being concerned with quantifying and modelling innovation and technological spillovers; the latter with university–industry linkages. This literature seeks to demonstrate that patent records are a '"window" on the "knowledge economy"' (Jaffe and Trajtenberg, 2002, p. 2). Obviously, this 'window' is not without its problems – and distortions.

First and foremost, only *certain forms* of knowledge and innovation are patentable. They must be codifiable (i.e. able to be fully disclosed), localizable (i.e. able to sustain a proprietary claim), have a technical application (i.e. a specific 'utility'), and embody a 'non-obvious inventive step' over and above the 'prior art'. For example, although the European Patent Convention specifically excludes computer software 'as such' from patentability, the European Patent Office (EPO) insists that no such exclusion applies to 'computer-implemented' inventions: much to the confusion—and consternation—of many working with software. Second, the *propensity to patent* potentially patentable knowledge and innovations varies significantly across time, space, sectors, types of firm, and, perhaps most importantly, jurisdictions (Cohen et al., 2002; Diallo, 2003). Although there is some evidence to suggest that there is a positive correlation between R&D expenditures and patenting rates (Freeman and Soete, 1997), the vast majority of firms appear to patent once, *if at all*, and only a small minority of firms hold multiple patents (Cefis, 2003). Third, patents concern *technologies* and *activities* (e.g. cutting, cleaning, sorting) rather than products or industries. This poses particular difficulties for researchers who wish to cross-reference *patent* classifications with *industrial* classifications, since the two are incommensurate and raise profound construct validity problems. Finally, patents are only *one* way of protecting intellectual property. Other forms of protection include secrecy, trademarks, design registration, and the assertion of copyright.

Arguably the greatest potential of patent data for researchers interested in the geography of innovation and the spatial structure of the 'knowledge economy' comes not from patent *citations*. The fact that patents cite other patents (along with other non-patent sources, such as academic papers) enables researchers to track the *circulation* and *transformation* of knowledge between innovations, inventors, firms, localities, regions, countries and sectors. In other words, patent citations have been taken to signify a *transfer* ('linkage' or 'spillover') of knowledge amongst innovators and technologies, and the spatial structure of patent citations can thereby assist in disclosing the *geography* of innovation. For example, Jaffe and Trajtenberg (2002) examined the patterns of USPTO (United States Patent and Trademark Office) patent citation amongst American, British, French, German and Japanese assignees as an indicator of international flows of knowledge, and reported evidence of geographic localization that fades slowly as knowledge diffuses over time (see also Jaffe et al., 1993; Stolpe, 2002). Hu and Jaffe (2003, p.

850) developed this approach to study the global diffusion of knowledge from the 'knowledge-rich' economies of the North (so-called 'world innovators') to the 'knowledge-poor' economies of the South. The basis for this work is the assumption that the 'frequency with which a given country's inventors cite the patents of another country is a proxy for the intensity of knowledge flow from the cited country to the citing country' (Hu and Jaffe, 2003, p. 852).

Here, we wish to highlight two crucial problems with the use of patent data in general, and patent citations in particular, as proxies for innovation and the circulation of knowledge: patents are *performative* rather than representational, and patent citations are *discriminatory* rather than referential. Despite appearances to the contrary, patents are not simply forms of codified know-how in a portable form. Nor are they a more or less opaque and distorted '"window" on the "knowledge economy"' (Jaffe and Trajtenberg, 2002, p. 2). Patents perform work: they claim, they cite, they delimit, they protect, they disclose, they block, they signify and they solicit attention (from investors, competitors, patent attorneys, and academics, amongst others). Most importantly, patents' *raison d'être* is to *discriminate* between who can and who cannot commercially exploit the inventions so claimed.

Citations form the cornerstone of both the econometric and scientometric analysis of patent records. Although citations are presumed to represent a transfer of knowledge this presumption is entirely misplaced. The legal basis for citations (whether by applicants, protestors or examiners) is *non*-disclosure of a flow, transfer or spillover of knowledge. To the contrary, they are discriminatory. Specifically, citations help the examiner to delimit and assess the patent claims by disclosing what is *not covered* by the grant, and to ensure that someone skilled in the art would be able to implement the invention as stated.[1] Accordingly, the USPTO *Manual of Patent Examining Procedure* states unequivocally 'There is no duty to submit information which is not material to the patentability of any existing claim' (Chapter 2000, §37 CFR 1.56). Similarly, the *Manual of Patent Practice* published by the UK Patent Office states 'The applicant is not obliged to describe or acknowledge the prior art, since the reader is presumed to have the general background technical knowledge appropriate to the art' (§14.83). In short, the 'closest' prior art is cited to delimit and assess the patent *claims* (concerning novelty, inventive step, utility, etc.), and not to signify a *transfer* of knowledge. This is why citations in EPO (European Patents Office) search reports are explicitly negative, identifying documents which either alone (marked 'X') or in combination (marked 'Y') 'destroy the novelty or inventive step of the subject-matter claimed'.

Although patents and patent citations do not disclose *transfers* of knowledge, they can be an inappropriate data source for economic geographers concerned with the knowledge economy. Rather than abandon patent records, we propose to shift the ground beneath them: from representation to performativity. In the next section we seek to demonstrate the value of a performative approach to patent records, which begins to take the *work* that they do seriously. We will do this by drawing upon the experience of the biotechnology and medical instruments, and computer-software industries in South Wales. We are interested in this *region* because it is relatively peripheral within the space economy of the UK and Europe, and has a history of resource- and technological-dependency that government policies seek to overcome. We are interested in these *industries* because they the Welsh Assembly Government sees them as important to the future of the Welsh economy, and they exhibit very different cultures of innovation and attitudes towards the protection and exploitation of intellectual property. Finally, our interest in *patents* crystallizes the ambivalence and tension within the so-called 'knowledge economy' between the need to share knowledge for collective learning, and the need to generate and protect intellectual property for commercial exploitation. Consequently, our entry into patent records is with respect to addressing how they are used to negotiate this ambivalence and tension.

Methodology

Our research consisted of five stages. First, the *population of firms* engaged in the two industries in South Wales was identified from company registrations, SIC (1992) codes and locational data. Most patent-based studies focus solely on the minority of firms that hold patents, and are therefore incapable of exploring the reasons why firms decide not to patent and the motivations for alternative methods of knowledge protection. Our study is not limited in this way. A total of 74 medical instruments and biotechnology firms, and 1015 computer software firms were identified within South Wales. Second, for each of these firms, a *patent search* was conducted using the web-based patent databases of the EPO, USPTO, other national patent offices, and the World Intellectual Property Office (WIPO); and patent applications, grated patents and expired patents noted for the period 1990 to 2002. We were especially interested in identifying the spatial and temporal distribution of the patents, and the location of the inventor, assignee, and the patent attorney handling the Welsh-assigned patents.[1] Third, we recorded the *citations* included in the patent documents, and differentiated (where possible) between those cited by the applicant, those revealed by patent office searches, and those cited by patent examiners (this differentiation is *impossible* for US patents prior to 2001, which creates yet more construct validity problems for the representational approach). In addition, while most patent-based studies rely exclusively on this 'front page' information, we also scanned all of the detailed patent descriptions and noted any additional references to patents and academic journals that were not cited on the 'front page'. Given their embedment within each innovation's technical description, these references may provide some of the otherwise elusive evidence of knowledge transfers and spillovers. Where possible, we also identified where the cited patents were assigned, and distributed them across four classes: the UK, the rest of Europe, the US and elsewhere in the world. Fourth, we carried out a *questionnaire survey* of 15 firms in each of the two industries in order to secure information on their technological focus, culture of innovation, and experience and attitude towards sharing and protecting their intellectual property. In the biotechnology/medical instruments industry, 12 of the 15 firms held patents in 2002, while no computer software firm held a patent at that time, although one firm had an application in-process. Finally, we conducted in-depth, *semi-structured interviews* with each of these 30 firms and with a number of patent attorneys and intellectual property specialists based in South Wales.

The High-technology Sector in Wales

Statistical information on the contribution of high-technology activities towards Welsh employment, establishments, GDP or exports is rare. The Welsh Assembly Government has established numerous policies over the past three years to promote a high-technology sector in Wales, particularly along the M4 motorway corridor which links Swansea, Cardiff, and Newport to Southern England. However, Statistics Wales has only begun to disaggregate UK economic statistics into detailed SIC categories for Welsh unitary authorities in the last year, with these data yet to be published. In an attempt to overcome this shortage of statistical context, the general data provided for Welsh high-technology activities (Office of National Statistics, 2002a) are supplemented by a detailed analysis of business registration data, providing what may be the most accurate picture currently available for medical/biotechnology and computer-software activities in South Wales.

The most recent data for Wales as a whole indicate that 135,000 people (11 per cent of the workforce) are employed in so-called 'high-technology industries', which includes manufacturing firms (75 per cent of high-technology employment) and service providers (Office of National Statistics, 2002a). However, by adopting the NACE classification (EU industrial classification system), these data overstate the extent of the high-technology sector in Wales by counting all employment in firms defined to be 'high-technology', many of which perform relatively little R&D. More informative may be the number of R&D employees in Wales, which accounted for 0.24 per cent of the labour force in 2000, compared to the UK average of 0.6 per cent, and an impressive 1.2 per cent and 1 per cent in the Eastern and South Eastern regions of England, respectively (Office of National Statistics, 2002b). Indeed, of the 12 Government Office Regions of the UK, Wales ranks last in its proportion of R&D employees in industry. Furthermore, due to several well-publicised closures or relocations of branch-plant facilities, employment in high-technology manufacturing has declined by 2.5 per cent since the mid 1990s.

As a component of the high-technology sector in Wales, the medical/biotechnology industry (comprising the manufacture of basic pharmaceutical products, preparations and medicaments, and medical and surgical equipment) is relatively small, employing 1800 people. R&D in natural sciences and engineering employs 1400 people, with a further 3900 workers employed in the computer-software industry (excluding those who are self-employed, estimated to be an additional 14 per cent) (Office of National Statistics, 2002c). Collectively, these industries account for just over 5 per cent of total high-technology employment in Wales. According to the Welsh Business Register (2002) South Wales was home to 74 medical/biotechnology firms, the majority of which (63 per cent) have been operating since 1990; and 1015 computer-software firms, 86 per cent of which were established in that period.

The geography of the medical/biotechnology and computer-software industries in South Wales reflects the dominance of its three cities: Cardiff, Swansea and Newport. These cities account for 56 per cent of medical/biotechnology firms and 49 per cent of computer-software firms, with the remainder of firms scattered amongst the towns in the region. Respectively, three quarters of computer-software patents and two thirds of medical/biotechnology patents are assigned to Welsh facilities. Of the latter, 75 per cent are assigned to companies located in Cardiff, reflecting substantial endogenous growth in high-technology industries within the capital city. In contrast, all foreign-assigned patents are owned by firms with facilities in small towns such as Pontypool, Chepstow, and Hengoed, which continue to rely upon external investment to provide high-technology employment. The Welsh 'stock' of patented knowledge in the medical instruments and biotechnology industry has increased from 23 to 392 patents since 1990 (see Table 16.1). Clearly, medical/biotechnology firms in South Wales are actively patenting their knowledge, with some firms patenting in vast quantities while most only have a few patents. In stark contrast, computer-software firms in South Wales have generated only 24 patents since 1990. This 'patenting gap' reflects different attitudes and practices of firms in these two industries towards the protection of knowledge and the benefits provided by patents.

The emerging knowledge-based economy of South Wales is supported by an ambitious high-technology strategy from the Welsh Assembly Government. At the heart of this strategy is the desire to 'increase the knowledge, research and development, and innovative capacity in all parts of the Welsh economy' and to increase 'the capacity of individuals, businesses and communities to acquire, adapt and apply knowledge' (Welsh Assembly Government, 2002, p. 11). The launch of the Technium© incubator programme in 2001 in Swansea, and the ongoing construction of nine more incubator developments across South Wales at a cost of £150 million, provides premises to small and new high-technology companies, and formal links to Centres of (Research) Excellence located throughout the constituent colleges and universities of the University of Wales. Further policy tools include: a £10 million 'Knowledge Exploitation Fund' to support research by Welsh SMEs; IP (Intellectual Property) Wales, which provides advice and financial assistance to firms seeking to protect their knowledge; and the Patent and Proof of Concept Fund (PPOC), established in 2002 to finance the early stages of the exploitation of ideas and products generated by university research in Wales (Welsh Assembly Government, 2003). Together, these policies amount to a new institutional infrastructure within Wales aimed at sponsoring the commercialization, exploitation *and protection* of knowledge by high-technology firms.

Having introduced the geography of these two industries within South Wales and their different propensities to patent, turn now to a critique of a representational analysis of patent records.

A Critique of the Representational Approach to Patent Data

This section provides a critical evaluation of the representational analysis of patent data. The following tables are derived from patent records (applications and grants) where the applicant/assignee is located in South Wales, irrespective of patent jurisdiction. The interest is in those patents over which high-technology firms in South Wales have ownership and control. The data only include those citations made by the applicant or their patent attorney and excludes citations made by patent examiners. Table 16.1 presents a summary statement of the citation of patent sources by *all* Welsh-assigned patents.

Table 16.1   Patent Citations in Welsh-assigned Patents: 1990–2002

	None	Self citation	UK	Europe	US	Rest of World	Total citations
Medical bio.	42 patents	35	9	26	96	31	197
Medical ins.	45 patents	188	13	66	65	3	335
Software	11 patents	0	0	0	0	0	0

Data in the *None* column refer to the number of Welsh-assigned *patents* that contain no citations. *Self citation* refers to cases where a Welsh firm cites its *own* patents (there were no cases of parent-subsidiary cross citation). In all other cases, data refer to the number of *citations* made by Welsh-assigned patents to patents held by *other* firms. *UK, Europe, US* and *Rest of World* refer to the location of the *assignee* of the cited patent, and *not* the location of its inventors, *nor* the cited patent's jurisdiction.
Sources: world-wide patent office websites.

Table 16.2   Journal Citations in Welsh-assigned non-US patents: 1990–2002

	Citations	Made by *No.* Patents	*Patents without data*[†]
Medical biotechnology	346	109	37
Medical instruments	2	190	48
Computer software	0	13	3
Totals	348	312	88

† Citations were either unavailable or untranslatable for some patent offices. Data from Welsh-assigned USPTO patents have not been included.
Sources: world-wide patent office websites.

Table 16.1 distils the structure of patent citation within Welsh-assigned patents, taken from the perspective of *ownership* (i.e. assignment), rather than from the perspective of either knowledge *production* (i.e. invention) or knowledge *protection* (i.e. jurisdiction). The data in Table 16.1 suggest two very different cultures of citation and seems to reveal the importance of both US-citations and self-citation, the latter suggesting the ability of some firms to appropriate and accumulate technological spillovers from internal research and development. Notably, 98 patents make no citations at all and there are relatively few citations to other firms within the UK. Both of these facts raise doubts about citations as evidence of a transfer of knowledge between firms, sectors and locations. Yet for a fuller sense of the different cultures of citation, one should also consider citations of non-patent sources, specifically academic journals (Table 16.2).

This table reveals a stark contrast in cultures of citation, in this case between medical biotechnology, and medical instruments and computer software. It suggests a strong university–industry linkage in the field of medical biotechnology. Crucially, interviews with firms and patent attorneys revealed that while patent attorneys typically search for prior art on behalf of the applicants using patent citation databases, they nevertheless rely on the applicants to provide *journal* citations. For this reason, journal citations may be a more reliable indicator of knowledge transfer than patent citations, especially in academic start-ups or university–corporate collaborations, where the initial stimulus for product development involves academic research (source: interviews with patent attorneys). Research using journal citations has been minimal to date and demands that researchers progress beyond the 'front page' of patent documents to read the patent descriptions where journal articles are cited; a place into which patent researchers seldom venture.

Table 16.3 presents the complete citation 'network' for *all* Welsh-assigned medical biotechnology patents. From a representational approach these data are taken as evidence of a network of knowledge flows that link South Wales high-technology firms with innovators elsewhere in the UK or worldwide. There is clearly a predominance of citations to US-assigned patents (49 per cent of total), potentially reflecting the dominance of US firms in developing the prior art in this industry. Equally striking is the scarcity of UK citations, suggesting that firms in South Wales' have adopted very little knowledge from the local or national economy.

Table 16.3   Patent Citations by Welsh-assigned Medical Biotechnology Patents: 1990–2002

	none	Self	UK	Euro	US	World	Total
Cardiff	*10 patents*	13	7	15	52	5	92
Hendy	*7 patents*	17	0	8	27	4	56
Hengoed	*12 patents*	1	1	0	3	18	23
Llanelli	*4 patents*	2	1	3	11	4	21
Pontypridd	*0 patents*	0	0	0	3	0	3
Swansea	*6 patents*	2	0	0	0	0	2
Tredegar	*3 patents*	0	0	0	0	0	0
Totals	*42 patents*	35	9	26	96	31	197

Note: there are no parent–subsidiary self-citations, and no information was available for 41 patents.
Sources: world-wide patent office websites.

A naive 'representational' assessment of this citation 'network' may infer a strong connection between South Wales and the US, perhaps involving international learning, technological complementarities or even research collaboration. Equally, a representational assessment implies a detachment of South Wales from domestic technological developments and that South Wales is far from being a 'learning region'. However, a patent *citation* 'network' must not be taken to represent a network of *knowledge*. That a third of Welsh-assigned medical biotechnology patents make no citations, and no citations are made in any of the Welsh-assigned computer-software patents, demonstrates the folly of a representational approach that infers a network of knowledge from patent citations.

The danger of mistaking citations for knowledge transfers is evident from the experience of one medical instruments firm. While this firm did not collaborate with any of the owners of the patents cited, they did collaborate with other firms, but crucially these relationships did not manifest themselves as citations in patent documents. Claims that patent citations can be used as proxies for knowledge flows or collaboration are questionable. Patent attorneys interviewed consistently disputed the link between patent citations and knowledge transfer. One attorney stated: 'I would say that generally [patent citations] didn't represent any wider transfer of knowledge ... [M]ost companies might be referring to something that has been found in the [patent] search and there will be no other contact whatsoever associated with it ... Very often the documents haven't come to light until after the invention has arisen.' This point is confirmed by another patent attorney: '[T]he first time the applicant is aware of citations is when the search report comes out. There is no ... interaction between our client – that would be the applicant – and the owner of the citation.'

Interviews with high-technology firms in South Wales reveal that few firms consult patent records to solve problems during the innovation process, and even fewer used patent records to identify potential collaborators, new markets or new areas for investment. The most common reason for consulting patent records was to check on the originality of potential products after the R&D process, to check the technical background of technologies, and to gain information on their competitors, none of which amounts to the quality of learning and problem solving at the heart of the innovation process. The frequent use of patent attorneys to conduct these searches (often retrospectively) further separates the innovation process from learning from patent documents. Thus, the claim that firms use patent records extensively as a method of learning is undermined, and the representational approach that infers a knowledge network from patent citations cannot be justified.

A Performative Appreciation of Patents and Knowledge Protection

The previous section illustrated the shortcomings of a representational analysis of patent data. Here we develop a *performative* approach to patents that moves beyond spatial and sectoral variations in the number of patents to acknowledge the role of patents in economic governance. Patents as product and patenting as a practice do far more than protect knowledge. Patents act within and upon corporate strategies, serve as a currency of the knowledge economy by which high-technology firms can be evaluated and are increasingly prominent in knowledge-oriented economic policies. The patenting process involves judgements about the cost, time, and rewards of applying for a patent, the risk of disclosing knowledge into the public domain, and the utility of alternative business strategies, such as secrecy, and therefore involves both economic motivations and cultural influences. Patenting is a contested business practice that provokes substantial dispute over which knowledge should *and should not* be subject to patent protection. An ongoing example is the dispute between large corporations (including Microsoft) lobbying for increased patent protection for computer software, and small firms (and indeed the UK Office of Government Commerce) that favour the proliferation of an open-source attitude towards software source codes (Thompson, 2003). While large corporations may be capable of extending their competitive advantage by patenting their intellectual property, small software developers perceive this practice to be a direct threat to their existence. As a recent interview with Bruce Perens, a key developer and advocate of open-source software argued, 'every small and medium sized enterprise is at risk regarding software patenting. That is a problem in Europe, because representatives to the European Parliament are pushing very hard for software patenting that would indeed shut out all small and medium businesses from the software development business' (Boyd, 2004). Ultimately, patenting is a legal process and subject to regulatory variations between and within legal jurisdictions that can significantly influence the rules and manner by which firms and regions compete and conduct themselves in the global economy (Rees and Doel, 2002). The contested and legal context of patent practice has received little attention from patent researchers to date. In response, Table 16.4 summarizes an agenda for a new, performative appreciation of patenting.

This approach recognises the importance of conventions and forms of business practice within an economy that become inscribed into 'normal' business behaviour over time through deliberate institutional practices and policies. National governments will typically be central to establishing the legal framework and procedures that underwrite the patenting process. However, regional governments may be important in developing an institutional framework that encourages patenting as business 'best practice'. In this regard, there is a need for research that explores the jurisdictional variations in patent criteria, patent awards and the revocation of patents. The case of South Wales illustrates the creation of an institutional framework promoting the patenting of knowledge, through policies including the Knowledge Exploitation Fund, IP Wales, and the PPOC Fund.

Although patenting is promoted in contemporary economic policy as good business practice and as a way of increasing the protected stock of knowledge within an economy, the medical and biotechnology industries and computer-software industries of South Wales exhibit very different attitudes towards patenting and cultures of innovation. Computer-software firms believe that patenting is not a mechanism available to them, despite the granting of over 20,000 patents by the EPO for computer-implemented inventions (Cook, 2002). Instead of patenting, interviewed computer-software firms relied upon protecting the expression and 'art-form' rather than an inventive principle, most notably using copyright (11 firms), non-disclosure agreements (11 firms), and trademark registration (8 firms). This is in stark contrast to the culture of patenting in the medical and biotechnology industry, where the substantial cost and time involved in research, development and testing encourages firms to patent their knowledge rather than risk losing intellectual property rights at the latter stages of product development. By contrast, computer software development typically costs much less, with our survey revealing an average R&D expenditure of £55,000 in 2002, compared to £400,000.

From a performative perspective, patents not only protect intellectual property rights (in fact they often fail so to do), but also perform other work within the knowledge economy. Patents function as signs to potential investors, as a tangible asset to current investors, and decoys and barriers to competitors. In the medical and biotechnology industry, for example, patents have become a form of currency wherein small firms involved at the discovery end of the innovation process seek to attract large corporate partners to finance product development and testing by selling or licensing their knowledge. Clearly, patents are crucial in enabling this partnership, as they not only protect intellectual property from exploitation by competitors but to advertise the firm's technological competence. In so doing they function as a kind of currency in the knowledge economy and provide a legal framework within which future entitlements and obligations are negotiated and designated. Additionally, interviews revealed that patents help high-technology firms to market their product, to attract or satisfy investor expectations and to serve as products in their own right. In the latter case, patents transform knowledge into a tangible asset that can be used as a bargaining tool or offered for sale should the firm be subject to a merger, acquisition or failure.

Patents and the patenting process are socially constructed and therefore subject to conflict. When challenged or violated, the fate of patents can result in a change in the technological strategy of firms. In interviews, respondents were largely critical of the level of protection provided by patents. Significantly, knowledge protection relies on the ability of a firm to enforce rather than obtain a patent. In reality the protection afforded to small firms is less than what large corporations are capable of when needing financing lengthy legal disputes. Interviews illustrate this point: five of the twelve firms that hold patents have experienced violation. Of these five, only one firm has successfully defended its patent rights to date (one dispute is currently in-process). In two cases, the violation resulted in a loss of the protection provided by the original patent, necessitating shifts in product focus and technological strategy. For another firm, the cost and time required to defend the patent in court were viewed as prohibitive and as a result the firm merged with its competitor and has seen product focus shift into new markets that it previously had no intention of serving. These cases illustrate the significance of patent violations for corporate strategy.

As a social construct, patents require constant maintenance. This involves defence of granted patents as well as the maintenance of patent regulations within and between jurisdictions. This maintenance necessitates the coordination, conscription, and inscription of a multitude of disparate elements, including laboratories and corporate R&D personnel, academic researchers, patent attorneys and search reports, patent documents, policymakers and politicians. Notwithstanding its diversity, this actor-network must be coordinated and maintained in the face of internal and external conflicts. The divergent attitudes towards the EU Directive to harmonize patent criteria for computer software, and the challenge to the patent system from open-source software, are examples of conflicts from within and outside of the actor-network associated with patents (Rees and Doel, 2002). Furthermore, great effort must be devoted to conscripting new elements into the actor-network, potentially including additional patent regulations, patent attorneys or firms seeking to patent their technology. Each individual or firm must be inscribed into the actor-network and must subscribe to specified forms of (problematic) practice. This can be exemplified with regards to university–industry collaboration, in which an academic researcher presents or publishes research findings, thereby placing them in the public domain and removing the possibility for patent protection by the corporation. In this case, the best practices of academia and industry are not compliant and require further inscription for the actor-network to operate effectively. Finally, actor-networks ideally require immutable mobiles, such as currency in global financial markets. As immutable mobiles, these can be traded throughout the network to generate further value and, through private ownership, can become concentrated in the hands of a few actors or widely dispersed. From this perspective, patents are a currency of a certain kind of actor-network that exists within the international knowledge economy.

Conclusion

Despite being widely utilized by researchers interested in the generation and dissemination of knowledge, patent records are an unreliable indicator of innovation and do not provide a meaningful window into the flows of knowledge between firms, technologies, regions, and nations. The representational analysis of patent records misses the varied legal frameworks and jurisdictional contexts in which patent practice takes place, or the discriminatory function of patent citations. Interviews with high-technology innovators and patent attorneys in South Wales reveal that patent searches are frequently performed by a patent attorney at the end of the innovation process, thereby reducing the potential for learning from patent documents and further undermining the representational interpretation of patent citations as a window on the knowledge economy. For these reasons, we reject a representational approach to the use of patent data, such as that adopted by econometric modellers. However, we do not discount the use of patent records out of hand, since non-patent citations, particularly of journal articles, can offer an indication of technology transfer from academic research to industrial application. This is expected to be especially relevant in the case of academic entrepreneurship and university–industry collaboration.

What is clear is that researchers need to focus less on what patents purportedly represent and more on what patents do, which is far more than protect intellectual property. In developing a performative approach, we suggest that patents and the process of patenting play a significant part in the governance of the knowledge economy. Patents provide firms with a tangible asset and a discernable value in the knowledge economy. Patenting can be a strategic objective of corporate research and development for one firm but a strategic constraint or threat for others. In contrast to the initial intent of increasing competition and innovation, the proliferation of intellectual property rights could reduce competition through corporate and knowledge concentration. Clearly, the way in which patents govern the knowledge economy is varied and extremely complex, but this complexity raises important questions for economic geographers that have until now been left unexplored.

Table 16.4   An Alternative Agenda for Research of Patenting in the Knowledge Economy

Theoretical approach	Principal arguments	Methodologies/research implications
Representational approach	Patents used as a proxy for knowledge transfer between firms, regions, and nations.	Econometric and scientometric modelling.
	Network of knowledge and collaboration 'read-off' from network of patent citations.	Patinformatics.
	Emphasis on tension between forces of localization and ubiquitification that forms of knowledge create	Studies of comparative and competitive advantage.
Performative approach	Patents are performative; a process rather than a 'finished product' Intellectual property rights (IPR) as a main component of policy agenda.	Expose 'work' patents do other than protect knowledge. Reveal the institutional infrastructure promoting the protection of IPR.
	Institutional infrastructure promoting patenting as 'good business practice'. Patent practice as form of regulation.	Expose contradictions of public policy regarding the disclosure and protection of knowledge. Reveal the influence and diversity of patenting cultures.
	Patenting as a business convention. Policy contradiction: knowledge as a public good versus private asset. Jurisdictional variations in patent criteria, process, and enforcement.	Reveal the difference that jurisdiction makes to the acquisition, violation, defence and deployment of patented knowledge.
	Patenting is a social construction.	
	Patenting (policy and practice) is contradictory, requiring maintenance. Patents require conscription and inscription. Patents are sustained by a network of actors (firms, researchers, attorneys).	Reveal changes in patent law and how these are contested. Investigate the contradictions of patenting practice and the strategies for its maintenance.
	Patents are an immutable mobile of capitalist accumulation (a currency of the knowledge economy).	Reveal and account for the alternative strategies for the protection and dissemination of knowledge (e.g. open-source computer software).

References

Acs, Z. J., Anselin, L., and Varga, A. (2002), 'Patents and Innovation Counts as Measures of Regional Production of New Knowledge', *Research Policy*, 31: pp. 1069-1085.

Boyd, C. (2004), 'Software Patents "Threaten Linux"', *BBC News Website*, http://news.bbc.co.uk/go/pr/fr/-/1/hi/technology/3422853.stm, January 23rd.

Breschi, S. (2000), 'The Geography of Innovation: A Cross-Sector Analysis', *Regional Studies*, 34(3): pp. 213-229.

Cefis, E. (2003), 'Is there Persistence in Innovation Activities?', *International Journal of Industrial Organization*, 21: pp. 489-515.

Cooke, P. (2002) 'Biotechnology clusters as regional, sectoral innovation systems', International Regional Science Review, 25,1: pp. 8-37.

Cohen, W. M., Goto, A., Nagata, A., Nelson, R. R., and Walsh, J. P. (2002), 'R&D Spillovers, Patents and the Incentives to Innovate in Japan and the United States', *Research Policy*, 31: pp. 1349-1367.

Diallo, B. (2003), 'Historical Perspectives on IP Protection for Software in Selected Countries Worldwide', *World Patent Information*, 25: pp. 19-25.

Freeman, C., and Soete, L. (1997), *The Economics of Industrial Innovation*, London: Pinter.

Griliches, Z. (1990), 'Patent Statistics as Economic Indicators: A Survey', *Journal of Economic Literature*, 27: pp. 1661-1707.

Hu, A. G. Z., and Jaffe, A. B. (2003), 'Patent Citations and International Knowledge Flow: The Case of Korea and Taiwan', *International Journal of Industrial Organization*, 21: pp. 849-880.

Jaffe, A. B., and Trajtenberg, M. (2002), *Patents, Citations, and Innovations: A Window on the Knowledge Economy*, Cambridge, MA: MIT Press.

Jaffe, A. B., Trajtenberg, M., and Henderson, R. (1993), 'Geographic Localization of Knowledge Spillovers as Evidenced by Patent Citations', *The Quarterly Journal of Economics*, 108(3): pp. 577-598.

Jung, S., and Imm, K.-Y. (2002), 'The Patent Activities of Korea and Taiwan: A Comparative Case Study of Patent Statistics', *World Patent Information*, 24: pp. 303-311.

Krugman, P. (1991), *Geography and Trade* Cambridge, MA: MIT Press.

Office of National Statistics (2002a), *Employment within the High-Technology Industries within the EU, 2000* (Statistical Bulletin: 95/2002) Statistical Directorate, National Assembly for Wales, Cardiff.

Office of National Statistics (2002b), *Research and Experimental (R&D) Statistics 2000* Economic Trends, #585.

Office of National Statistics (2002c), *Annual Business Inquiry, 2001*.

Rees, K. G., and Doel, M. A. (2002), 'Networks of Knowledge: The Circulation and Regulation of Knowledge in High-Technology Industries', Paper presented to the Dynamics of Economic Space Conference of the International Geographical Union, Johannesburg South Africa, 29th July–3rd August, 2002.

Santangelo, G. D. (2002), 'The Regional Geography of Corporate Patenting in Information and Communications Technology (ICT): Domestic and Foreign Dimensions', *Regional Studies* 36(5): pp. 495-514.

Slater, P., Twyman, P., and Blackman, M. (2000), 'The *Smart* Way for Patent Information to Help Small Firms', *World Patent Information*, 22: pp. 337-341.

Stolpe, M. (2002), 'Determinants of Knowledge Diffusion as Evidenced in Patent Data: The Case of the Liquid Crystal Display Technology', *Research Policy* 31: pp. 1181-1198.

Thompson, B. (2003), 'UK Tests Open Source Waters', *BBC News Website*, http://news.bbc.co.uk/go/pr/fr/-/1/hi/technology/3181108.stm, October 10th.

Welsh Assembly Government (2002), A Winning Wales: The National Economic Strategy of the Welsh Assembly Government, Cardiff: Welsh Assembly Government.

Welsh Assembly Government (2003), *A Winning Wales: Annual Report 2002–2003*, Cardiff: Welsh Assembly Government.

Worgan, A., and Nunn, S. (2002), 'Exploring a Complicated Labyrinth: Some Tips on Using Patent Data to Measure Urban and Regional Innovation', *Economic Development Quarterly*, 16(3): pp. 229-236.

Chapter 17

Regions as Institutions, Inter-regional Firms and New Economic Spaces

Roger Hayter

Introduction

Before the mid-1960s, economic geography qua industrial geography was strongly regionally focused and examined the spatial distribution of activities, industries and factories with little reference to their corporate organization. Since then, heralded by the geography of enterprise, the firm has become a central unit of investigation in economic geography (McNee, 1965; Krumme, 1969; Hayter and Watts, 1983; Dicken and Thrift, 1992; Maskell, 2001). The organization of industrial activity is recognized as a vital dimension for explaining location dynamics and regional development. The literature routinely distinguishes between inter-regional firms, especially giant multinational corporations (MNCs), and small and medium sized enterprises (SMEs) as different types of institutions with distinctive structures, strategies and location behaviour. Indeed, economic geography's analytical embrace of 'the firm' (and industrial organization) was principally stimulated by the power of MNCs in using location as a competitive weapon and orchestrating new institutionalized, occupationally-based spatial divisions of labour (Pred, 1974; Fredricksson and Lindmark, 1979). In this view, regional development has become strongly dependent on the priorities and preferences of MNCs.

For several decades, the economic geographies of firms and inter-firm relationships have been subject to increasing, diverse theoretical scrutiny and have been empirically explored in a variety of research designs. In contrast, the idea of regions has received less attention. Britton (1974, p. vv) noted decades ago that a focus on the firm in enterprise geography 'would weaken ... geographical output'. This concern reflected underlying spatial ambiguities in defining firms and the remarkably varied, geographically non-contiguous nature of corporate spatial systems. Britton (1976; 1980; 1999) went on to pioneer understanding of the structure of branch plant economies. Failure to give conceptual equivalence to both firm and region has weakened the understanding of geographical expression of behaviour. Hence regions remain under-theorized and are often portrayed as geographically defined spaces firms organize and integrate. As statistical units regions are useful (and self-justifying) for revealing differences among and within themselves. While economic geography is replete with studies emphasizing regional context, local cultures, local bargaining and local adaptation that indicate that regions are more than simply (permeable) containers for mobile capital, the idea of the region lacks the same significance and respect that it had prior to the 1960s. While attempts to formally explicate how regions behave and why do exist, they are rare (Patchell, 1996).

This chapter seeks to empower the *idea* of regions by interpreting them as institutions. This objective is not the same as claiming power for regions nor is it meant to demean the importance of firms as institutions. However, if the latter is well documented, the interpretation of regions as institutions is under explored. The point of departure is Holmén's (1996) metaphor of regions as 'meeting places' of endogenous and exogenous or local and global forces that mutually combine to create local economies that are unique (Johnston, 1984). Global-local dynamics are explicitly interpreted as interdependent instituted processes in which the local and the global affect each other. Indeed, the one cannot be understood without reference to the other. Even the most insistent globalizing institutions require local presence becoming a part of local habits and customs. Even the most insistent local institutions cannot ignore global forces. Moreover, this role is not limited to a few 'leading edge' regions but applies generally, including to what are termed, not without ambiguity, 'new economic spaces'.

As institutions, regions differ fundamentally from firms, especially inter-regional firms and MNCs. Given a broad conventional concept of regions as geographically contiguous and politically defined territories within nations, two observations are important. First, for regions planning, problem-solving and location adjustment is geographically constrained. Firms, in contrast, have much broader planning horizons that are potentially global in scope. Second, regions are more complex and unruly institutions than firms. While firms have specific business mandates, regions are multi-institutional characterized by internal conflict and fragmentation that can affect regions as well as cooperation and integration. Regions have to 'sort out' a wide variety of alternative institutional values, and this process is geographically constrained. Economic, social and political institutions are interdependent, and firms cannot ignore these interdependencies as they plot their strategies. In this regard, much contemporary economic geography has become *too* fixated on the firm. The current emphasis on production chains and firms and their suppliers (that is, other firms) captures this fixation while recent pleas to develop a theory of the firm are not new and are similarly circumscribed (Maskell, 2001). The interpretation of regions as institutions is also a plea to encourage economic geography to broaden its institutional vista (Martin, 1994).

The chapter has three main sections. Section One develops the idea of regions as institutions in a way that is consistent with the 'institutional turn' suggested by Martin (2000) and Barnes (1999) and follows what is known as 'dissenting institutionalism' (Hayter forthcoming). The other sections elaborate on this theme in the context of two new economic spaces. The second section examines the new auto industry spaces in the US mid-west (and south) and focuses specifically on the hybrid factories created by Japanese transplants (Liker et al., 1999). The hybrid factory specifically illustrates how local and global institutions interact to create regionally distinct forms of operation. The third section focuses more generally on the idea of (newly) 'contested resource peripheries' that feature complex clashes of institutional forces that are either seeking to retain vested interests or comprehensively remap resources according to their own values (Hayter, 2003; see also Hayter et al., 2003). Contested resource peripheries graphically illustrate the need for economic geography qua industrial geography to broaden their institutional vision.

Regions as Institutional Meeting Places

Regional geography once stood at the centre of geography, at least of human geography. For geography faculty, the teaching of regional geography was a widespread expectation, regional field trips routine and regional classifications and regional texts important. In the paradigm of areal differentiation, regions were envisaged as complex historically formed unique entities that required synthesis of the social and physical factors shaping human life to be understood. Indeed, regions were uniquely shaped by distinct cultures, habits, values, tastes, speech and so on, and thus strongly implied the idea of regions as institutions. As highly differentiated landscapes, the wider 'situations' of regions, for example as represented by early patterns of settlement from 'outside' and contemporary patterns of trade, were invariably recognized within the areal differentiation paradigm. The focus was largely on the internal characteristics of regions, and on their integration or synthesis. This focus readily connected with the rapidly emerging professions of urban and regional planning. However, the regional approach was also marred by over-emphasis on description, the a-theoretical treatment of regions as largely self-contained entities and the failure to address significant socio-economic issues in a coherent problem solving way.

Since the mid-1960s, however, a tidal wave of nomothetic approaches has repositioned regional geography. New approaches sought to more systematically focus on specific kinds of economic, social, urban and environmental processes that were not contained by any particular regional boundaries. Various kinds of formal theory and research designs were now adopted to systematically investigate processes. Regions remained classified, for example, as cores and peripheries, but were generally not at the centre of conceptual elaboration. Indeed, in the theoretical developments regions became 'given' conditions across which the really interesting processes could be investigated. In neoclassical location and land use theories, for example, regions are conceptualized as homogenous plains or isotrophic surfaces over which Homo Economicus rationally roams in search of optimal spatial structures. Similarly, in Marxian landscapes regions became more or less implicit landing posts for the transformations of various circuits of capital.

With respect to the geography of enterprise, Krumme (1970, p. 318) recognized that big corporations had become so powerful as to be 'states without states', belonging 'to so many political jurisdictions that they seem to be practically independent of all of them'. He further argued that the power of giant corporations at the national level was even more evident at the regional scale, where they are more open and vulnerable than nations to the discretionary location priorities of inter-regional and multinational corporations. Beyond recognizing their openness and vulnerability, however, the geography of enterprise has been primarily focused on understanding 'the firm', especially the giant firm rather than the region.

Whatever the differences, neoclassical, Marxian and geography of enterprise approaches tended to treat regions in theoretically casual or implicit ways. Many caveats can be made to this statement and there have been several pleas to resurrect and rejuvenate regional geography (Bradshaw 1990; Holmén 1996). By and large, however, economic geography's engrained systematic orientation has continued to conceptually privilege individual decision-making actors, notably the firm (in whatever sector of the economy), and regions are not seen as especially pro-active or intrinsically interesting. Even within economic geography's institutional and cultural turns, regional context is often dismissed. Peck and Miyamachi (1994), for example, portray Japanese industrialization as a minor variation on (western-inspired) regulation theory. Sayer (1997, p. 22) interprets Japanese production systems similarly. In contrast, others interpret Japan as a remarkable story uniquely created by distinctive interactions of global-local or exogenous-endogenous factors.

Dissenting institutionalist economist, Hodgson (2001) has emphasized the importance of historical specificity that claims time periods are both unique and connected. He also believes geographic differences are significant – that regions are both connected and fundamentally different. This view is consistent with Barnes' (1996) idea about local models and Storper's (1997) regional worlds of production. Metaphorically, Holmen's (1995, p. 58) representation of regions as '"meeting places" for both endogenous [local] and exogenous [global] processes' effectively captures a global economy of regions that are connected but different. Global processes create these connections, and their differences result from global and local interactions. Global processes also have beginnings that are typically locally specific. Moreover, the global-local dynamics that create unique regions are instituted and interactive in which global institutions are controlled outside the local, even though the local is geographically defined. Indeed, in this view, regions are themselves institutions, albeit complex ones. As 'meeting places', regions are where institutional habits, routines, values and conventions are shared *and* debated.

Regions are clearly more complex institutions than firms primarily because they organize the interactions of multiple institutions that may be complementary or in conflict (Martin, 1994). Thus regions are territories where there may be widely held common values, processes of valuation and regulations, modes of thought, distinct groves to local life and potential sites of considerable conflict amongst groups regarding what habits and conventions should be. In this regard, regional government and planning authorities are formal institutions that are mandated to pro-actively meet the diverse needs of their populations, by synthesizing ('sorting out') global-local dynamics into patterns of land use and activity patterns that underlay local production and consumption systems. Admittedly, some plans work out better than others and conflict and fragmentation can characterize regions as well as integration and cooperation. Regionally mandated governments and planning institutions, for example, may not properly represent or be competent enough to properly deal with all the diverse values within their territories. Ultimately, regions as institutions are not only represented by governments and planning authorities.

In general, regions comprise a wide range of inter-related institutions associated with particular (and instituted) global-local dynamics. Regions do not, or rarely, speak with one voice and they are not autonomous. But in one way or another they are pro-active and global institutions do not simply have their way with otherwise passive regional containers. Even in an age of globalization global institutions need to be grounded and accommodate regional needs.

Moreover, all regions play institutional roles. In this regard, new economic spaces are potentially significant to the extent they reveal, indeed facilitate, new forms of instituted global-local dynamics. Admittedly, the theoretical elaboration of new economics spaces is imprecise. In practice new economic spaces refer to the emergence of new forms of manufacturing and related service activity in already settled regions not previously known for such activities. The rise of high tech electronic activities in Silicon Valley, and in many other previously non-industrial areas, is often cited in this context. New economic spaces need not be only associated with new high tech activities; South China has become a massively important new economic space for many industries while the location of auto investment in the US South and mid-west represents a shift to new economic spaces for the auto industry. Typically, new economic spaces are associated with manufacturing or service sector activities. Yet the resource industries provide distinct, instructive forms of new economics space. Thus in the case of resource industries new economic spaces may be literal 'empty spaces' or sparsely settled spaces. Moreover, for many resource industries their existing economic space is being completely re-defined by new forms of aggressive resistance from indigenous (aboriginal) peoples and environmental non-government organizations (ENGOs).

The creation of new economic spaces reflects the interplay of local-global processes that are implemented by various institutions that in thought and action interdependently engage local and global perspectives. Thus new activities require property rights of one kind or another, impose and draw upon local institutions, and once established, become part of the local structure distinct local-global relations. Even on the periphery, where resources are immobile and geographically extensive, the export-driven exploitation of Baldwin's (1956) hypothetical 'empty lands' characterized by no prior local actors, requires that resource rights are defined and allocated (mapped) as a basis for 'local' settlement and the accumulation of 'institutionalized' (vested) interests.

Hybrid Factories: Japanese FDI in the US

Whatever their boundary-spanning and scale-jumping abilities, global institutions typically require local presence in some form and this presence is typically shaped by local context. Global localization, for example, means that corporations become global by establishing branch plant that extends their conventions and structures to new regions where local habits in turn modify corporate conventions (Mair, 1994).

The hybrid branch factory is a related, specific illustration of this synthesis and testifies to the importance of the interactive adaptation between the local and the global. Many countries and regions around the world seek FDI (foreign direct investment), not simply to provide jobs, but as a source of know-how and to replace established local traditions with new ones based on best (technological and organizational) global practices. Simultaneously, to maintain viability, MNCs adapt to local tastes, work practices, religious beliefs, managerial attitudes, environmental conditions and regulations. In practice, branch plants are 'hybrids' of imported and local practice, as studies of Japanese investments in Asia (Itagaki, 1997) and the US (Liker et al., 1999) have revealed.

Within the US, several Japanese auto firms have invested in green field sites in small communities and in States, or at least regions within States, such as Ohio, Kentucky and Tennessee, that were previously non-industrial. Mercedez Benz and BMW have followed this trend to the southern states Alabama and North Carolina, as will Volkswagen in the near future, while General Motors (GM) built its 'Saturn' plant in a small community in Tennessee. In all cases, one major attraction of the new economic space was the potential to facilitate new forms of labour relations not possible in the old industrial auto spaces of Michigan. While GM retained a unionized workforce, subject to their agreement on new working conditions, the Japanese transplants have typically hired non-union labour. State governments and local communities have been extremely supportive of the new investments. Even so, for the Japanese firms a US location meant a completely different regional and cultural context from their home base in Japan. For the US national government, states and communities, the Japanese auto firms offered a different kind of production system. Indeed, the Liker et al. (1999) study was sponsored to assess the contributions of Japanese production systems to the competitiveness of the US industry.

This assessment argued that it was first necessary to understand the Japanese production system as practiced in Japan and then examine which components of that system were being transferred to the US. They conceptualized Japanese production systems in terms of four hierarchically embedded layers, namely shop floor production systems, factory level management and organization, corporate systems and the institutional fabric of Japanese society as whole. Each of these layers has specific attributes. For example, shop floor systems feature broad job classifications, team work, kaizen and strong quality standards while factories are typically tightly connected to long term, stable, hierarchically organized supplier relations that involve mutual learning commitments. Each level taken individually, and especially when taken in combination, defines a highly distinctive Japanese production system.

As Liker et al. (1999) recognize, Japanese production systems are not homogeneous. In this regard, the Toyota system may be taken as a classic type of core firm based production system around which there are variations within and beyond the Japanese auto industry (Sheard, 1983; Hayter 1997, pp. 349-372). Japanese production systems are also dynamic. Thus Toyota's hierarchical, structured, stable, geographically concentrated, innovation driven production stem that Sheard analyzed had taken several decades to construct, and has continued to evolve. Nevertheless, in the 1980s across many industries Japanese production systems were considered to define global best practice and there was widespread interest in gaining access to this organizationally based know-how.

In a general sense, the transfer of Japanese production systems from Japan to foreign countries is shaped by industry and product contexts, by the mode of transfer (direct foreign investment, joint venture, licensing), and by host country characteristics. Regardless of the specific influence of these factors, however, the transfer of Japanese production systems can be problematic. Thus the implication of embeddedness is that the layers within Japanese production systems are complex, multi-faceted, culturally defined and mutually interconnected institutions. Moreover, host countries comprise their own embedded, layered institutional arrangements. That is, host countries are not simply containers passively awaiting the arrival of 'given' foreign practices. Indeed, local institutions may wish to adopt, modify or resist attempts to impose globally imposed practices. The hybridization of operations results from a problematic interaction between local and global institutions as they both seek to accommodate to each other.

Adler (1999), for example, compares the human resource management (HRM) practices introduced by Toyota at NUMMI, a joint venture with General Motors in California, and its wholly owned green field factory in Kentucky (TMMK). At both plants, work organization, as measured by job classification, team work, job rotation and role of supervisors, and individual and organizational learning methods, as measured by training, suggestion boxes, quality control circles and information sharing, were judged similar to Toyota's practices in Japan. With respect to employment relations, however, adaptation to some form of American practice occurred. Indeed, even though the Kentucky plant was non-union, employment relations attributes such symbols of unity, labour relations, grievance procedures, discipline, personal selection, wages and benefits, were classified as close to the characteristics of 'an American union substitution model' (USM) (Adler, 1999, p. 107), while employment security, promotion and health and safety combined features from this model with Toyota's practices. At NUMMI, employment security, labour relations, grievances, discipline, promotion, and health and safety combined the conventional United Auto Workers (UAW) practices with Toyota practices. Symbols of unity reflected the USM model, personal selection a UAW-USM combination, and wages and benefits, the UAW model. Similarly, Pil and MacDuffie (1999) explored in more detail problem solving activities, the influence of teams on various work practices, forms of contingent compensation and supplier relations.

Japanese transplants in the US have therefore not been clones of Japanese practice but have formed hybrids between Japanese and American practice. In effect, these hybrid factories are bargains between the global institution of the Japanese MNC and local institutions such as American labour. Once established, hybrid factories become both global and local institutions. TMMK, for example remains under Toyota's control and its behaviour can be modified to meet the needs of the parent corporation. But the branch plant is also part of the daily life within Kentucky and its behaviour shaped by local attitudes. Indeed, there may be initiatives undertaken in Kentucky that Toyota can exploit elsewhere. An interesting issue is whether the hybrid factories have been successful from the perspective of long run development. Florida (1996) strongly suggests the answer is positive. He has claimed that the American Manufacturing Belt has been rejuvenated especially as a result of the adoption of new thinking in managerial attitudes, labour relations and the organization of innovation and production, especially those evolving from 'best practice' Japanese experience in new green field factories unfettered by old attitudes (Florida, 1996). In this view, Japanese FDI directly creates 'high performance organizations' and 'demonstration effects' that create virtuous processes of cumulative causation.

Hybrid factories are not inevitably consistent with local development, however. There are no mechanical rules to define a priori what constitutes 'appropriate' forms of hybridization and corporations can impose inappropriate practices on regions while regions can reject potentially important best practices from elsewhere (Soyez, 1988). As Soyez documents, in Nova Scotia's forest industry, attempts to introduce Swedish best practices to the region were often resisted by local groups as inappropriate by local foresters, and others. The firm also failed to appreciate local conditions. Indeed, there were was little agreement between the Swedish firm and local groups on how to accommodate to one another and the desired impacts from FDI for local development were not as expected in this case. In the context of developing countries, it should the problem of creating hybrid factories by FDI is complicated considerably by technology transfer issues.

Contested Resource Peripheries: Different Kinds of New Economic Spaces

Resource peripheries are not usually cited in relation to new economic spaces and are indeed marginal to theorizing in economic geography in general (Hayter et al., 2003). Yet industrialization has always been dependent upon the exploitation of resources and this exploitation has historically pushed the margin of settlement to all parts of the globe, no matter how remote. Resource peripheries continue to define important, fascinating new economic spaces and their structure, and restructuring is contingent upon instituted local as well as global dynamics.

In his classic article, Baldwin (1956) talked about export-based resource exploitation in two types of new economic space. The first refers to the exploitation of an empty land by immigrant entrepreneurs. The second refers to the establishment of capital-intensive 'plantation' economies by MNCs in the context of a dense indigenous population engaged in traditional activities. The purpose of Baldwin's analysis was to reveal the superiority of the immigrant entrepreneur model over the foreign-owned plantation model for local development. He argued that in the latter model local inputs were typically replaced by affiliated inputs from foreign sources, while decision making autonomy was restricted. In contrast, Baldwin argued that broadly based entrepreneurship was conducive to the development of local sources and to investments that diversify the economy in the long term. While Baldwin's (hypothetical) analysis referred to agriculture, it applies generally to all forms of export-based resource-based exploitation and can be readily extended to different types of scenarios.

Baldwin's framework is instructive because it formally recognizes that the exploitation of new economic spaces requires the establishment of regionally based institutions that define the global role of the local (or of the region). In the entrepreneur immigrant model, the entrepreneurs become the vested interests that define the 'classic' form of local institutions rooted in locally-based decision making and property rights. Moreover, successful regional diversification depends on entrepreneurial ability to sustain export markets and re-allocate export income locally. The plantation model also requires local property rights, access to dedicated infrastructure and a local workforce.

In the last several decades, there has been an emergence of widespread, possibly systemic conflict among resource peripheries reflect realities not anticipated in Baldwin's framework. In general, contemporary contested resource peripheries reveal at least two broad types of new economic spaces. First, in areas not hitherto exploited from the Amazon to Siberia, new resource development, export-based resource projects are facing new and renewed opposition from indigenous peoples and environmental groups. Indeed, the very notion of an 'empty land' has been undermined by the critical reactions of even relatively tiny impoverished populations to resource projects. This opposition to industry has frequently been conjoined and/or led by ENGOs who wish to preserve rare, yet surviving habitat. Second, environmental and indigenous conflicts have arisen in already established resource-based regions, effectively re-defining them as economic spaces. Over vast areas of the 'new worlds' of North America, Australia and New Zealand and South Africa resource exploitation both by entrepreneurs and large corporations often proceeded as if the land was empty. There were significant variations in how aboriginal populations were treated in these lands at the time of settlement. However, a capitalist landscape and institutions became deeply embedded in these regions and indigenous populations were typically marginalized in the process. Yet, across these regions, which are among the most advanced in the world indigenous concerns and rights, invariably involving the use of resources, have gained renewed vigour over the past several decades. Indeed, ENGO opposition to resource industries in these same rich countries has been extremely strong, focused and powerful.

The new political economy of resource peripheries has been further profoundly complicated by what may be described as 'perverse neo-liberalism'. Neo-liberalism qua globalization anticipates declining trade barriers. Such a trend is welcome for vested industrial interests in resource peripheries that depend on access to distant markets. In fact, resource-based exports have often long enjoyed relatively free access to the world's major markets. In reality, many resource peripheries have found their exports restricted directly and indirectly by the major markets of the world, namely the US, Japan and the European Union (EU). The most publicized cases are the many extremely poor developing countries whose agricultural exports have been undermined by a combination of tariff barriers and massive subsidies to farmers within the US, Japan and the EU. The latter countries have 'justified' these restrictions on the basis that exports from poor countries are 'unfair' in that they take advantage of low labour and other costs, and additionally restrict inward direct foreign investment. Yet, progress towards higher wages may be predicated in part on export income while, as noted, Baldwin long ago warned of the dangers for local development arising from the foreign controlled plantation model. Moreover, rich resource peripheries have also found their exports to major markets restricted on occasion. A graphic example of perverse neo-liberalism is provided by Canada's softwood lumber exports that enjoyed duty free access to US markets for almost four decades but which have faced punishing restrictions since 1983 (Hayter, 2000).

Elsewhere, in Australia and New Zealand, if neo-liberalism has not been perverse, it has still posed severe problems of structural change (Le Heron and Pawson, 1996; Stringer, 2001). In these countries resource exploitation was predicated on duty free access to British markets. However, this access was abruptly restricted on the UK's entry in to the EU in the 1970s. Consequently, for the past two decades, Australian and New Zealand exporters across the resource spectrum have been seeking new export markets, especially in Japan and Asia. This transformation has in turn required, and indeed is defined by, wholly new instituted global-local processes.

Within economic geography resource peripheries are typically deemed to be rather uninteresting 'slippery' spaces, basically export dependent, their fortunes buffeted by global forces, and much less fascinating than the diverse, 'sticky' places of core regions (Markusen, 1996). The reality is different. Resource peripheries are complex regions featuring clashes among powerful institutional forces, represented by aboriginalism, environmentalism, neo-liberalism as well as by vested industrial interests. The very intensity of these clashes confirms that geography matters in resource peripheries. The nature of the institutional clashes underlying contested resource peripheries varies around the globe. In the case of British Columbia's forest economy, US-based trade lobbies, ENGOs and Aboriginal Peoples are trying to convince the provincial government to remap the forests according to their own particular values (Hayter, 2003). The re-mappers share a dislike for the status quo, but diverge over solutions. Thus US interests seek privatization, the ENGOs promote conservation and aboriginal peoples are demanding treaties that re-assign the forests to them. Indeed, these rival claims have sustained a 'war in the woods' that is over two decades long. Meanwhile, British Columbia's provincial government desperately contemplates a range of new institutional solutions which include treaties, parks, community forests, market auctions, different types of tenure, industry working circles, and privatized forests. That solutions have yet to be found only confirms the importance of the creation of socially acceptable local institutions.

The industrial structuring and restructuring of resource peripheries has therefore become extraordinarily complex and the influence of new forms of instituted global-local dynamics created by cultural, environmental and trade politics cannot be ignored. Clearly, the geographical scope of debates on how to use resources is not confined to resource peripheries themselves. Indeed, these debates are globally extensive and are often bewildering (Soyez, 2002). But these spatially unbounded politics are also attempts to remap instituted rights within resource peripheries. This re-mapping is inherently problematic because it requires regions to synthetically engage in normative judgments in how to adjudicate competing, often globally supported claims representing different values, social legitimacies and responsibilities. Moreover, this synthesis, and the various associated forms of policy experimentation, is not just about the firm. Other institutions are vitally important and these institutions interact and clash in unique ways within regions. Within resource peripheries, the restructuring of industry can only be understood with reference to a multiplicity of institutional voices and these multiple voices express themselves in regionally unique ways.

Conclusion

Regions are complex institutions, not mere porous containers or contexts, as they are so often at least implicitly portrayed in economic geography and especially industrial geography. As institutions, regions proactively and reactively mediate, experiment and synthesize, albeit not always successfully, among diverse institutional interests. From an analytical perspective, there are (instituted) processes that define the uniqueness of regions than can only be understood from a multi-institutional perspective within regions. This claim is not to deny the importance of focusing on inter-regional firms and other important actors as they criss-cross regional boundaries. Indeed, such geographically unbounded work is vitally important if their geographical behaviour and their connections among regions are to be understood. But such perspectives are dominating economic geography and over-defining (geography's) meaning of globalization and new economic spaces. The tremendous flurry of work on regionally anchored industrial districts provides important caveats to this claim. This literature, however, which remains largely focused on firms and inter-firm relations, has tended to reduce regional difference by the classification of industrial districts into relatively few types. This, of course, does not address regions not featuring interesting industrial districts.

This chapter suggests that systematic, cross-boundary analyses of firms and other actors needs to be complemented by multi-institutional, regionally focused studies to uncover significant geographic relationships that would other wise be missed. The themes of hybrid factory and contested resource peripheries, especially within the context of new economic spaces, have been briefly introduced to indicate the potential of such regional approaches. Both hybrids and contested resource peripheries require nuanced knowledge of regionally defined institutional clashes and synthesis. Both themes raise fascinating policy issues concerning appropriate forms of (local) institutional behaviour and structures.

References

Adler, P. (1999), 'Recontextualisation and Factory-to-factory Knowledge Transfer from Japan to the United States: the Case of NSK', In Liker, M. Fruin, M. and Adler, P. (eds)

Remade in America: Transplanting and Transforming Japanese Management Systems. New York: Oxford University Press.

Allenby, B. R. (1999), *Industrial Ecology*, Upper Saddle River, NJ: Prentice Hall.

Baldwin, R. (1956) 'Patterns of Development in Newly Settled Regions', *Manchester School of Economics and Social Studies*, 24: pp. 161-179.

Barnes, T. J. (1987), 'Homo Economicus, Physical Metaphors, and Universal Models in Economic Geography', *The Canadian Geographer*, 31: pp. 299-308.

Barnes, T. J. (1996), *The Logics of Dislocation: Models, Metaphors and Meanings of Economics Space*, New York: Guilford Press.

Barnes, T. J. (1999), 'Industrial Geography, Institutional Economics and Innis', In T.J. Barnes and M. Gertler, *The New Industrial Geography: Regions, Regulations and Institutions*, London: Routledge, pp. 1-22.

Barnes, T. J. (2001), 'Retheorizing Economic Geography: From the Quantitative Revolution to the "Cultural Turn"', *Annals Association of the American Geographers*, 91: pp. 546-65.

Barnes, T. J., Hayter, R. and Hay, E. (2001), 'Stormy Weather: Cyclones, Harold Innis, and Port Alberni, British Columbia', *Environment and Planning A*, 33: pp. 2127-2147.

Bradshaw, M. (1990), 'New Regional Geography, Foreign Area Studies and Perestroika', *Area*, 22: pp. 315-322.

Britton, J. N. H. (1974), 'Environmental Adaptation of Industrial Plants: Service Linkages, Locational Environment and Organization', In Hamilton, F.E. I. (ed.) *Spatial Perspectives on Industrial Organization and Decision-making*. London: Wiley, pp. 363-392.

Britton, J. N. H. (1976), 'The Influence of Corporate Organisation and Ownership on the Linkages of Indusrial Plants: A Canadian Inquiry', *Economic Geography*, 52: pp. 311-324.

Britton, J. N. H. (1980), 'Industrial Dependence and Technological Underdevelopment: Canadian Consequences of Direct Foreign Investment', *Regional Studies*, 14: pp. 181-200.

Britton, J. N. H. (1999), 'Does Nationality Still Matter?', In Barnes, T. and Gertler, M. (eds) *The New Industrial Geography*. London: Routledge, pp. 238-264.

Castells (1996), *The Rise of the Network Society*, Oxford: Blackwell.

Dauvergne, P. (1997), *Shadows in the Forest: Japan and the Politics of Timber in Southeast Asia*, Cambridge, Mass: MIT Press.

Florida, R. (1996), 'Regional Creative Destruction: Production, Organization, Globalization and the Economic Transformation of the Midwest', *Economic Geography*, 72: pp. 314-334.

Fredriksson, C. G. and Lindmark, L. G. (1979), 'From Firms to Systems of Firms: A Study of Interregional Interdependence in a Dynamic Society', In F. E. I. Hamilton and G. J. R. Linge (eds), *Spatial Analysis, Industry and the Industrial Environment*, 1: pp. 155-86. New York: Wiley.

Freeman, C. (1988), 'Japan: A New National System of Innovation?', In G Dosi, C. Freeman, R. Nelson and G. Silverberg (eds), *Technical Change and Economic Theory*, pp. 330-48. London: Frances Pinter.

Freeman, C. (1992), *The Economics of Hope*, London: Pinter.

Fruin, M. (1992), *The Japanese Enterprise System*, Oxford: Clarendon Press.

Hayter, R. (2000), *Flexible Crossroads: The Restructuring of British Columbia's Forest Economy*, Vancouver: UBC Press.

Hayter, R. (2003), 'The War in the Woods: Globalization, Post-Fordist Restructuring and the Contested Remapping of British Columbia's Forest Economy', *Annals of the Association of American Geographers* 96.

Hayter, R. (2004), 'Dissenting Institutionalism as a Framework of Economic Geography: The Embeddedness, Evolution and Differentiation of Regions', *Geografiska Annaler*, pp. 95-115.

Hayter, R., Barnes, T. and Bradshaw, M. J. (2003), 'Relocating Resource Peripheries to the Core of Economic Geography's Theorizing: Rationale and Agenda', *Area*, 35: pp. 15-23.

Hayter, R. and Le Heron, R. B. (2002), 'Industrialization, Techno-Economic Paradigms and the Environment', In R. Hayter and R. Le Heron (eds), *Knowledge, Industry and Environment: Institutions and Innovation in Territorial Perspective*, London: Ashgate, pp. 11-30.

Hodgson, G. M. (2001), *How Economics Forgot History*, London: Routledge.

Holmen, H. (1995), 'What's New and What's Regional in the "New Regional Geography?"', *Geografiska Annaler*, 77 B: pp. 47-63.

Itagaki, H. (ed.) (1997), *The Japanese Production System: Hybrid Factories in East Asia*, London: MacMillan.

Johnston, R.J. (1984), 'The World is Our Oyster', *Transactions of the Institute of British Geographers*, 9: pp. 443-59.

Krumme, G. (1969), 'The Geography of Enterprise', *Economic Geography*, 45: pp. 30-40.

Krumme, G. (1970), 'The Inter-Regional Corporation and the Region', *Tijdschrift voor Economicsche en Sociale Geografie*, 61: pp. 318-33.

Lee, R. and Wills, J. (eds) (1997), *Geographies of Economies*, London: Arnold.

Le Heron, R. and Pawson, E. (eds) (1996), *Changing Places. New Zealand in the Nineties*, Auckland: Longman Paul.

Liker, J., Fruin, M. and Adler, P. (eds) (1999), *Remade in America: Transplanting and Transforming Japanese Management Systems*, New York: Oxford University Press.

Mair, A. (1994), *Honda's Global Local Corporation*, New York: St. Martin's Press.

Markusen, A. (1996), 'Sticky Places in Slippery Space: A Typology of Industrial Districts', *Economic Geography*, 72: pp. 293-313.

Martin, R. (1994), 'Economic Theory and Human Geography', In D. Gregory, R. L. Martin and G. E. Smith, *Human Geography: Society, Space and Social Science*, Basingstoke: Macmillan, pp. 21-53.

Martin, R. (1999), 'The New "Geographical Turn" in Economics: Some Critical Reflections', *Cambridge Journal of Economics*, 23: pp. 65-91.

Martin, R. (2000), 'Institutional Approaches in Economic Geography', In E. Sheppard and T. J. Barnes, *A Companion to Economic Geography*, Oxford: Blackwell, pp. 77-94.

Martin, R. (2001), The Geographer as Social Critic – Getting Indignant about Income Equality, *Transactions, Institute of British Geographers*, 26: pp. 267-72.

Maskell, P. (2001), 'The Firm in Economic Geography', *Economic Geography*, 77: pp. 329-344.

Patchell, J. (1996), 'Kaleidoscope Economies: The Processes of Cooperation, Competition, and Control in Regional Economic Development', *Annals of the Association of American Geographers*, 86: pp. 481-506.

Peck, J. and Miyamachi, Y. (1994), 'Reinterpreting the "Japanese miracle": Rgulationalist Perspectives on Post-1945 Japanese Growth and Crisis', In Le Heron, R. and Ock Park, S. (eds) *The Asian Pacific Rim and Globalization*. Aldershot: Ashgate, pp. 37-59.

Pil and MacDuffie (1999), 'Transferring Competitive Advantage Across Borders: A Study of Japanese Auto Tranmsplants in North America', In Liker, M. Fruin, M. and Adler, P. (eds) *Remade in America: Transplanting and Transforming Japanese Management Systems*. New York: Oxford University Press.

Sayer, A. (1997), 'The Dialectic of Culture and Economy', In Lee, R. and Wills, J. (eds) *Geographies of Economies*. London: Arnold, pp. 16-26.

Sheard, P. (1983), 'Auto Production systems in japan: Organization and location Features', *Australian Geographical Studies*, 21: pp. 49-68.

Soyez, D. (1988), 'Scandinavian Silviculture in Canada: Entry and Performance Barriers', *The Canadian Geographer*, 32: pp. 133-40.

Soyez, D. (2002), 'Environmental Knowledge, the Power of Framing and Industrial Change', In R. Hayter and R. Le Heron (eds), *Knowledge, Industry and Environment: Institutions and Innovation in Territorial Perspective*, Aldershot: Ashgate, pp. 187-208.

Storper, M. (1997), *Worlds of Production*, Cambridge, MA: Harvard University Press.

Stringer, C. (2001), 'Globalization of the New Zealand Forestry Industry: The New Impact of Japanese Linkages', In R. Hayter and R. Le Heron (eds), *Knowledge, Industry and Environment: Institutions and Innovation in Territorial Perspective*, Aldershot: Ashgate, pp. 253-272.

Chapter 18

Potential and Limitation of New Industrial Policy in Korea: Fostering Innovative Clusters

Ji-Sun Choi

Introduction

Korea suffered from the 1997 IMF financial crisis, although it had been considered one of the most successful countries newly industrialized countries (NICs) in Asia during the 1980s. This prompted government-led industrial restructuring. The new administration that took office in 2003 has continued to reform the existing inappropriate economic structure, seeking to develop South Korea into an economic hub of northeast Asia in the 21st century. To this end, the government has targeted balanced national development, along with promoting new economic growth.

Balancing national development between the Greater Seoul Metropolitan Area (GSMA) and provincial regions is a formidable challenge. Many policies since the 1970s have attempted to relieve the over-concentration around the GSMA. Despite persistent efforts these policies have been unsatisfactory. For example, although the growth rate of the employment of manufacturing industries in the GSMA decreased, the decrease in the growth rate contributed to the increase in the growth rate of manufacturing employment only in the Chungcheng area located immediately adjacent to the GSMA, rather than leading to more geographically balanced national development across the whole country (Choo et al., 2002, p. 133). Contrawise, statistics indicate that the over-concentration around the GSMA did not decrease as much as it was expected. About 57 per cent of the manufacturing firms with more than 5 employees were concentrated in the GSMA, while it only occupied about 12 per cent in terms of land area at the end of 2000 (MOCT, 2002, p. 104). Nonetheless, the concentration remains high. Of the nation's top 100 companies, 91 are headquartered in the GSMA. The percentage for public enterprises headquarters in the GSMA is 83 per cent (ACRPT, 2003, p. 1). In addition, the growth of knowledge-based economy results in the re-concentration of knowledge-intensive industries around the GSMA because the area is full of competitive high-quality human capital as well as ICT infrastructure.

As a way to relieve the over-concentration around the GSMA and to boost the regional economy, the present government is trying to develop region-specific strategic industries and support regional innovative clusters, building on the concepts of National Innovation System (NIS), Regional Innovation System (RIS) and innovation clusters, introduced by the previous administration of Kim Dae-Jung (1998–2002). Regional Innovation System (RIS) and innovative clusters in particular have become central in policy discussion. They were adopted as tools by which regional competitiveness and regional innovative capacity could be improved.

This chapter offers an interpretation of how Korean industrial agglomeration policies have been developed and examines the potential and limitation of current new innovative cluster policies to establish successful RIS. The chapter begins with the theoretical background of innovation clusters and the historical trajectory of industrial agglomeration policies in Korea. This is followed by a review of the contents of cluster polices after a new administration took office in 2003. Potential problems that may be caused by current industrial innovative cluster policies are discussed, before consideration of the policy implications.

Background on Innovative Cluster Policy

'An innovative cluster' is the word on every policy maker's lips these days in Korea. Innovative cluster policies aim to improve regional economies by encouraging physical co-location among local firms and building formal and informal networks. This concept appears to be a powerful motivation for transforming the landscapes of existing economic spaces, and has been popular since the early 1990s (Rosenfeld, 2001). The introduction of innovative clusters is particularly attractive to local governments because the policy is expected to promote indigenous regional growth and to improve regional competitiveness (Lee, 2001, p. 308). Yet, the recognition of the fruits of firms' physical agglomeration is hardly new. Why then a surge in popularity?

Marshall (1922) first mentioned the advantages of the agglomeration of the firms in the same and related industries (Hayter, 1997, p. 330). Marshall's work was rediscovered when Piore and Sabel (1984) dealt with flexible and specialized industrial districts in Italy. Since then, industrial districts have been highlighted again from various perspectives. Diverse types of industrial districts were identified and their characteristics and influences on existing economic spaces were researched (Park, S. O., 1996). Key academics such as Michael Porter have raised the profile of policy pertaining to industrial clusters. According to Porter (1998, p. 78), clusters are geographic concentrations of interconnected companies and institutions in a particular field. They are made up of upstream and downstream industries, complementary industries, government bodies and other related institutions. Although the definition and the elements of clusters are still debatable, Porter's view of clusters is appealing to policy makers and business managers.

The debate on clusters and industrial districts over the last decade has been more focused on the role of innovation as facilitator than as cost minimizer. As innovation is regarded as a result of the interaction between tacit and articulated knowledge, the construction of common values and norms becomes essential for sharing various knowledge among business actors. The limit of the transfer of such knowledge among remote business actors enhances the importance of regional innovative capacity, which helps firms to improve the innovative capability through collective learning processes (Lawson and Lorenz, 1999).

The advent of the knowledge-based economy idea in the 1990s gave new life to the innovative cluster notion. In the knowledge-based economy knowledge is regarded as more important than traditional production factors such as land, labour and capital. The source of wealth has moved from national assets (i.e. land and relatively unskilled labour), to tangible created assets (i.e. buildings, machinery and equipment, finance), to intangible created assets (i.e. knowledge and information of all kinds) (Dunning, 2000, p. 8). Knowledge-intensive industries tend to be geographically congregated in a few locations, rather than dispersed across the country (Park, S. O. and Choi, 2000, p. 9). For example, as one of the most representative knowledge-intensive activities, advanced producer services have been clustered in Seoul, especially in three local areas within Seoul (Park and Nahm, 1998). The tendency toward the local clustering of knowledge-intensive industries results from the difficulty in transferring cumulated tacit knowledge and local know-how across space (Audretsch, 2000).

From Industrial Complexes to Innovative Clusters in Korea

Initial Development of Industrial Complexes

Within the context of Korean government policy before the 1980s industrial complexes were just the agglomerations of production activities. The establishment of initial industrial complexes was the result of industrial sectoral policies to promote several strategic industries. Ulsan Industrial Complex was established in 1962, in accordance with the first Five-year Economic Development Plan. Export industrial complexes were established under the Export Industrial Estate Development Promotion Law (1964). Industrial Site Development Promotion Law (1973) encouraged the development of heavy and chemical industrial complexes (Park, S.O., 1991, p. 83). These policies attempted to agglomerate manufacturing plants in specific areas geographically for the rapid industrialization based on the external economies of scale. The policy direction added to the bipolar industrial concentration in the GSMA and the Southeastern Area.

Over the same period the Korean government enacted laws in terms of industrial spatial polices to reduce a regional economic disparity between the areas along the axis of Seoul-Busan (from the northwest to the southeast) and the axis from the northeast to southwest of Korean peninsula. National industrial complexes, local industrial complexes, and agricultural and industrial complexes were designated and developed under several laws by central and local governments. The Local Industrial Development Law (1970), the Free Export Zone Establishment Law (1970), and the Industrial Distribution Law (1972) were enacted. The Farm Household Income Source Development Law (1983) sequentially enabled the designation and development of rural industrial complexes. The Industrial Placement and Factory Construction Act (1990) replaced the Industrial Placement Act (1975) and the Industrial Complex Management Act (1977). The Act simplified the complex industrial location related Acts and supported firms to easily determine the establishment of new factories and the relocation of existing factories.

Development of High-technology Industrial Complexes

In addition to the establishment of the industrial complexes pertaining to production functions, local high-technology industrial complexes have been established since the late 1980s. The history of high-technology industrial complexes dates back to the Seoul Research and Development (R&D) Complex located in Hongneung in Seoul (Park, J.R. et al., 1999; Kwon, 2002). The Korean government pushed the agglomeration of various research institutes for the improvement of R&D efficiency in the late 1960s. Daedeok Science Town was then established in Daejeon in the early 1970s as a way to decentralize R&D capability to provincial areas and has evolved as the most successful R&D complex in Korea. The above two complexes placed more importance on agglomerating diverse types of R&D institutes without focusing on industrial agglomeration.

The central and local governments intended to actively stimulate regional technological capabilities in the late 1980s and the early 1990s. Seven Local High-Technology Industrial Complexes were founded and the clustering of high-technology industrial firms was encouraged. However, despite these efforts, most had difficulty in attracting high-technology industries. The following reasons have been identified (Kwon, 2002, pp. 92-93): Local governments failed to get sufficient financial support to complete the development of Local High-Technology Industrial Complexes; The number of high-technology industrial firms was not enough to maintain the Local High-Technology Industrial Complexes in provincial areas, because most local firms were related to only mass production and assembly industries; Local governments concentrated on building physical infrastructures and did not give enough consideration to improving innovative networking among related actors inside the complexes and to establishing advanced producer services for encouraging firms' innovation.

Boom of Creating Innovative Clusters in Korea

Many existing industrial complexes have adopted the concept of innovative clusters since the late 1990s. Industrial complexes with only production functions have added R&D, and R&D complexes have included production functions. They commonly endeavor to improve local networking among innovative actors inside the complexes and global networking with external actors.

Several ministries also plan to establish specialized innovative clusters, which fit well with the unique goals of each ministry (Table 18.1). The Ministry of Commerce, Industry and Energy (MOCIE) supports Technoparks and plans to support Knowledge-based Industrial Clusters. The Ministry of Finance and Economy (MOFE) has devised policies related to cluster creation including Free Economic Zones and Special Regional Development Zones (SRDZs). Similarly, the Ministry of Science and Technology (MOST) has plans to establish Regional R&D Clusters, Daedeok R&D Special Zone and Science Research Complexes. Since 1996 The Ministry of Culture and Tourism (MCT) has formulated policies to establish Cultural Technology (CT) Centers. The Ministry of Information and Communication (MIC) has also implemented a policy pertaining to Regional Soft Towns since 1999. In addition, new types of Local High-Technology Industrial Complexes have been established since 2000 by some local governments with the help of the MOCIE and the MOCT. Furthermore, New Local High-Technology Industrial Complexes accept innovative cluster policies. They mainly concentrate on searching for the way to increase in the innovative capability of local high-technology innovative firms through a strong local and global networking.

Table 18.1   Examples of Plans for Creating Innovative Clusters in Korea (2003)

Mainly-related ministry	*Policy*	*Note*
Ministry of Commerce, Industry and Energy	Technopark Projects	Act on the Support of Industrial Technology Complexes
	Knowledge-based Industrial Clusters	Industrial Cluster Promotion and Factory Construction Act
Ministry of Finance and Economy	Free Economic Zones	Act on Designation and Operation of Free Economic Zones
	Special Regional Development Zones	Planning to propose a law, which will go into effect in 2004
Ministry of Science and Technology	Regional R&D Clusters	About 20 clusters will be supported by 2008 (nationwide)
	Science Research Complexes	About 3 complexes will be supported in 2004
	Daedeok R&D Special Zone	Planning to propose a law in 2004
Ministry of Culture and Tourism	Cultural Technology Clusters	Basic Act on Development of Cultural Industries
Ministry of Information and Communication	Regional Soft Towns	Act on Development of Software Industries

Source: Websites of each Ministry and related internal materials (2003).

The MOCIE began constructing Technoparks in late 1997, in order to establish growth centers for the development of NIS (Kwon, 2001, p. 47). The Technopark is seen as an advanced type of initial industrial complexes. The MOCIE enacted the Industrial Cluster Promotion and the Factory Construction Act at the end of 2002, substituting the existing Industrial Placement and Factory Construction Act. The new Factory Construction Act deals with the development of innovative clusters and plans to promote the clusters of knowledge-based industrial firms. This act is differentiated from earlier legislation because it is not simply focused on the agglomeration of industrial sectors, but also on the encouragement of systematic cooperation among the actors in industrial complexes.

The CT clusters of the MCT attempt to create synergistic effects by putting together firms, universities, research institutes and venture capital pertaining to cultural industries in specific areas. Likewise, the MIC Regional Soft Towns also promote the agglomeration of firms, research institutes, universities, venture incubating facilities, venture capitals and public authorities related to computer software and information technologies. The MCT CT clusters and the MIC Regional Soft Towns share a common goal to encourage formal and informal networks among the actors within clusters, over and above physical proximity. Although these types of clusters were encouraged between 1998 and 2000 they have been further strengthened by the new administration.

Free Economic Zones of the MOFE are defined as the area that is developed with the aim of improving the business environment for foreign-invested enterprises and the living conditions for foreigners. These zones are expected to contribute to balanced national development, going one step further than existing Free Export Zones. Furthermore, SRDZs are introduced. According to the MOFE, they are modeled on the Japanese Special Zones for Structural Reform. SRDZs aim at cutting through regulations and providing a good environment for constructing diverse types of innovative clusters related to region-specific products. SRDZs are not limited to industrial clusters, but include such special zones as R&D, tourism, urban beautification, and venture firms. Local governments are encouraged to apply for SRDZs with their own specific items. The relaxation of regulations is an essential part of SRDZs.

The plan to establish Daedeok R&D Special Zone by the MOST is part of developing South Korea into an economic hub of northeast Asia in future. The government expects that the harmonization between a very high level of R&D and high-technology based industrial functions inside Daedock area will create an ideal type of innovative clusters, akin to Silicon Valley. The MOST also plans to establish Regional R&D Clusters and designate Science Research Complexes in 2004. These Regional R&D clusters are intended to activate regional R&D capabilities for region-specific industries in provincial areas. Examples of clusters that already exist or are under construction are illustrated in Figure 18.1. Five types of industrial clusters are presented: Local High-Technology Industrial Clusters, Cultural Technology Clusters, Regional Soft Towns, Technoparks and Free Economic Zones.

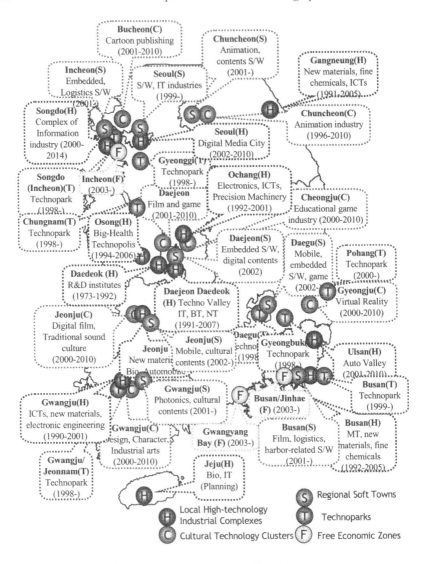

Figure 18.1   Examples of Cluster Policies by Region

Source: DIP (2003), MCT (2003), Kwon (2001), Kwon (2002), MOFE (2003).

Overview of New Innovative Cluster Policy in Korea

The new government's policy seeks to grow innovative clusters for balanced national development and the improvement of national competitiveness (Table 18.2). New opportunities are provided to underdeveloped regions through physical infrastructure, and more importantly, enhancing local networks among innovative actors based on the development of innovative clusters. Autonomous local governments as well as central government ministries are expected to play crucial roles in developing knowledge-based innovative industrial clusters. This section briefly summarizes the plans devised by the MOCIE, which is mainly responsible for balanced national industrial development.

The MOCIE fundamentally aims to integrate production, science and technology, and business supporting systems into an innovative cluster for establishing RIS, in regions that have self-supporting innovative capacity (Figure 18.2). Several industrial policies have been established for this purpose (Yun, 2003). First, production, science and technology (R&D institutes, universities, and laboratories, etc.), and business-support (financing, logistics, and marketing, etc.) are gathered in a specific region for establishing innovative clusters, based on hardware infrastructures such as existing industrial complexes, highways, harbors and airports. The networks among innovative actors in regions are supported and strengthened. The areas where knowledge-based industries are already (or will be) agglomerated are designated as Knowledge-based Industrial Clusters upon application by local governments to the central government. Regulations are relaxed and local firms with innovative capability are supported. Physical social infrastructures are also built with the support of the central government.

Table 18.2   New Directions for Regional Development Policies (2003)

Regional Development	*Previous policies*	*New policies*
Policy goal	Building industrial complexes	Spatial diffusion of innovative clusters
Measurement	Establishing physical infrastructure (Hardware)	Establishing Regional Innovation System (Software)
Promoting system	Focusing on individual policy programs	Focusing on institutional and systematic support as packages
Procedures	Unilateral support from central government (Top-down)	Enhancement of the role of autonomous local government (Bottom-up)

Source: DPBNDPT (2003: 5).

Table 18.3   Financial Self-support Index of Local Governments

(Unit: No. of Local Gov't, per cent, Reference year: 2002)

Types of Local Gov't Distribution	Total	(%)	Metropolitan city and Provinces	City	County	Autonomous District
Total	248	100	16	74	89	69
Less than 10%	4	2	-	-	4	-
10~less than 30%	116	47	7	26	76	7
30~less than 50%	77	31	1	19	8	49
50~less than 70%	31	13	5	18	1	7
70~less than 90%	16	6	2	10	-	4
90% or more	4	2	1	1	-	2

Note: Index=(Local Tax + Non-tax Revenue)/(Total Budget of General Account) * 100.
Source: MOGAHA (2003).

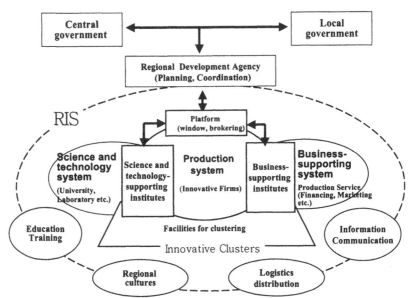

Figure 18.2   Policy Model for Regional Innovation System based on Innovative Clusters

Source: Kim (2003).

Regional Development Agencies (RDAs) are likely to be introduced. They are known to play crucial roles in holding up various supporting programs systematically. Another important role of RDAs is to coordinate related policies by the ministries of central government and each local government and to get rid of duplicate policy promotions. RDAs comprise experts on industries, academics, research institutes, local press and NGOs. They are expected to select regional competitive industries and to manage the financial support from the central government for promoting them. Local universities and colleges are supported as the nuclei to build innovative clusters and to enhance the networks among local innovative actors. The capability of R&D and commercialization of local universities and colleges are intensified through the support of researchers and technological equipments. The new organizations that encourage technology transfer between local universities and local industrial firms are constructed inside local universities and colleges.

Fiscal support programs for region-specific industries in provincial areas and metropolitan cities are expanding. Plans involving more than one province or metropolitan city are also encouraged. A 'Plan Contract' system has been introduced to guarantee a stable relationship between central and local governments, considered vital for the successful development of local industries. Subsidies for balanced national development are available to help firms move to provincial areas. Collective logistics centers covering more than one province are being built, promoting regional industrial development. Finally, existing industrial complexes are re-developed as growth poles for the creation of regional innovation. This is in line with the introduction of Complex Innovation System (CIS), which was introduced by Korea Industrial Complex Corporation (KICOX, 2001). In addition to new innovative cluster, efforts are being made to transform existing industrial complexes into innovative clusters.

According to MOCIE's plan, the new era of localization will proceed step-by-step on a long-term basis. During the first stage (2003~07), RIS will be fostered with hardware and software infrastructure. The fruits of the newly constructed RIS are diffused at the second stage (2008~12). Income differences may be reduced between the GSMA and provincial areas. Self-supporting regional economic systems will be completed cyclically at the final stage (2012~17).

In addition to the promotion of local innovative clusters, local technology innovation centers are envisaged (Kwon, 2001, p. 125). Thus, the MOCIE supports Technology Incubating Centers (TIC), Technology and Business Incubators (TBI) and Technomarts. The MOST also supports Science Research Centers (SRC), Engineering Research Centers (ERC), Regional Research Centers (RRC) and Research Information Centers. MIC supports the Centers for University Venture Startups and the Centers for Information and Communication Research, and centers relevant to Small and Medium Business Administration (SMBA) including BI, Consortia of Industry, academics, research, the Centers for University Venture Startups and the Centers for SMEs.

A Blind Faith in the Potential of Innovative Clusters?

Most local governments and the central government in Korea have made the effort to reinvigorate regional economies with industrial innovative cluster policies. The words 'cluster' and 'innovation' have dominated Korean society with the advent of the knowledge-based economy and the prevalence of cluster and RIS theory. Many local governments are desperate to create their own unique clusters and RIS. Unfortunately, however, in many cases the creation of innovative clusters is still focused on the creation of large buildings. The emphasis on hardware infrastructures may lead to the construction of the production complexes that were far from local governments' original intention.

A major side effect faced by Korea is the overheated competition for creating new clusters. Koreans seem to have a fantasy of the '-Valley' notion, in an attempt to capture through association the perceived successes of Silicon Valley. The dream is an idealistic development of innovative clusters with flawless collaboration among innovative actors inside their innovative clusters. In many cases, however, it is hard to find a clear difference in local plans. Although most local governments seem to recognize the importance of invisible well-organized networks and collaboration for the success in their clusters, the measures used are sometimes superficial.

Another problem comes from the fact that most local governments are eager to attract only promising new industries. After the Kim Dae-Jung administration (1997–2002) placed much importance on six promising new technologies, otherwise known as 6T, including IT (Information Technology), BT (Bio Technology), NT (Nano Technology), ET (Environment Technology), CT (Culture Technology) and ST (Space Technology). 6T terminology is readily found in the report on the creation of regional innovative clusters. The introduction of a knowledge-based economy has heightened interest in the promise of the new. Many local governments have included at least one of the new technologies in their local strategic industries. Some local governments simply follow the fashion and choose some of the industries without adequately considering their regional characteristics. Sometimes less importance is placed on the advancement of existing traditional manufacturing industries. Even when local governments do not insist on the new technologies, they often select the industries in vogue, with which they have little experience.

The effort to create new local clusters is often undertaken with disregard to the plans of neighboring local governments. Rather, the policy directions for creating innovative clusters sometimes duplicate those of regional neighbours. Local governments do not seem to consider wide areas that cross specific regional boundaries and the harmonization among clusters. Even though the central government plans to construct supra-regional clusters that connect several local clusters, collaboration is unlikely to be sincere.

According to the data collected, a small number of regions are favored for innovative clusters, despite the initial intention to promote the diffusion of innovation into diverse types of provincial areas. Such metropolitan cities as Incheon, Daejeon, Jeonju, Gwangju, Daegu, Busan and Ulsan, all with large populations, feature as locations for clusters (Figure 18.1). The effort to create innovative clusters was limited to a few regions that already had considerable capability in terms of human as well as social capital. It is related to the problems regarding over-investment in specific regions and the failure of balanced national investment.

The new administration's policy for balanced national development begins with the diffusion of power to local governments. Local governments are expected to play pivotal roles in devising and managing local innovative clusters. The central government emphasizes that local governments should bear the main financial responsibility. In reality, however, the financial self-support index of Korean local governments is not as high as expected (Table 18.3). About 47 per cent of local governments have a financial self-support index of less than 50 per cent. Therefore, ways of increasing local governments' financial self-support should be framed first.

Concluding Remarks

This chapter attempted to summarize the historical development of industrial cluster policies in order to understand current innovative cluster policy and think about the potential and the limitation of the new innovative cluster policy as a path to industrial and regional economic development in Korea.

In the early industrialization of Korea, the development of various industrial complexes played a critical role in national economic growth. In the initial stage of industrial complexes, the complexes were simply the agglomeration of manufacturing plants. In the evolutionary development of the complexes, some have taken on innovative clusters to some degree by adding diverse functions together beyond a simple production function and enhancing networks among the actors with different functions. Before the 1960s, the Korean government placed more importance on sectoral policies than locational ones, in order to progress the Korean economy as quickly as possible. As the national economy has increased in size, the issue of balanced national development has become important for total national economic growth. Although industrial complexes began to be built as a choice for developing several strategic industries at the initial stage, they later became accepted as a major measure of locational policies to promote regional economic development.

The construction of industrial complexes was favored because they seemed to guarantee a quick and visible success in regional economic growth. Recognition of the importance of R&D activities led to the building of industrial complexes focusing on R&D function. The importance of local high-technology industrial complexes accelerated in the 1980s and 1990s. Since the end of the 1990s, RIS and innovative clusters have been the buzzwords for regional development. Many types of policies have been planned and carried out by the ministries of the central government and local governments. However, even though they attempted to embody their own unique policy goals, their policies were largely undifferentiated.

Thus, anxiety about the feasibility and future of those policies should be raised. The overheated competition to create new clusters and the adherence to new promising industries without thought to regional fit may cause serious problems. Harmonizing with neighboring local clusters should not be forgotten. The heavy burden to show quick and visible success has encouraged goving top priority to physical infrastructure, instead of concentrating on long-term plans for encouraging local and global networks among innovative actors. But perhaps most crucial is the low level of the financial self-support index of Korean local governments which prevents them from functioning as the main bodies to implement innovative cluster policies and RIS.

References

ACRPT (Administrative Capital Relocation Project Team) (2003), *The Need for Administrative Capital Relocation and its Present Condition (in Korean)*, Administrative Capital Relocation Project Team of the Korean Government, Available at: http://www.newcapital.go.kr.

Audretsch, D. B. (2000), 'Knowledge, Globalization, and Regions: An Economist's Perspective', In J. H. Dunning (ed.), *Regions, Globalization, and the Knowledge-Based Economy*, New York: Oxford University Press, pp. 63-81.

Choo, S., Moon, M.-S. and Jeong, J-H. (2002), 'Regulations for the Capital Region and Metropolitan Knowledge-Based Industrial Development', *Journal of the Korean Regional Science Association*, 18(3): pp. 127-138.

DIP (The Center for Digital Industry Promotion of Daegu) (2003), *Internal report on the spatial distribution of Regional Soft Towns*, Daegu: DIP.

DPBNDPT (Diffusion of Power and Balanced National Development Project Team) (2003), Regional development based on specialization in Korea (in Korean), Report to the Presidential Transition Team of the Korean Government.

Dunning, J. H. (2000), 'Regions, Globalization, and the Knowledge Economy: The Issues Stated', In J. H. Dunning (ed.), *Regions, Globalization, and the Knowledge-Based Economy*, New York: Oxford University Press, pp. 7-41.

Hayter, R. (1997), The Dynamics of Industrial Location: The factory, the Firm and the Production System, Chichester: John Wiley & Sons Ltd.

KICOX (Korea Industrial Complex Corporation) (2001), *Plans for Complex Innovation System (in Korean)*, Seoul: KICOX.

Kim, S.-B. (2003), *Construction of Regional Innovation System for Balanced National Development in Korea* (MS PowerPoint material, in Korean), Workshop for Balanced National Development in Korea, Presidential Committee on Balanced National Development, the Ministry of Commerce, Industry, and Energy.

Kwon, Y.-S. (2001), *Model Technopark Project and Building the Regional Innovation System in Korea* (in Korean), Anyang: Korea Research Institute for Human Settlements.

Kwon, Y.-S. (2002), 'Development of Local High-Technology Industrial Complexes in Korea' (in Korean), *Kukto*, Korea Research Institute for Human Settlements, 252: pp. 84-98.

Lawson, C. and Lorenz, E. (1999), 'Collective Learning, Tacit Knowledge and Regional Innovative Capacity', *Regional Studies*, 33(4): pp. 305-317.

Lee, K. (2001), 'From Fragmentation to Integration: Development Process of Innovation Clusters in Korea', *Science, Technology and Society*, 6(2): pp. 305-327.

Lee, K. (2003), 'Promoting Innovative Clusters Through the Regional Research Centre (RRC) Policy Programme in Korea', *European Planning Studies*, 11(1): pp. 25-39.

Marshall, A. (1922), *The Principles of Economics*, London: Macmillan.

MCT (Ministry of Culture and Tourism) (2003), Internal report on Strategies for Constructing Cultural Technology Clusters (in Korean), MCT.

MOCT (Ministry of Construction and Transportation) (2002), *A Handbook of National Land Development* (in Korean), MOCT. (available at http://www.moct.go.kr).

MOFE (Ministry of Finance and Economy) (2003), *Korean Free Economic Zones are the Future of the Northeast Asia* (in Korean), MOFE. (available at http://www.mofe.go.kr).

MOGAHA (Ministry of Government Administration and Home Affairs) (2003), Statistical Yearbook, MOGAHA. (http://www.mogaha.go.kr).

Park, J.-R., Park, Y.-K. and Song, Y.-P. (1999), Suggestions for the Efficient Development of Local High-Technology Industrial Complexes After the IMF Bailout (in Korean), Seoul: Samsung Economic Research Institute.

Park, S. O. and Choi, J.-S. (2000), 'Development of Knowledge-Based Industry for Promoting Growth: Theory and Policy Issues' (in Korean), *The Korean Journal of Regional Science*, 16(2): pp. 1-25.

Park, S. O. and Nahm, K.-B. (1998), 'Spatial Structure and Inter-Firm Networks of Technical and Information Producer Services in Seoul, Korea', *Asia Pacific Viewpoint*, 39(2): pp. 209-219.

Park, S. O. (1991), 'Government Management of Industrial Change in the Republic of Korea', In D. C. Rich and G. J. R. Linge (eds), *The State and the Spatial Management of Industrial Change*, London and New York: Routledge.

Park, S. O. (1996), 'Networks and Embeddness in the Dynamic Types of New Industrial Districts', *Progress in Human Geography*, 20(4): pp. 476-493.

Piore, M. and Sabel, C. (1984), *The Second Industrial Divide: Possibilities for Prosperity*, New York: Basic Books.

Porter, Michael E. (1998), 'Clusters and the New Economics of Competition', *Harvard Business Review*, November-December, pp. 77-90.

Rosenfeld, S. A. (2001), 'Backing into Clusters: Retrofitting Public Polices', Presented at John F. Kennedy School Symposium, Harvard University, March 29-30.

Yun, Y.-S. (2003), 'Region-Specific Development through Industrial Clusters', *Nara Economy*, 2003–2004, Korea Development Institute, pp. 29-33.

Chapter 19

Academic Economic Geography and Sites of Economic Geography Practice: Examples and Reflections from New Zealand

Richard Le Heron

I find it odd that various discussions of the nature of geography pay such scant critical or reflective attention to the ways in which different geographical knowledges generated across such a wide array of institutional bases course through our own disciplinary structure. It is years since Foucault taught us that knowledge/power/institutions lock together in particular modes of governmentality, yet few have cared to turn that spotlight on the discipline of geography itself (Harvey, 2000, p. 6).

Introduction

This chapter explores where economic geography might go were economic geographers to explicitly confront the nature and effects of their academic work. My argument is as follows. Economic geographers could do more than study old and new economic spaces: we could actively *engage* in their creation through the ideas, methods and techniques we use in teaching, research, writing, consultancy and advisory roles. What is needed is more conscious reflection on how economic geography, at large, consists of discourses and practices with differing potential for impacts and creative change in societal settings. Economic geography is interpreted here as a community (FitzSimmons, 2004) of academics, students, practitioners and other supportive actors who are doing two main things: *representing* the world through models, analysis, narratives and other approaches and *presenting* these representations in a wide variety of ways in different contexts. An important first step in moving economic geographers into a more reflexive position is to appreciate, write about and teach about the varied sites in which economic geography is being practiced.

This chapter is premised on a particular reading of recent reflections on economic geography (Clark et al., 2000; Johnston, 1995, 1997; Lee, 1997; Leyshon, 1997; Scott, 2000) which attempt to revitalise the subject area by seeking understanding from what might be called 'intellectual histories' of the subject.

These reviews have three major shortcomings. First, they fail for the most part to address economic geography as an activity area that is constituted as a heterogeneous and changing community of knowledge workers. The common assumption that at different times and places the subject can be treated as relatively homogeneous deflects attention away from the range of contributions springing from the field. Second, and more importantly the reviews are internally skewed, in so far as they privilege the academy as *the* site in which economic geography knowledge is produced and used. This conceptual limitation closes off economic geographies constructed in contexts outside the academy, whether produced by 'trained' geographers or by others using or independently developing geographic methodologies. Third, commentary generally omits discussion of the practices and methodologies that distinguish the subject. In particular, this shortcoming means that the written record of thinking in the subject is the favoured evidence in any assessment of the subject area's health and future. In spite of sensitivity to the social construction of disciplinary knowledge, the practices of knowledge constitution seem to escape critical attention.

The chapter has four parts. It begins by identifying a number of concerns that suggest new directions in thinking will have to underpin the making of new economic geographies The concerns suggest some elements of a new conceptual mapping of economic geography. This opening section leads into a broad-based discussion of economic processes in their institutional settings. The section takes a catholic stance towards economy, conceptualising the economic as inter-linked with social, cultural and institutional and political processes and interwoven with a range of ecological, energy and material processes. This view re-situates and widens what might be considered the work of economic geography, in terms of where the practices and practitioners of geographic knowledge of the economic may be found. Following Harvey (2000) a wide range of 'sites' of economic geography practice are identifiable – sites of important calculative activities relating to the nature, direction and extent of investment. The chapter then moves to the New Zealand scene. Two sections, one offering a national commentary and the other providing some Auckland examples, illustrate how an interpretation of economic geography as both knowledge and practice helps us uncover a deep accumulation of geographic knowledge and expertise.

A different Conceptual Mapping (of where 'economic geographies' fit)

At least three very practical concerns form grounds for attempting an alternative mapping of economic geography's discourses and practices. The examples trigger some as yet unasked questions, which might begin to re-direct efforts of economic geographers.

*   *Concern 1* Recent geography graduates (at least in New Zealand) often make two comments: 'I found it so hard to immediately use my economic geography' and 'I had to learn so much when I got my first job after university'. These comments encourage questions such as 'What *translations*

do economic geography graduates have to make when they go from academia into other workplace settings?' and 'What preparation do they have for *engaging in different kinds of economic geography practice*?' These questions go *beyond* the usual debate which focuses on relevancy, especially for policy (Martin, 1999, 2001). The issue of interest is the scope and nature of practices embodied by economic geographers that might give a broader understanding of the subject being enacted. There is thus a gap to be bridged, between the world of academic economic geography (regardless of the porosity of its borders) and the many worlds of things economic and geographical encountered outside the academy.

• *Concern 2* Long-in-the-career geographers, when asked by academics to give words of encouragement to students about careers using geography almost always couch their remarks (unsurprisingly) in terms of 'geography as they knew it'. This prompts a different line of inquiry. 'What are the kinds and content of economic geography stories/knowledges that are circulating?' 'How are these knowledges being defended or rejected in conditions and contexts very different to those in which they originated?' 'How do these narratives affect and effect the work economic geographers wish to complete?' Indeed ex-students of geography occupy many worlds of geography, in New Zealand and abroad. They write policy documents, develop strategy in agencies, generate advertisements for the media, undertake market research, head corporations and government organisations, implement planning procedures, lead community activities and so on. In very real ways economic geography is not just representing the social world through textual output, it can be said to be constitutive of it through the actions of its practitioners.

• *Concern 3* Harvey (2000, p. 4) contends that there are many primary sites for the production (I would add *and consumption*) of geographical knowledges and that the qualities of such knowledges vary from site to site. His list includes (1) the state apparatus, (2) military power, (3) supra-national institutions, (4) non-governmental organisations, (5) corporate and commercial interests, (6) the media, entertainment and tourist industries, and (7) education and research institutions. This list can be extended. Immediate additions include indigenous institutions, religious institutions, households and families, community groupings, political organisations and so forth. Harvey concludes that 'geography as a discipline is situated at the confluence of a vast array of geographic discourses, constructed at quite different institutional sites with often seemingly incomparable (and some would argue incommunicable) rules of operation' (Harvey, 2000, p. 5). Seeing sites as windows into the worlds of economic geographies raises other questions ranging from 'In what ways and which recent economic geographies have travelled or not travelled into these diverse sites?' to 'What conditions made possible the resurrection of early traditions (now largely rejected within economic geography) in new guises in some sites? One well known example is Paul Krugman's outline of a new economic geography in economics which draws heavily on the canons of 1960s-1970s regional science. New economic geographies are likely to be facilitated by the fact that many economic geographers now move across different spheres and geographic borders in their lifetime. Academic representations of this world are increasingly out of kilter with the realities of where and how geographers practice.

The three concerns begin to reveal how little we currently know about geographic discourse and practice. We have few studies of economic geography *beyond* the education and research site. We can hazard a guess that the large numbers of economic geography graduates over 'the great half century', to use Allen Scott's (2000) phrase, are re-telling economic geographies with few connections between the 'generations' of discourse and practice which underlie the subject's intellectual trajectories. Our understanding of how and which economic geographies travel where is remarkably limited. In many respects, these dimensions force recognition of the *distinction between what is performed in the name of economic geography and what is practiced but is not necessarily named as economic geography.* These interpretive challenges demand new responses in the universities.

Clark, Feldman and Gertler (2000, p. 6) see economic geography as a field of research at the heart of the emerging global economy, where 'Space becomes not less important but more important with the passage of historical time, not just because it is a domain of strategic resources offering ever more subtle opportunities for economic contestation and differentiation, but also and concomitantly because of its reassertion as a medium of social and political action, that is, as a constantly changing assemblage of territorial interests in the new global economy' (Scott, 2000, p. 33). What if we take seriously the claim of Clark et al. that the globalising economy should be a key focus, and ask: 'How might a graduate of economic geography from any educational or research institution, anywhere, perform *in* the worlds or sites of the emerging globalising economy?' This is of course both a deliberately loaded and liberating question. It is loaded in that it decentres the conventional raft of accounts about economic geographies that are textual statements, and focuses instead, on economic geographies as being constituted by the actions of practitioners, whoever and where ever they might be. It is loaded in so far as begins where most mainstream accounts end, with what might be done with the 'knowledge', in this case of economic geographies. It is liberating, in sense that it does not privilege how the future may or may not be made. No template of economic geography is given, merely an acknowledgement of a particular passage of education, training and socialisation labelled 'economic geography'. Moreover it pauses, leaving the future open. In doing so it encourages a look at how a graduate might fare and consideration of whether different learning situations and pathways of experience might be worth exploring.

Wider Investment Processes and Sites of Knowledge and Calculation

Harvey's (2000) vision of a broader understanding of the multiple work of economic geography, however, needs to be taken further, by situating the practitioners and practices of economic geographic knowledge in relation to societal processes. This is a strategic step in re-conceptualising economic geography. Harvey's vision points to both investment and state processes that are interconnected with the spheres of production, reproduction and consumption. This perspective highlights the allocation of resources to do particular work *and* the governing of work, interpreted broadly. Much academic economic geography has investigated industries, enterprises and regions, with a strong industrial bias, with little regard for a great many other economic activities, territorial arrangements and organisational forms. The concern here is that *all* activities, state, commercial, community and individual and so on, are constituted directly or indirectly through processes pertaining to investment and governance. Particular sites – as indicated in the previous section – are more or less important, at different times and places. Importantly, it is not unreasonable to expect to find a diverse set of economic geographies wherever one looks.

Why the concern over sites and the work that is attempted at different sites? Jessop's (1990) concept of strategic sites sharpens up the interest on those sites which by virtue of their 'conditions of choice' (Grafstein, 1992, p. 3) affect directions of change. This thinking suggests that a more active consideration of how economic geographers engage in strategic sites may be an important research frontier. More recently Jessop (2001, p. 1217) amplifies his position, arguing that 'institutions matter because they are seen ... as the points of crystallization of social forms, as defining the rules and resources of social action, as defining opportunity structures and constraints on behaviour, as shaping the way things are done, as path-dependent path-defining complexes of social relations, as macrostructural matrices of societies and social formations.' But improving the capacities of economic geographers as actors in institutional contexts requires more attention to how societies work on themselves. *A pre-condition to capacity building is grasping the dual positioning of institutions; in investment fields in which governmental rationalities are deployed and in governing domains where investment logics are also applied.* State and investment processes are rarely unproblematic, featuring contradictions, dilemmas, tradeoffs, geographically uneven patterns of injustice and exploitation and so forth that surface as political struggles. Indeed (Hayter, 2004, p. 110) concludes 'The central normative challenge for economic geography, as dissenting institutionalism, is to define and celebrate good, creative or legitimate regional differences while seeking to contribute to institutions that will reduce bad, destructive and illegitimate regional differences'.

But are there insights and capacities that economic geographers passing out of the academy might bring to strategic and operational activities? Harvey (2000) is again a valuable guide. He suggests four themes in geographic knowledges around which 'strong ideas might cluster'. His highlights are: cartographic identifications, measures of space-time, concepts of place/region/territory, and environmental qualities and relations to nature. Although he observes that 'any search for an alternative to neo-liberal globalization must search for a different kind of spatio-temporality' and 'social and political projects are always ecological and environmental projects', he leaves undeveloped the notion of situated knowledges and practices (Le Heron, 1975; Le Heron and Pawson, 1996; Larner and Le Heron, 2002). In a similar vein, Barnes, Hayter and Hay (2001, pp. 2127-2128) write 'Our claim is that spatial and temporal processes cannot be theorized in the abstract, but must be set within the context of particular kinds of economies, institutions, commodities and places', while Herod and Wright (2001, p. 2091) acknowledge that 'theories of political economy developed on the economic margins incorporate different conceptions of space and time than do those fashioned at the economic core of the world economy' (a theme further developed in Appadurai (1999), Hayter, Barnes and Bradshaw (2003), Le Heron and Stringer (2003), and Yeung (2001, 2002, 2003a,b). At stake as well is the assumption that the academy is really *the* innovative site for interpreting and developing the road maps of new economic geography.

Context thus remains of paramount importance. As Larner and Le Heron (2002, p. 419) identify, 'What goes with this is constructing the empirical and the political anew. Representational knowledges that codify structural processes are sorely needed, for these highlight boundary conditions for action. So too is non-representational knowledge or learned-in-action intelligence'. They go on to say 'This puts a premium on performativity, the spectrum of connecting or asssociative practices' (e.g. networking, project management) which might make a difference and lead to movement towards alternatives. At present much associative activity underwrites existing political configurations. New questions spring to mind: 'What subjectivities and socialities do existing economic geographies privilege and what limits to representation, presentation and performativity do these qualities impose?' 'How might additional skills (potentially, derived from knowledge about subjectivity and sociality associated with the projects of economic geography) such as negotiation, facilitation, project management, event management, project-team roles (Grabher 2001, 2002) be used to perform economic geographies in new ways?' We simply have only rudimentary knowledge about these aspects of practice.

Having established that geography and economics combine at many sites, and that knowledge from this interconnection is potentially implicated in governmental and investment calculations and behaviour, the next sections go on to provide illustrative examples of the terrain that economic geographers occupy in New Zealand and Auckland, New Zealand's largest metropolitan area.

New Zealand Examples

This section is an impressionistic 'mapping' of where economic geographers and economic geography are placed in the New Zealand economic and institutional landscape. At the outset it must be acknowledged that the exercise is at best indicative. The intention is to offer a preliminary overview of how an investigation of sites, knowledge and activities might be approached.

Whatever the approach, some sites will be discerned to have greater visibility or importance over others. This is unavoidable. The aim is to show that by posing positioning questions, practices that relate to shaping new economic spaces will be centred in discussion and analysis. The nature and level of contributions by economic geographers in making decisions or economic geography knowledge in informing decision making can then be ascertained.

For each of site, particular organisations can be identified in which geographers carry out economic-related tasks about relationships in space, place and location. A summary for the mid-1990s for Wellington and Auckland illustrates a density of geographers across much of the economy (Table 19.1). The table was compiled by systematically contacting geographers known to be working in particular organisations in these cities and preparing a list of staff with geography degrees. While this is an imperfect method, it nonetheless establishes the breadth of employment of geographers. It has since been supplemented by career profiles prepared by Geography Departments in New Zealand (Pawson, 1999; Milicich and Stringer, 2001). Note: summaries have also been developed in other countries as well, but the common feature there, as in New Zealand, is the failure to analyse the performative dimensions of the subject in terms of different sites.

A limited survey of the websites and recent publications of four government departments in August 2004 (The Treasury, Ministry of Economic Development, Ministry for the Environment and Work and Income New Zealand) provides information on the nature of the 'geographies' being shaped or shaping internal and external relationships of these institutions. For example, Treasury has in recent years been attempting to understand the significance of New Zealand's size and location in the globalising world economy. Working papers in 2004 covered topics such as 'Global connectedness and bilateral economic linkages – which countries?' and 'Theory vs Reality: Making environmental use rights work in New Zealand', each involving geographic treatment of economic ideas, including reference to agglomeration, regional difference and population features. The Ministry of Economic Development promulgates a conception of the region, forming at the interface of top-down intervention and bottom-up community and social development. In practice this is expressed as a normative understanding of regional difference, with the regionalisation being used to identify those regions that have been 'left behind' and need to catch up. Their treatment of regional difference in text and in practice differs little from earlier generations of regional policy in New Zealand (Franklin, 1978; Le Heron, 1987). In 2004 Work and Income New Zealand differentiated new economic spaces in New Zealand in their 'red-lining' of locations where beneficiaries would not be able to move to while receiving a benefit because the town did not have a local economic base with sufficient employment opportunities. The final example relates to the move by the Ministry for the Environment into research on urban spaces and infrastructure, ecological footprints, the calculation of total economic value by assigning monetary valuation to ecosystem services, sustainable land management practices and oceans policy development. In this instance the Ministry is involved in delineating new organising principles that might enter into the re-configuration of the economic and the shaping of new economic spaces through modified or redirected investment processes.

Table 19.1   Some Organisations Employing Geographers – 1996

Auckland	Wellington
3M New Zealand	Barrett Fuller
Adis International	Civil Aviation
Air New Zealand	Comalco New Zealand
Auckland International Airport	Department of Conservation
Auckland City Council	DOSLI
Bales Advertising	ENZA
Bestwood Ltd	Hiliary Commission
Beca Consultants	New Zealand Historical Atlas
CM research	Hutt Valley CHE
Communicado, Auckland	Immigration Service
Connell Wagner	Inland Revenue Department
Consolidators International	Department of Internal Affairs
Department of Conservation	Meat Industry Association
DOSLI	MERA
Forsyte research	Meterological Services
Hames Sharley	Ministry for the Environment
Information Tools Ltd	Ministry of Agriculture and Forestry
Institute Environmental Health and Forensic Science	Ministry of Commerce
Kingett Mitchell	Ministry of Energy
KPMG	Ministry of Transport
Manukau City Council	Ministry of Foreign Affairs and Trade
Meteorological Office, Whenuapai	Mobil Oil
Ministry for the Environment	New Zealand Defence Force
Ministry of Housing	New Zealand Manufacturers Federation
New Zealand Wine Institute	New Zealand Mining Association
New Zealand Customs	New Zealand Post
NIWA	New Zealand Qualifications Authority
North Shore City	New Zealand Tourism Board
Royal New Zealand Navy	Prime Minister's Department
Reg Price and Associates	Public Health Commission
Sheldon and Partners	Resource Management and Environmental Planning Consultants
Statistics New Zealand	Robert Young Tellfer
Tradenz	Department of Social Welfare
Tonkin and Taylor	Statistics New Zealand
TVNZ	Te Puni Kokiri
UniServices	Tourism Resource Consultants
Waitakere City	TransRail
Watercare Services	Treasury
Woodward Clyde	Wellington City Council
Works Consultancy, Auckland	

Such survey is of course illustrative and only draws attention to the fact that economic geography is being performed at the sites. It does not say anything about the actions of economic geographers. Nevertheless it indicates that a mixture of ideas abound, from traditional, contemporary and cutting edge economic geography, as practiced in the academy and outlined in standard textbooks and journals. Whether these ideas are present because economic geographers have been informing the debates, whether they are being attributed to other disciplinary sources, or whether they are being re-invented in situ, simply can not be ascertained from the investigative approach used here. This said, the scoping exercise suggests too much about the practices of economic geography is unknown and indicates a priority area for research, on economic geography.

Auckland Examples

How economic geographers are able to do work (assuming an active intentionality guided by knowledge gained in the universities) and the manner in which they are put to work (reflecting their assignment to work in particular jobs) depends greatly on the political projects in any context. In New Zealand under the 5th Labour government, the state has been reasserting itself in various forms. This is highlighted with distinctive surges of interest in governing – around for instance such concerns as markets, competition, industries and connection to the rest of the world. These governmental urges are underpinned by rationalities that encourage or fuel the identification of manageable political projects. That is, investment strategies and allocations are framed in terms of narratives that mobilise, energise and satisfy political supporters. Thus, investment processes become contested arena as they mesh into or are enmeshed by political initiatives. These can be quite diverse (Table 19.2), with coherence at the national level and more localised expressions in Auckland.

Table 19.2 provides an illustrative schematic for the New Zealand and Auckland scene. It uses concepts familiar to economic geographers but assembles and positions them differently. Moreover, it recognises the formative influences of the geographical literature *and* the employment roles of practicing geographers. The specifics shown hint at the range of governmental pressures shaping investment in Auckland. They should be seen as neither a complete listing of influences nor necessarily a connected list. Moreover, the placement of the concepts in the table does not imply particular equivalence in or amongst the columns and rows. The table is merely a device to illustrate the idea that economic geographies and economic geographers might be associated and associate on new terms. This assemblage attempts what Thrift (2004, p. 82) regards as the emphasis of understanding performative knowledge, 'inventing new relations between thought and life'.

Table 19.2   Mapping of Recent Governmental Dimensions Relating to Auckland

Governmental moments	Governmental rationalities	Economic geography literature	National Political projects	Specific sites (at which economic geographers working)	Politicised projects in Auckland	Involvement of Economic Geographers
Market making	Globalisation	Yes	Market liberalization privatization	Treasure/Prime Ministers Department	Infrastructure Auckland	Yes
International competitiveness	Competition state	Yes	Creative Industries Creative Cities	Trade NZ/Industry NZ/Min Econ Dev	Knowledge Wave Designer fashion	Yes
Industry making	New economy	Yes	Clusters Incubators	Industry NZ/Skills NZ/Local Government	Competitive Auckland	Yes
Connectivity	Regional Development Community Development	Yes	Partnership	Local government/Industry NZ/Department of Labour/CEG	AREDS	Yes

Acknowledgement: The basic form of this figure was proposed by Nick Lewis and has been developed through discussion with Nick and Wendy Larner.

Conclusions

The chapter opened with a quote from Harvey reminding geographers that Foucault's ideas about knowledge production, power and relations and institutions should be used when examining the discipline. The chapter has explored economic geography and economic geographers in such terms. The approach has been to consider the work of the academy as but one site of economic geography practice, where both cognitive knowledge about substantive issues and performative knowledge about how to be an economic geographer can be acquired. In exploring the approach it is apparent that past traditions of critical internal review on the nature of the subject make few steps in the direction of what Thrift (2004) calls non-representative knowledge. This is hardly unexpected given the general unwillingness of economic geographers to embrace the constitutive dimensions of practices.

Where next then? Getting to know economic geography through greater dialogue with different practitioners is probably going to be the most productive way forward. This is a many-sided project, in which no site or group of economic geographers or practitioners of economic geography should be ascribed pre-given roles, capacities or qualities. Indeed, how economic geographers connect into different institutional environments becomes a matter of much interest, for as Thrift (2004) contends, the interplay between the subjectified individual economic geographer and the wider environment will always impact greatly on where the doing of economic geography takes the subject area.

The chapter has argued that insight into the cognitive and performative dimensions of economic geography will come from seeking *in-site* awareness and a-where-ness of practices. In a very real sense, this is a journey of discovery where newly understood spaces of economic geographic practice will summon new practices of economic geography.

Acknowledgements

Wendy Larner, Nick Lewis, Edwin Massey, Mike Roche, Juliana Mansvelt, Jon May and Steffen Wetzstein provided critical and helpful comments on a paper that formed the basis of this chapter. Their perceptive suggestions and questioning is greatly appreciated. The efforts of Russell Prince, who undertook research relating to the contemporary government scene, are gratefully acknowledged. Needless to say, I am responsible for the views finally offered in the chapter.

References

Appadurai A. (1999) 'Globalization and the research imagination', *International Social Science Journal*, 51, pp. 229-238.
Barnes, T. (2001a) 'Retheorizing economic geography: From the quantitative revolution to the "cultural turn"', *Annals of the Association of American Geographers*, 91, pp. 546-565.

Barnes, T. (2001b) 'In the beginning was economic geography – a science studies approach to disciplinary history', *Progress in Human Geography*, 25, pp. 521-544.

Barnes, T. (2002) 'Performing economic geography: two men, two books, and a cast of thousands', *Environment and Planning A*, 34, pp. 487-512.

Barnes, T., Hayter, R. and Hay, E. (2001) 'Stormy weather: cyclones, Harold Innes, and Port Alberni, British Columbia', *Environment and Planning A*, 33, pp. 2127-2147.

Clark, G., Feldman, M. and Gertler, M. (2000) 'Economic geography: Transition and growth', In Clark, G., Feldman, M. and Gertler, M. (eds) *The Oxford Handbook of Economic Geography*, Oxford: Oxford University Press, pp. 3-17.

Fitzsimmons, M. (2004) 'Engaging ecologies', In Cloke, P., Crang, P. and Goodwin, M. (eds) *Envisaging Human Geographies*, London: Arnold, pp. 30-47.

Grafstein, R. (1992) Institutional Realism: Social and Political Constraints on Rational Actors, New Haven: Yale University Press.

Grahber, G. (2001) 'Locating economic action: projects, networks, localities, institutions', *Environment and Planning A*, 33, pp. 1329-1334.

Grahber, G. (2002) 'Fragile sector, robust practice: project ecologies in new media', *Environment and Planning A*, 34, pp. 1911-1926.

Harvey, D. (2000) Cartographic identities. Geographical knowledges under globalization. Paper distributed to the 29th International Geographical Union Congress, Seoul, South Korea, 16 August, for Symposia 3. Post-modern societies: Culture, Space and Place.

Hayter, R. (2004) 'Economic geography as dissenting institutionalism: The embeddedness, evolution and differentiation of regions', *Geografiska Annaler*, B, 86: pp. 95-115.

Hayter, R., Barnes, T. and Bradshaw, B. (2003) 'Relocating resource peripheries to the core of economic geography's theorizing: rationale and agenda', *Area*, 35, pp. 15-23.

Herod, A. and Wright, M. (2001) 'Theorizing space and time', *Environment and Planning A*, 33, pp. 2089-2093.

Jessop, B. (1990) *State Theory: Putting Capitalist States in their Place*. Cambridge: Polity Press.

Jessop, B. (2001) 'Institutional re(turns) and the strategic-relational approach', *Environment and Planning A*, 33, pp. 1213-1235.

Johnston, R. (1995) 'Geographical research, geography and geographers in the changing British university system', *Progress in Human Geography*, 19, 3, pp. 355-371.

Johnston, R. (1997) *Geography and Geographers: Anglo-American Human Geography Since 1945*, London: Arnold.

Larner, W. and Le Heron, R. (2002) 'From Economic Globalisation to Globalising Economic Processes: Towards post-structuralist political economies', *Geoforum* 33, 415-419.

Lee, R. (1997) 'Prologue. Economic geographies: Representations and interpretations', In Lee, R. and Wills, J. (eds) *Geographies of Economies*. London: Arnold, pp. xi-xiv.

Lee, R. (2002) 'Nice maps, shame about the theory? Thinking geographically about the economic', *Progress in Human Geography*, 26, 3, pp. 333-356.

Le Heron, R. and Pawson, E. (eds) (1996) *Changing Places. New Zealand in the Nineties*. Auckland: Longman Paul

Le Heron, R. and Stringer, C. (2003) Review of Hayter, R. Flexible Crossroads. The Restructuring of British Columbia's Forest Economy, *Economic Geography*, pp. 215-218.

Lewis, N., Larner, W. and Le Heron, R. (2003) 'Governmentalities and industry: The co-constitution of New Zealand designer fashion', unpublished manuscript.

Leyshon, A. (1997) 'Introduction: True stories? Global nightmares, global dreams and writing globalization', In Lee, R. and Wills, J. (eds) *Geographies of Economies*. London: London, pp. 133-146.

Martin, R. (1999) 'The new "geographical turn" in economics: Some critical reflections', *Cambridge Journal of Economics*, 23, 1, pp. 65-91.

Martin, R. (2001) 'Geography and public policy: The case of the missing agenda', *Progress in Human Geography*, 25, 2, pp. 189-210.

Milicich, M. and Stringer, C. (2001) 'Geographers: People Going Places', *New Zealand Journal of Geography*, October 112, pp. 34-36.

Pawson, E. (ed.) (1999) *GeoJobs*. Hamilton: New Zealand Geographical Society.

Scott, A. (2000) 'Economic geography: The great half-century', In Clark, G., Feldman, M. and Gertler, M. (eds) *The Oxford Handbook of Economic Geography*, Oxford: Oxford University Press, pp. 18-44.

Thrift, N. (2000) 'State sovereignty, globalization and the rise of soft capitalism', In Hay, C. and Marsh, D. (eds) *Demystifying Globalisation*, New York: St. Martins.

Thrift, N. (2004) 'Summoning life', In Cloke, P., Crang, P. and Goodwin, M. (eds) *Envisaging Human Geographies*, London: Arnold, pp. 81-103.

Yeung, H. (2001) 'Redressing the geographical bias in social science knowledge', *Environment and Planning A*, 33, pp. 2-9.

Yeung, H. (2002) 'Doing what kind of economic geography?', *Journal of Economic Geography*, 2, pp. 250-252.

Yeung, H. (2003a) 'Practicing new economic geographies: A methodological examination', *Annals of the Association of American Geographers*.

Yeung H. (2003b) 'Theorizing economic geographies of Asia', *Economic Geography*, 79, 2, pp. 107-128.

Index